FOOTPRINTS OF
A QUEER HISTORY:
LIFE-STORIES FROM GUJARAT

FOOTPRINTS OF A QUEER HISTORY: LIFE-STORIES FROM GUJARAT

Maya Sharma

YODAPRESS

YODA PRESS
79 Gulmohar Enclave
New Delhi 110 049
www.yodapress.co.in

ISBN 978-93-82579-35-9

Editors in charge: Arpita Das, Himadri Agarwal and Chitraksh Ashray
Typeset in Adobe Caslon Pro, 11/14.4
By MSourcing
Published by Arpita Das for YODA PRESS

Contents

Preface

This book is the result of a convergence of various developments in the larger women's and queer movements: from the national and local level, down to Vikalp (Women's Group) in Vadodara, Gujarat; marked by personal journeys, political consciousness, socio-legal struggles, friendships, and love; to put on record within the larger historical processes our humdrum and unexceptional acts of everyday-living, that are pierced with the pain of stigma and silence as we go about living our ordinary lives.

This book is also an attempt to tell the story of an organisation, the story of Vikalp. When many of these stories were first penned, we used different terms to describe people than the ones we would use these days, for we did not know any better. Often the term used by families or neighbours in the village for trans men was 'chokri chokro che' (woman who is man). For many reading these stories, these descriptors and local labels may cause some discomfort. For example, in the two stories of Mansa and Mataji, the individuals are described as women, and Mataji's marriage is mentioned as a marriage between 'two women'. Readers are right to feel that it is wrong to assume that the individuals in the story identify as women, and perhaps both/none of them do so. Similarly, in the story of Mansa, we did not know her preferred identity for certain. But as stories, this is how they first appeared before us. In Mataji's story, the gender of the individual changes once a month. At first, I tried to insert notes to explain how or why this had happened, but the technicalities began to distract from the story and the individuals themselves. Therefore, I preferred to use the pronoun 'they' as it was used by most people around them, signifying the respect they enjoyed locally (in many Indian languages, the plural pronoun is often also used to show respect), and also because I felt that the usage of 'they' captured well the gender change within which Mataji lived their daily life.

In two other stories, trans men refer to themselves as lesbians for many years. Using the language used by the characters themselves, and the public (and even ourselves) during the time before knowing any better, is relative to the context and used simply as a method of storytelling. Later as our understanding developed, we used the pronoun 'he' and trans men in deference to the choice of the subjects, also changing the terminology in the narratives written earlier. Therefore, these stories sometimes use both the identities: 'lesbian' and trans man. The evolution of language and terminology from the beginning to the end of the book is again a stylistic choice to reflect our journey of learning as an organisation and the evolution that has taken place both within the queer and non-queer communities in this regard.

In one of the stories mentioned above, the name is not written, and instead appears as a _____. The individual in this story does not relate to or refer to their given name and did not want it printed. These decisions throughout the book are not uniform, but I am of the opinion that they accurately represent the fact that neither are the experiences, realities, opinions and desires of those who appear within it.

The Story of these Stories

While this book is the result of a coming together of queer people from Sabrang and other activists in Vikalp, the creation of a book was never the intended idea. Until July 2009, the queer community was an illegitimate child of the state. And so, as a community, we often came together to relieve our isolation and meet others like ourselves. Having a community softened the daily hardships that came with the choices made to live as our true selves, and the anxieties of facing the ordeal of an unevenly paced legal journey. The need to politicise came to us consciously and compulsorily, as a need to lobby and advocate for the diverse experiences of the queer community.

It is critical that we acknowledge the positive changes that have come about since we began our work. What is most striking about the decades of the 1990s and 2000s is the pace and the nature of uneven changes that have taken place: from the first public protest on Delhi's streets organised by AIDS Bhedbhav Virodhi Andolan (ABVA) against the harassment of gay men in 1991; to the raging controversy that followed when the film *Fire* (1999), that depicted two women in love, was banned; to the increasing number of attendees at Pride parades across different cities across the country; the filing of a historic PIL for the reading down of Section 377 in 2001; and the remarkable judgement of the Delhi High Court in 2009 in which Section 377 was read down, following almost a decade of struggle. Four years later, however, the judgement was reversed by the Supreme Court. Yet, 2014 saw a landmark judgement from the Supreme Court itself, granting transgender persons the right to self-identify. And finally, in 2018, the Supreme Court read down Section 377 and homosexuality was decriminalised in India. Of course, the rapid pace of change seen within the last few years has been heartening, but the situation of queer community is one that is still characterised by ambiguity, silences, and contradictions. Any realisation of the recent changes is happening at a highly disparate degree between the metropolises on the one hand, and the smaller towns, and rural, tribal areas of the country on the other.

When Vikalp began its work on sexual health in 2002, the raging controversy surrounding the film *Fire* and the debate concerning the presence of 'such women in our pristine culture' had not yet trickled into the far interiors of the rural and tribal areas of India. As the queer community began to engage legally and the numbers at Pride parades continued to swell, we realised that the interiority of subjects living away from urban societies remained enigmatic, almost invisible. A book such as this thus hopes to change this narrative, by offering some inclusivity, a bridge across the disparity, as it were.

I have been asked why this book of stories largely focuses on trans men, in the same way that our meetings also currently focus on this group. In my own journey, the discovery of the term 'lesbian' as a form of validation was a means for rejoicing; yet, the inadequacy of the word was soon realised when one began to work in the field. Many in the community lived within shifting identities, and some completely refuted the identity of 'lesbian' because the word connoted the female gender. And whilst trans women were now being taken into account by the government-run sexual health programmes, the term 'transgender' was not even commonly used to refer to trans men. As we looked around us and within the queer movement, those amongst us identifying as trans men could find no conversations around themselves. Although these new government programmes began to create some kind of legitimacy surrounding gender issues, they rarely acknowledged the presence of transmasculine persons. I wanted to record the experiences of those on the outer margins of an already marginalised group. It makes sense here to provide a definition of 'trans' as 'an umbrella term for people whose gender identity differs from the sex they were assigned at birth, outside the binary genders of female and male. The term transgender is not indicative of gender expression, sexual orientation, hormonal makeup, physical anatomy, or how one is perceived in daily life.'[1]

Within the traditional systemic arrangements of hetero-patriarchal structure, marriage and reproduction become the prime functions of human beings. As a result, desire encoded in

[1] 'Definitions.' Definitions – TSER. https://transstudent.org/about/definitions/.

this duality justifies the categorisation of same-sex loving people as 'deviant', and these oppositional binaries and perspectives of gender roles compound the invisibility of trans men. The onus of 'reproduction' deriving from the gender at birth comes to rest heavily on trans men, thus giving way to narratives that differ from those of trans women early on in life: socialisation to perform feminine roles, mobility restrictions and compulsory dress codes and forced marriages. Whilst working on the ground, we began to gather a sense of these significant differences and disparities: between rural and urban, between trans women and trans men, and countless other intersections. We wanted to make some kind of attempt at recording these differences that reflected lived realities.

In a survey carried out by Vikalp, it was found that 40 per cent of trans women surveyed were married in Chhotaudepur (a rural tribal area during the time of study) compared to 80 per cent of those who were living in Ahmedabad (the largest city in Gujarat). In contrast, a survey of 50 trans men undertaken in Gujarat found that only 18 per cent were married. In a cultural context where greater coercion existed for women, the trans men group held several more layers of untold, interconnected stories, as we discovered down the line.

Surveys did nothing to unravel these layers for us—a sense of loss overtook us as stories slipped by.

Through meetings and moments of sharing, it was realised that there were many complex issues within our lives best expressed through personal narratives and story-sharing. Families and communities often create stories that seek to explain the non-normative. These stories win legitimacy through the enactment of affirmative silences, collaborative assents, and nods. With each member prodding the other to go on, or picking up where the other left off, the sharings snowball and become a performance of a collective that repeats and ritualises to recover, reclaim, and reconnect a part of their 'own' for/to the rest. While the survey

conducted by Vikalp, produced as a shared effort of the community, had left those involved with a sense of 'this is not a sense
of who I am' upon its completion, it had also unwittingly high-
lighted the need for telling and sharing stories. Above all, it was
our stories that held us together in rapt attention and made us
empathetic and understand one another better. It became clear
that stories have in them that magical spin that reaches right into
the inner recesses; as a result, what began as a natural corollary
to mitigate isolation gradually grew into a conscious goal to document detailed stories.

For those marginalised voices rarely heard, only stories truly
and fully capture their day-to-day reality. The thing about stories is that they echo universal emotions, and so can be used to
change attitudes and perspectives. Stories talk to us in words,
and words, in one's own surroundings, say more than the tex-
tual meanings attached to them. They transcend the limitations
of defining human experiences and show the impossibility of
telling the whole truth and nothing but the truth. Stories reach
numerous levels encompassing narrators, listeners, subjects and
contexts; they arouse the imagination for that untellable tale and
leave room for the inarticulate to attempt those spillages of reality that can only be sensed.

Philosophies aside, there were also pragmatic reasons for
using the story form: I am not an academic, but I love to listen
to stories told to me and I often write them down. Some of these
stories were written down as precisely that, for my own love
of writing, while others were a response to my documentation
work for an organisation. I have written stories before; however,
the difference between this and the earlier work is that, when
I look back now, I find that those were fragments, little pieces
that I could intrude upon, interrupt. Ethically, in those stories, I
found myself in a conflicted place. But here, I was living my life
with the community on a daily basis, and over time trust and
love had built up gradually. Thus, it was relatively simpler to

talk about our lives together, creating a much greater possibility of going deeper. In the previous work, I had to go out and 'find' protagonists to write about; whereas those who appear in these stories took their own initiative to find Vikalp. But most importantly, these stories came into fruition because they wanted to be told.

The writing of these stories has not been linear or chronological. Some of these stories span a period of nearly 10 years within a larger narrative of an organisational journey and us knowing one another. Others are only as long as our visit lasted in the field. Some stories came out of a crisis, the disjuncture caused in daily life after a couple's elopement and its immediate aftermath. And some revolve around exploring faint whispers of 'two women living together....' Most were fed to me in small bites, here and there, and I wrote and recorded them in the same manner. The stories have been gathered through face-to-face conversations, letters, phone calls, experiences shared during community meetings, and retold documented events of organisational interventions. They were all later fact-checked, even while being colourised by the tellers' own perspectives, and of course, mine too. These are their stories, the parts willingly shared with us, and the parts which I heard and understood. The details within the scenes that I visited often indicate truths unspoken, which is why such details are mentioned: they might be tightly closed curtains, a particular silence, or some kind of behaviour that dropped hints of concealed realities. Really, this is also a story of collecting stories.

As a narrator of stories that were told to me, I hovered between being an insider and an outsider, and sometimes both. An insider in the sense of belonging to the sexually marginalised, and queer, community: a lesbian and non-academic activist involved with the community's struggles, both giving and taking support. And also, an outsider: to trans men, trans women, and sex workers.

So, I don't claim that I know it all, but this book is an effort to put together our stories. It may still only be a fragment. I don't claim that it is the only truth. But it is some part of the truth, out there, for us; for posterity, for people to know the struggles that we have been through. Collectively, these individual stories tell the story of our organisation, and our organisation's story collectively tells the story of a movement. And perhaps there will be a better day when we can look back and gratefully acknowledge the struggle of the people here who made the path easier for our future generations.

Maya Sharma
5 January 2022
Ahmedabad, Gujarat

Acknowledgements

This book is the result of a synergy built over time between members of our diverse queer communities, with myriad efforts put in by many different people at different points of time. I gratefully acknowledge those community members who shared their life-stories with me and willingly agreed to have them recorded at the risk of facing untoward consequences. Though I happened to record the stories told to me, those who shared their stories are as much the authors of each of their narratives. I respectfully acknowledge them and all my other queer community members who listened patiently to what had been recorded and written. Humbled and a million-fold enriched, I know that no word of thanks can quite capture the trust that I was reposed with, the generosity in sparing time for me on many occasions; when I fumbled for the right word in translation, they sought its appropriateness through their experience, unfolding the complexities of language, tradition and culture and found words that legitimised queer experiences. These suggestions and subsequent questions that came my way gave me a deeper insight. Inadequate though these words of grateful acknowledgement may be, I thank you all.

I wish to acknowledge the support Vikalp as an organisation gave me and particularly Indira Pathak, who appears in various stories as an activist initiating action. His critical suggestions opened up knots of a layered reality that besets our daily lives. It was because of his support that I, as a lesbian woman, was able to overcome my fear of writing on trans masculine lives. Prem, Pallu, and Kiran—thank you for being with me, challenging and prodding me on, in the writing of these stories.

This book would not have seen the light of day without Roisin Seaton's support in editing, her belief when I doubted and hesitated, and above all her methodological approach in sorting out the stories from a pile of documents that had accumulated over the years. She brought the stories together, gently making me let go of them, thereby relieving me of an excess attachment. Thank you so much, Roisin.

To Aniruddhan Vasudevan, who patiently read through several of these stories in the midst of his PhD, giving me invaluable suggestions, and along with Sayan Bhattacharya encouraged me to reach that evasive full stop we call the finishing line. Thank you both so much. Your support meant a lot then and continues to do so now.

Mario Da Penha was the one who introduced me to Musa Suhag and Nighat Gandhi who translated and explained to me the Urdu words. Together, both of them made the magical story come alive for me, showing me the many places in which possibilities live. I thank you both.

Dr L. Ramakrishnan's appreciation of my writing and willingness to read through a few other stories meant a lot. Thank you, Ramki.

Many thanks to Andra Bosneag who pulled out the different stories, incidents, and interventions written over time from different files. She organised them and pulled out the idea from cold storage that I would one day put them all together. She began the process for me.

Lily Goldschmidt, Marni Wolf, Siddharth Narrain and Tanvika Gulyani—thank you all so much for all the many different ways in which you helped to make this book happen.

Individually, all of you have been such warm critics. I learnt a lot from you. And thank you, Maninderjit Singh, for your conversations during COVID times.

I am indebted to Arpita Das and her team at Yoda Press who meticulously read through the manuscript and finely wove it together. And thank you, Chitraksh, for always asking and answering and being there as an ally.

1

My Story

The individuals within these pages have shared a lot with us, and I too had shared my story with them. In order to give the reader some sense of those years of sharing, and also as a method that emerged over time, I unburden myself here as I did then in sharing some of my personal experiences, events that played a role in me recognising my sexuality and the cumulative events that led me here, to give context and reason as to how I came to Gujarat.

Back in school, as an adolescent, my love for a teacher was easy to camouflage. Unfortunately, it could not last long beyond school. In college, I learnt that two women who loved one another were labelled 'cooing pigeons', and they were mocked and commented upon. I locked away the memory of the woman I had loved on dark staircases. Once, she came to visit me in my marital home and I was a good host, without meeting her eye. But now, when she is no more, I miss her. I am left with the pang that I did not go back and tell her that it was she who showed me that the love I held for her, and another classmate who did not reciprocate, was nothing to be ashamed of, an affirmation that her religion condemned as sinful. She interpreted many things differently and also taught me to cross lines while seeing their many meeting points.

By the 1990s, I was falling in love with women all over again. Being in a metropolis made it possible to speak of this love, though still in whispers. The taste of the forbidden 'L' word was new for me, and exciting. We wrapped it and its comforting secrecy around ourselves. From nothing at all, here was now a word that existed outside us, validating us. The central park in Connaught Place was that one spot we knew by word of mouth to be a favourite haunt of our community and the policemen. Back then in 1992, I was one of those who marched on Delhi streets in the protest organised by ABVA against police harassment of gay people. I walked then as an anonymous activist from a women's group, a closeted lesbian, fearing that if seen I would by association suffer the label of being 'one of them'. I hoped no one would see through me.

While engaged in advocacy work, as a volunteer with CALERI (Campaign for Lesbian Rights), a Delhi-based autonomous group formed in 1998 in response to the violent protests against Deepa Mehta's film *Fire*, we experienced a dearth of material depicting women's same-sex love. In order to get our voices heard, I realised it would be useful to produce evidence that would validate the presence of people 'like us'. I began to explore the idea of research, undertaking field trips in the northern parts of the country. At the Human Rights Conference in 2002 organised in Panchgani, I found the opportunity to share what I had encountered during my research treading deep into rural areas of Rajasthan, and into silences of safety. One story, in particular, acted as a catalyst: both inwardly on a personal level, and outwardly in consequences that ultimately led to the creation of this book.

In a landscape of gender roles and codes, Babu Maharaj stood out as an 'oddity' dressed in dhoti and kurta, with a pen in the upper pocket, her 'maleness' and way of being simultaneously covering and uncovering the fissures in gender binaries. I first heard of her described by another activist as 'Babubai'. The name itself aroused my interest; 'babu' is the generic term of address for a man, and 'bai' is a generic term of address for

women. The activist described her as having short hair and living with a woman. Despite warnings that she may not want to
meet me at all, I managed to track her down and made my way
to her home. As the second man I had asked about Babubai in
the village led me to her door, I remember feeling eager, yet anxious and uncertain. The woman who opened the door had a pale
complexion and a sturdy build. I noticed that her breasts were
bound with a cloth. Hurriedly I introduced myself, referencing
my group and the specific co-worker who had told me about her.
She offered me a handshake that I can never forget: strong, firm
and warm.[2]

There was another woman in the house, her name was Sita.
I had previously been informed that she was a widow. I told
the pair I was collecting stories of women who had managed to
remain single. After offering and bringing me tea, Maharaj explained, 'We are Ramsnehi *bhakts* (followers of a religious sect);
our lives revolve around worship and singing *kirtan-bhajan*
(hymns).' I asked why they had not attended the women's group,
at which she began to swear. 'At the meeting [on women's health]
I went to, they showed dirty pictures, talked about sexual organs
and having children [...] What have I to do with such matters?
It was so disgusting; I wished the ceiling would collapse upon us
[...] I have had enough of such topics.'

Listening to her speak, I felt that she had rejected woman-
ness.[3] All of my inquiries into her personal life and my constant
reference to 'single women' aggravated her, and soon the mood
of the conversation turned hostile. I became aware of the couple's
gaze and how they were scrutinising me, surely wondering why
anybody would come all the way from Delhi just to meet them. I
knew they would never admit to having a same-sex relationship

---

[2] Sharma, Maya. 'She Has Come from the World of the Spirits...': Life Stories of
Working-Class Lesbian Women in Northern India.' In *Women's Sexualities and
Masculinities in a Globalizing Asia*, 254. New York: Palgrave Macmillan, 2007,
p. 254.
[3] Ibid.

because of their sectarian affiliation, which accommodated them as a unit on the condition of silence and denial. I was asking the wrong questions, too abrupt and inappropriate. My focus on their single status had made them distrustful. The conversation proceeded in a way that ended up with me leaving. I was uneasy, having a premonition of something worse to come.[4] I had gone about interviewing Maharaj in such a self-absorbed manner that I didn't realise that I was disturbing something serious, something that was very strong and also very delicate.

I took a window seat on the bus that would take me back. Just as I settled in, I locked eyes with Maharaj outside the window. She told me this bus would take very long, and to take the next one instead. As I made my way off the bus, the driver warned, 'Don't be misled by Babu Maharaj's words. Go back to your seat.' I soon understood that she was trying to lure me off the bus. I was in deep trouble as she demanded through the window 'give me what you are writing!' There was a huge scene, both of us talking and shouting together, until it finished with her tearing out the pages that I had written and storming off.[5] She had caused a disjuncture at so many levels that I carried her picture in my mind's eye for a long, long time afterwards. It was an unforgettable experience of understanding the risks and the necessity of silence in the place where a subject was located. It threw up the ethical dilemma of writing about somebody that does not want to be written about; yet, I chose to narrate it, as I could see no other way to break the cultural silences.

It was this story that I shared at that Human Rights Conference. This was my first-of-a-kind experience, in going into the rural interiors, and for that reason many people at the conference were interested. Also, it was obvious that here was a woman who did not identify with the label of 'woman' that her body subscribed to. Despite receiving appreciation at the conference,

---

4 Ibid., p. 256
5 Ibid., p. 257.

the news of what I had shared reached the union office before I did. When I went to the office after a few days, it bristled with a tension so taut that I could barely keep my balance. I was hauled up for lowering the image of the institution, and my defence that I did not represent the union at the conference cut no ice. Unions never ask their officer bearers to leave, but from then on it was no longer easy to work there. At this time, I had already begun working closely with Vikalp, and carrying out research in rural Gujarat with their support. And so, when the door closed at the union, I set myself free and devoted myself to researching alongside Vikalp, and moved permanently to Gujarat.

2

Recalling Rainbows in Gujarat

As India's most westerly state, wrapped in 992 miles of coastline, the diversity of climate, landscape and inhabitants found in Gujarat is hardly a surprise; indeed, it is a state in which you can never find yourself more than 100 miles from the sea.[6] The Gujarati language, its many dialects, and accents are an ode to history: conquerors, traders, merchant communities passing through or settling in Gujarat, a corridor from west Asia to the high seas. The seeds of Gujarati—found in Sanskrit, Prakrit, and even adopting some Persian and Arabic words—were sown during the Chalukyan period, and the language became increasingly popular when it was used by Hindu and Muslim saints to express themselves.[7]

The Gujarat of today came to be in 1960, a time in which it was not uncommon for states to go through mergers and divisions.[8] Following the success of the 'Mahagujarat' movement, led by students and prominent figures, mainland Gujarat, Kutch and Saurashtra detached from Bombay and tied themselves together with a common language. Even today though, Gujarat is rarely

---

[6] Pathak, Devavrat Nanubhai, and Deryck O. Lodrick. 'Gujarat.' Encyclopedia Britannica. 1999. britannica.com/place/Gujarat#ref280954.
[7] Yagnik, Achyut, and Suchitra Sheth. *The Shaping of Modern Gujarat: Plurality, Hindutva, and Beyond*. Penguin Books, 2005, p. 15.
[8] Ibid., p. 227

viewed as a single entity and can be divided into four subregions, geographically and socially.

'Kutch' translates literally as something that is intermittently wet and dry; a fitting name for the most north-westerly part of both Gujarat and India, which houses the world's largest salt flats, transforming into a white desert as the water dries up in between monsoons. The southern shores of Kutch face Saurashtra, lying on the opposite side of the gulf. With the Gulf of Kutch to her north, and embraced by the Arabian Sea to both the south and south-west, Saurashtra boasts of such fertile land that it earned itself the name 'good country', which its Prakrit name, Sorath, translates to. Eastern Gujarat is the most densely populated and urbanised subregion: Ahmedabad, the state's former capital, has emerged as an economic hub and is India's fifth-most populous city. The plains that surround Ahmedabad and other cities, such as Vadodara and Surat, are both agriculturally productive—an industry which employs about half of the state's workforce—and highly industrialised, though managing to remain relatively free from labour unrest by following approaches favoured by Gandhi, the world's most famous Gujarati and the father of our nation. The mountains and green pastures running through Southern Gujarat form an area known as the Eastern Adivasi Belt, portions of which are populated almost entirely by tribal people. Tribal and oppressed-caste peoples together form about one-fifth of the state's population, while three-fifths of Gujarati residents are rural.

India's colonial past presents complex changing, shifting, and integrating realities that run in oppositional, criss-crossing, and parallel streams. The Gujarat of that time reflects similar cross-currents, experiencing equally the widespread influence of colonialism and the social reform movement of the nineteenth century that led to the sanitisation of arts, literature, culture, and life in general. However, with India being the vast country that it is, and with such a widely dispersed population, large numbers of people managed to remain untouched by the influences of ideologies formulated by colonists and nationalists: While a traditional moral conservatism was being reconstituted, it had limited impact on the ground.[9] Weaving through these ideological intersections were subaltern voices and traditions creating yet another site of resistance. Pockets of people continued to live their daily lives as they were, based around beliefs, practices, traditions, and rituals that had been handed down through generations, some of which are still visible within Gujarat's tribal and rural areas.

One example of this can be seen in the month of March. When the harvests are done and the granaries are full, amidst blossoming trees and flowers, diverse categories of tribal communities converge in central areas to celebrate and sell their products. It is during this *mela* (fair) that the boys and girls of the community are able to browse and select their partners to then go off and elope together, without any parental interference whatsoever. Then there is also the tradition known as *ghar jamai* (house husband) amongst the Tadvis in the Narmada district: for families who have borne only daughters, the bridegroom is allowed to come and live in the familial home of the wife, and the land continues to be in the wife's name. In a survey by Vikalp, we were surprised to learn that ownership of land in these areas was largely still with the women. Men who go to live in their wives' homes are not seen as 'any less of a man' for being a *ghar jamai* but instead an asset to families dependent on the produce from their land.

In three villages of Chhotaudepur—namely Surkheda, Ambada, and Sanada—it is the bridegroom's sister who heads the wedding procession, marries the woman, and takes home the bride for her brother; a practice that has evolved to overcome a 'curse' upon the village in which men would lose their lives if

[9] Gupta, Charu. *Sexuality, Obscenity and Community Women, Muslims, and the Hindu Public in Colonial India*. Permanent Black, 2001, p. 85.

they themselves went to fetch the bride. It is also no strange sight in these areas to see women out ploughing the fields, and it is well known that tribal areas have better sex ratios as compared to the national averages.

What I share as a socio-historical background of Gujarat is naturally sketchy and limited as it is learnt through field visits; I make no pretence of academic analytical work. I am simply sharing what I have seen in small vestiges of tradition—practices that differ from dominant-caste patriarchal structures—that challenge our norms and allow us a glimpse into the diversity within these 'outer' communities. Of course, the *Sanskritisation* process, economic factors and others have brought in many changes, but we were still able to witness several customs that continue to illustrate the uneven influences and processes of changing intersections.

An attempt to unearth any 'queer' stories, histories, art forms, or expressions existing in Gujarat is valid, both because these are stories that demand to be told and they also debunk the notion that trans and genderqueer identities are a 'western' phenomenon. Despite the sanitisation of many aspects of culture, it is still possible to trace footprints of 'queerness' in Gujarat's history, especially if we consider the notion of 'queer' to encompass 'not merely about [...] LGBT persons, but about loosening up the rigid structures of caste, gender and compulsory sexuality' which so far is the most fitting definition of the word that I have found, expressed as such by Arvind Narrain: it's about questioning notions of purity, muddying rigid boundaries and opening out a space for those at the margins of hegemonic structures which make up our society.[10]

Bhavaai is a form of folk theatre that has existed in Gujarat for a long time, a tradition in which men perform the role of female characters, dressed in female clothes. The art of Bha-

---

[10] Narrain, Arvind. 'Queering Democracy: The Politics of Erotic Love.' In *Law Like Love: Queer Perspectives on Law*, edited by Alok Gupta and Arvind Narrain. New Delhi: Yoda Press, 2011, p. 3.

vaai is rooted in the non-normative, stemming from dissent with the mainstream views of a caste-ridden society. The originator of Bhavaai was excommunicated from his own caste after rescuing a girl from a non-dominant caste and claiming her as his daughter. Some of the Bhavaai plays present a scathing review of the caste-ridden social structure: people belonging to different levels of social strata, ranging from king to knave, are portrayed in Bhavaai.[11] However, Bhavaai too suffered a setback under the social-reform movements of the colonial times as 'litterateurs, both Hindu and Muslim, launched puritan campaigns to cleanse the precolonial Indian literature',[12] a trend captured eloquently in the story 'The One Who Creates' by Nanabhai Jebaliya, found in Gujarati school text books. The tale is of an anxious Brahmin school master, who asks a Bhavaai performer to leave after the first day of his performance, due to fears of the 'influence' it could have on his students. The story does not mention what particular adverse influences the play would have had on the learners. Instead, we must infer from our own knowledge of Bhavaai and its dialogues—often imbued with double meanings—what the school master feared.

Amidst these emerging trends of morality and puritanism, there is evidence of a countermovement in which 'erotic consumerism became a part of the publishing boom in Uttar Pradesh, surreptitiously disturbing the dominance of clean literature'.[13] Perhaps it was within this context that the Gujarati book *Chumban Mimansa* was published by S.S. Mehta and Brothers of Kashi in 1929. Offering erotic pleasure,

---

[11] Claus, Peter J., Sarah Diamond, and Margaret Ann Mills. *South Asian Folklore: An Encyclopedia: Afghanistan, Bangladesh, India, Nepal, Pakistan, Sri Lanka.* Routledge, 2003, p. 63.

[12] Sharma, Pandey Bechan. *Chocolate and Other Writings on Male Homoeroticism.* Translated by Ruth Vanita. Durham & London: Duke University Press, 2009, p. xxxi.

[13] Gupta, Charu. *Sexuality, Obscenity and Community Women, Muslims, and the Hindu Public in Colonial India.* Permanent Black, 2001, p. 50.

Chumban Mimansa describes the history, development, and methods of kissing. It was subsequently translated into Hindi and, interestingly, the cover stated that it was meant only for private circulation—apparently to meet the moral injunctions that both Victorian Britain and the nationalist leaders had put out against any 'obscene production of material'.[14]

One of the earliest published pieces of literature on same-sex love in Gujarat appeared in *Janmabhoomi*, a nationalist newspaper, as part of a daily series in 1936. Written by Zaverchand Meghani, *Niranjan* was an attempt to shed light on the 'untouched corner of sexual perversion', as per the author. The decades between the 1860s, when the British imposed Section 377 criminalising homosexuality, and the writing of the novel *Niranjan* was more than enough time for the stigma and shame evoked by the law to spread its influence far and wide. Ideals of marriage, procreation, and the family unit birthed shame and stigma around same-sex attraction: 'a homophobia that was marginalised and ineffective in precolonial society became dominant in the course of the nineteenth century, especially amongst the educated class'.[15] Half a century later, we do find themes of same-sex relationship/ attraction in Gujarati literature again. A novel published in 1992, *Mira Yagnik Ni Dayari*, written by Bindu Bhatt, is based on the attraction between two women living in a hostel. It was translated to Sindhi and even won a Sahitya Akademi award. It was also awarded the Goverdhanram Tripathi Award in 1993. In 2011, Kaajal Oza wrote the novel *Purna Apurna*, which dexterously weaves the story of a trans man within a complex social milieu.

Meghani was perhaps amongst the first authors in Gujarat who wrote a work in an era when homosexuality was intensely contested. The late nineteenth-century imposition of Section 377

[14] Gupta, Charu. *Sexuality, Obscenity and Community Women, Muslims, and the Hindu Public in Colonial India*. Permanent Black, 2001, p. 54.
[15] Sharma, Pandey Bechan. *Chocolate and Other Writings on Male Homoeroticism*. Translated by Ruth Vanita. Durham & London: Duke University Press, 2009, p. xxxi.

of the Indian Penal Code made it possible at the time to criminal-
ise sex between two adult men. The story, named after the main
character, follows a same-sex attraction between a professor and
a young hosteller, Lalwani. We see Niranjan's first interaction
with Lalwani as a kind of duty-bound affection, slowly flowering
into friendship and later maturing into love; what stands out in
the book is all its complexities refusing a singularity of interpretation. The latter half of the story is indeed about same-sex attraction, despite the fact that the physical sexual aspect remains
unstated in the narrative which deftly steers clear of the shame
and stigma around same-sex attachment.

Meghani's book followed the publication of *Chocolate* by Pandey Bechan Sharma 'Ugra', which openly spoke about homo-erot-
ic love and physical attraction between men; the 'Chocolate' here
is a colloquial subcultural code, which he 'briefly brought into
wider circulation by his usage in the title'.[16] Meghani and Ugra
both wrote on a similar theme in different states, Meghani in Gujarat and Ugra in Uttar Pradesh, but they did so in literary forms
that varied. Ugra wrote openly and explicitly, not refraining from
telling us of the deep yearnings of lovers, mentioning kisses and
hugs. The stories are told in the voice of a strong, disapproving
narrator representing the condemnation of mainstream society.
Ugra was strongly advised against publishing the stories, advice
he did not heed. On publication, *Chocolate* received both appro-
bation and praise.

A decade later in his story, Meghani resisted naming the
relationship overtly, instead leaving it ambiguous, even in the
thoughts of the protagonist, as Niranjan is shown to be uncom-
prehending of the intense surge of feelings that Lalwani evokes.
Perhaps Meghani was following an age-old tradition best described by Vanita and Kidwai in the following words: 'in most
cases when such attachments are documented or represented in
history, literature, or myth we have no way of knowing whether

---

[16] Ibid., p. xxx.

they were technically "sexual" or not'.[17] Meghani also felt compelled to share that although he based his other stories on personal experiences, he had nothing personal on which to base the
story of *Niranjan*. He may have had good reason not to divulge
the source from which the story sprang.

The story was published as a book in 1941. In the preface to
the second edition, Meghani notes that the story was received
well both by the general public and by regional critics. He does
not deny us the truth, though, that the ending in the second edition is quite different from that of the first. The original story
concludes with Niranjan dissolving his marriage; however, in the
second edition, he marries the woman he has been engaged to.
Meghani tells us that 'people who were deeply interested in the
nuances of the story met me personally, while others wrote and
rebuked me that such an end did not integrate or weave in well
with the rest of the story. This criticism stayed in my heart. I also
felt that it was a mistake. The consequence is evident in the last
two chapters.' Even though the novel ends on the social reformist
ideal of a heterosexual marriage, it would be erroneous to assume that Meghani was simply subscribing to this ideal. Perhaps
it is critical to read the protagonist's decision as also emanating
from a sense of profound disappointment when Lalwani refuses
to go along with him, making the novel a reflection of a lived
reality for many queer people, both past and present.

Of course, stories don't just exist within the pages of books.
There are numerous less well-told and even little-heard stories
about same-sex couples who find ways to love and live with one
another, and women who manage to find pathways through
which they can break out of the patriarchal system, dismantling
it in ways that remained invisible, enabling themselves to live
how they wished. For instance, we have heard of brothers from

---

[17] Vanita, Ruth. 'Preface', In *Same-Sex Love in India Readings from Literature and
History*, edited by Ruth Vanita and Saleem Kidwai. Macmillan India Limited,
2001.

tribal, Dalit, and religious minority communities with whom their sisters had talked of their love for women, and so these siblings drew a pact with each other: the brothers would marry their sisters' girlfriends, and because remarriage in these communities is not a taboo, the brothers could marry again, which would still allow the two women to live together. There were other women who had acquiesced to a heterosexual marriage in full knowledge that they would swiftly return home. Such an action, while arousing suspicion about their character, nonetheless facilitated a life lived in close companionship with their 'friend'. Same-sex marriages have also been performed by pundits in temples away from the censoring eyes of the larger society. All the time, in these many ways, women who loved women and trans persons have crafted out spaces for themselves either by pushing the boundaries within given structures or by simply refusing to fall in line, making it evident that like in many other structures of 'patriarchy', negotiation is possible within intersecting realities. Several of these multiple realities are constantly in flux and bear upon one another while defining as well as differentiating experiences. No oppression or domination can uniformly be labelled as greater or lesser. The waves recede and return.

Similar stories also exist in the royal households of Gujarat. Prince Manvendra Singh Gohil, in an interview with me, shared a story about a princess who was married during the pre-independence years. As a young teenager, she had shown traits of typically 'masculine' behaviour. Growing up, it was not her habit of chain-smoking and drinking—quite a common practice amongst the women in Rajput royal families—that caught everyone's attention, but rather her 'manly behaviour', and a 'certain independence' that marked her out. The princess was well known for her hunting skills. Sitting astride a horse, with a hat that barely allowed her short crop of hair to peep out, feet clad in hunting boots placed firmly in stirrups, she rode out, looking straight ahead and responding with alacrity to the villagers' calls of SOS when leopards and bears damaged crops and attacked human beings. Such was her bearing and behaviour that those who recalled her remarked, 'That one, she was no woman'. This princess was married during the pre-independence years, and even during the years spent with her husband she was known not to behave like a typical 'wife' might be expected to; moving around freely, socialising in and outside her community 'unveiled', and rarely seen in the traditional garb of a Rajput princess except on public festivals and functions.

Not long after her marriage, she left her husband to return home to her paternal state. Some say that her husband also preferred members of the same sex, and had fallen in love with a Muslim man who lived on the estate that his wife's parents ruled. It seems that each of them found their love along Gujarat's river banks, amidst the richly endowed forests green with thick trees, home to wild animals and a source of livelihood to the tribal people who lived there. The princess acquired her own bungalow and chose a tribal woman to act as her live-in housekeeper. Whispers circulated within the family that the tribal woman had cast some kind of profound magical spell over the princess, having bewitched her so completely that even they had to first approach her if they wished to speak with the princess or seek a favour from her. The princess invited her closest friends and relatives to attend a ritual performed by her and the tribal woman, which was conducted in a temple of the Goddess Amba that still stands today. An attendee of the ritual told Manvendra that it was a form of a marriage ceremony between the two women. This event took place somewhere in the 1960s.

Not much is known about the tribal woman, other than the fact that she was a rebel like the princess. She organised workers in her community to strike, which were seen as 'disruptions' that delayed production, caused losses, and led to closures of textile factories in the region. The two women built a relationship lasting three decades, sharing a home adorned with specimens of taxidermy, remnants of the princess' hunts, including an upright black bear with a drinks tray balanced in his outward-facing paws, and other eccentric decorations. Several years later, the princess remortgaged the country bungalow and had to move back to her in-laws' house, where it was said she met her death by smoking; one night, a burning cigarette butt fell on the mattress where she lay and the slow, smouldering fire engulfed her. Some others say she was deliberately put to sleep to maintain family honour. Ironically, on the day of her funeral, the whole town was closed, markets and banks shut, businesses suspended, in order to pay homage to her.

It is safe to assume that there would have been several 'gay' royals throughout the ages, but not many of them were publicly 'out' until the Gujarati prince Manvendra Gohil. Manvendra was brave enough to reveal his sexuality, despite initial family hostilities accusing him of sullying the royal family's honour, and an equally hostile reception from some amongst the public. Gujarat has also been home to one of the first few artists who openly claimed his homosexuality in India: Bhupen Khakhar. Khakhar used his art to tackle some of India's most taboo subjects, such as the incessant Hindu-Muslim conflict, as well as the invisibilisation of homosexuality.[18] It was in Vadodara that he found his art style and a supportive community of artists who encouraged him to make Gujarat his home. As a gay artist, his paintings openly explored themes of gender definitions and identity, a rare subject in those days.[19] He created a stir in the world of art, and amongst all of us in the community as well.

Away from palaces and celebrities, there are many more gender queer stories told of times both past and present in Gujarat. Queer narratives that are passed down within our communities may rarely find a place in the annals of histo-

[18] 'Smashing India's Sexual Taboos.' October 29, 2002. http://news.bbc.co.uk/2/hi/entertainment/2372697.stm.
[19] Hyman, Timothy. *Bhupen Khakhar*. Chemould Publications and Arts, 1998.

ry, their presence erased from the maps and the newer world that throngs the street, but these stories live on in the collective memory of our community, passed down through word of mouth. Our stories survive us. An elder in our community once told Sylvie, a trans woman activist, the tale of a temple and a community of *kinnars* who once lived in the place where the spectacular building of the Vadodara Court stands today. Ensconced inside the inner sanctum of this temple, Bahuchara Mataji[20] watched over her community of *kinnars* who congregated every day in the quiet of the temple to offer her prayers and seek her protection. The temple was located here till Maharaja Sayaji Gaekwad III asked for the land to be given to him so that the Nyay Mandir could come up here in memory of his wife. This is how the temple of justice came to be located in Vadodara in the place that was once inhabited by the kinnar community and their goddess. Behranpur is where the *kinnar* community now lives.

Another layered story of gender lies buried in the *dargah* of Hazrat Musa Suhaag[21] at Shahibagh in Ahmedabad. It is a story replete with signs and symbols that we would in our present time call 'queer'. However, I refrain from naming it so; suffice it to say that the story is embedded in the non-normative. Musa Suhag[22] belonged to a revered Sufi order, the Suhrawardi Silsila (lineage). As per the story, when Musa first visits Nizamuddin Auliya's shrine, he is filled with contempt for the women singing in gratitude at the fulfilment of their wishes. As a result, he

---

[20] Bahuchara Mataji is one of the Hindu goddesses who is worshipped by the transgender communities in India. There are several different folk stories told in relation to her. Several of them dwell on gender transformation, creating a space outside the binary.

[21] It was from Mario Da Penha that I first heard the story of Musa Suhag. I gratefully acknowledge him and Nighat who translated much of the content from Urdu to English.

[22] The meanings of 'suhag' include auspiciousness, love, and caring. A woman whose husband is alive is known as a 'suhagan'. Thus, the word 'suhag' denotes a blessed and auspicious state of conjugality for a woman.

is punished. The articulation of the punishment comes to him through a revelation in a dream. He is forbidden from visiting Medina, the city where the Prophet is buried. Unable to see what he has done wrong, Musa seeks help from another holy man, who upon deep meditation tells him that he had hurt the sentiments of Nizamuddin Auliya by his contempt for women when he had visited the mausoleum in Delhi. The holy man advises Musa to return to Nizamuddin Auliya's *dargah* and beg his forgiveness, before planning to visit the Prophet's tomb in Medina.[23]

It is at this juncture that a transformation occurs in Musa. Before going to the shrine, Musa shaves his beard and moustache, dons women's clothing and wears bangles on his wrists. When he hangs a *dhol* (drum) around his neck, he resembles those very women whom he had ridiculed at Nizamuddin's shrine earlier. In this state, he arrives at the shrine and starts circumambulating Nizamuddin's tomb. While doing this, he is blessed with a shower of divine illumination (*tajillyat-e-rabbani*), which is so powerful that Musa falls to the ground and loses consciousness. During this state of unconsciousness, the divine secrets (*asrar-e-ilahi*) are revealed to him. The veils (*hijabaat*) separating him from God are lifted in an instant, and Musa's consciousness is transformed/raised to a much higher level.[24]

From that day onwards, Musa's life changed. He shed his masculinity, dressed like women, wore bangles, and started living with the *hijras*, singing and dancing and doing *dhamaal* (ecstatic dance performed by devotees at shrines) like them. The story does not end here. It is said that Musa happened to visit the city of Ahmedabad with his *hijra* family once and continued to sing and dance with them. The *ulema* (religious scholars) of the city were disapproving of his ways, and they forcefully dressed him in

[23] YouTube. December 25, 2020. https://www.youtube.com/watch?v=dMKWH-D7P2MA.

[24] YouTube. December 28, 2020. https://www.youtube.com/watch?v=CwEaRN-Qyni0.

white as befitted a holy man, and dragged him to offer prayers at a mosque. As soon as the Imam (prayer leader) started reciting the prayers in the mosque, however, Musa's white apparel miraculously turned into a bright red one. Everybody was shocked. Musa explained it thus: 'My *khavind* (husband) is immortal. He can never die. So why are these people trying to turn me into a *bewa* (widow) by dressing me in white?'[25]

On hearing the story, I wondered if Musa's journey to Nizamuddin Auliya's *mazaar* had more to do than to bow in prayer to the saint. Unbidden and unconsciously, Amir Khusro's verse rose in my mind:

> 'Khusro has given himself to Nizam
> You made me your wife when our eyes met.'

There are many other stories which the queer community in Gujarat has interwoven with their general beliefs in order to validate their relationships. There is a belief, for instance, that while standing in the Mahi River, which diagonally slices Gujarat from its south-west to north-east, you can tell nothing but the truth. It is said that two women, standing hand-in-hand and knee-deep in the river with their faces turned to the rising sun, can make a promise of staying together forever, even as they drink the river's water cupped in their palms.

Others conceal their love; they tattoo the names of their beloved under shirtsleeves and collars. Others still need not be so secretive. Tucked deep in an interior village in a district of the Saurashtra region during one of our home visits there, we heard the story of the affirmation a queer couple had received from their dominant-caste community of landowners in the year 2010. As evidence of the acceptance of their parents and community, the elderly parents of the couple told us that the entire community in the village had stood witness to their transmasculine son and

---

[25] YouTube. December 28, 2020. https://www.youtube.com/watch?v=CwEaRN-Qyni0

his wife taking a round of the fire in their first Holi celebration, a ritual symbolising the couple receiving an affirmation as man and wife in front of the whole community.

An introduction to queer Gujarat would not be complete without a mention of Maitri Karaar. Although sounding far-fetched, it is not wholly untrue to claim that 'official' same-sex unions were happening in Gujarat almost 50 years ago, preceding even the 'world's first-ever legal recognition of same-sex unions' in Denmark in the late 1980s. Maitri Karaar, literally translating to 'friendship contract', implies a real 'legal recognition', stamped and signed by court officials. Of course, the legal entitlements and civil rights it could have offered remain wholly ambiguous compared to official same-sex unions in Denmark and other Western countries, but still, in the queer community, to have a pocket of India make such a remarkable claim is an enormous thing, especially when one thinks of the little freedom women have generally enjoyed in the country.

These ruptures with mainstream tradition reveal the resil-ience of people and communities determined to present alter-natives to the norm. It is through these narratives that we get a sense of a multilayered Gujarat and its queer strands, alive as the spoken and the unspoken, written and performed, lurking parallel and on the underside, its faint lines visible in spite of the wide-sweeping dominant influences over time.

3

You Write, and I Will Tell

Until a few years ago, Chhotaudepur was in the Vadodara district, located in central Gujarat; it is now a district in itself, right on the border of Madhya Pradesh. It is largely populated by the Rathwa tribe, with an undeniably rural landscape; it has also retained some traditions that bear the mark of times past like the weekly *haat* held in the heart of Chhotaudepur. The *haat* is a splash of brilliant colours. On Wednesdays, crowds throng the streets, scrutinising and bargaining for daily necessities like spices, household goods, clothes, slippers, and utensils, all arrayed invitingly in open stalls. Jute bags and mats line the street on which a variety of vegetables lie in small heaps. The customers can buy any one or many of these vegetables without the hassle of a weighing scale. A way of 'market-ing' handed down through the generations. This, then, was the ancient crossing at which a bunch of us activists in Vikalp first encountered Shashi.

I had stooped down to pick up tomatoes at the same time as Shashi did, also making for the same heap. Our heads bumped against each other's and our hands touched. As we were bent low in close proximity, a whiff of sweat enmeshed with the familiar smell of a dolomite crushing unit introduced Shashi to me as one of the workers whom we were reaching out to through our programme on sexual health in collaboration with the government of Gujarat. I looked up to see a pair of eyes filled with the irrepressible mirth of a child. We laughed in unison and I watched her gracefully fade into the market crowds, but not before we had asked her where and when we could meet Shashi's employer. 'You know where it is, just outside Ekalbara village, opposite the old *mahuva* tree. Ask for Hanifbhai. He is in the factory around 11 a.m.'

The next day we met Hanifbhai. Surprisingly, he was cordial and met us with a smile on his face; surprising because of the 'notoriety' we had acquired after filing a PIL regarding the safety of workers. As an organisation, we were suspect. He asked us to visit the following week. The delay in giving us an appointment was clearly a way to verify the truth about our partnership with the government.

The next week found us at Shashi's workplace. As we walked alongside the grey-white dolomite stones piled on the sides of the broken road, we found an explanation for the white pall of dust ahead and all around us; even the treetops and roofs were cloaked in white powder. These stones quarried from a village nearby are dumped outside the factories, and here they are crushed into powders of varying thickness for different uses such as glassmaking, toothpastes, and soaps.

On our way back out of the factory, we spotted Shashi. But she did not meet our eye. On the days that followed, Shashi was reluctant to join the meetings. A few weeks later, when she did start joining the meetings, she would sit quietly. We continued to visit regularly and meet the workers. Sitting under the *mahuva* tree, outside the crushing unit, or at a quiet tea stall, over several weeks as other workers' lives slowly began to unfold, Shashi too began to talk. However, she initially chose to talk about the 'safe' parts of her life that had no bearing on her gender identity and sexual preference. 'Here, in Chhotaudepur, I was born in a village right here, in my father's house. A midwife came to help my mother deliver. I am the first child. My parents are followers of Raimuni. He is the "religious messenger" of our tribal beliefs and religion. My father was…well, he was not steadfast in his relationship with my mother. When I was a little over two years old, my mother left him…' She looked away briefly, and then continued matter-of-factly, 'My father got married to some other woman and brought her home. After that, my mother could no longer live there. Often, they would all argue and fight. This was the breaking point. Even earlier she had known about my father's relationships with other women, but she had turned a blind eye. This time, however, another woman was actually living in her house. I suppose it must have been hard for her. So, she went to her maternal home and took me with her. Then my parents separated. After my mother left my father, she lived with her parents and worked in the fields on daily wages and raised me. By the time the actual separation happened amongst our respective community members, I was old enough to understand what had happened. My mother and I share a special relationship, and I would gladly do anything for her. She has suffered so much, but I admire her courage. I had the option to return to my father and live with him and his wife, and I thought about it, but decided against it. I love my mother more than I do my father. I was raised by my mother.

'As soon as my mother got her separation endorsed by our respective relatives, my maternal grandparents and an uncle pressured my mother to get married again. She married a young man from a nearby village. He too was a farmer like my father. Now I live with my stepfather, my younger brother, and his wife. I love my siblings.'

She continued, 'My stepfather did send me to school. I must have been seven or eight years old then, and all I could think of was playing all the time. I had no interest in studying or going to school. My second father did not like nor care for me. His behaviour was stepfatherly towards me. It hurt me intensely at the time. I felt hated, often spurned and rejected. Relatives and neighbours often made remarks that pierced my heart. "That woman there," they would say, and the woman they pointed to was my mother, "That woman there has brought with her another man's son." And they would say within my earshot, deliberately, "There goes the one born of another man."

'When I look back, I feel my childhood was so dark, with little laughter and even less warmth or fun. My stepfather paid no attention to me. He thought I was no good at anything, and especially since I showed no inclination to read and write. My father, I mean my stepfather, insisted that I go out to graze the cattle in the forest. I think it was around this time that my younger brother was born. I am fond of him. I got to watch him as he grew into a toddler, then a young man, and now he is married. I used to take care of him while my mother worked. As the days passed, I grew up somehow. We all do.'

Shashi spoke lovingly of her village to us saying, 'Whatever the odds, Chhotaudepur is where I belong; Jamla is the village from where I come. It is only about two kilometres from here.'

She looked away from us and seemed to be counting. 'In the village, families live in *fediyas*. I was counting these to let you know the number of people living in our village. There are around 200 families; we all know one another and we know our hills, trees, seasons and our farms, my people, my language. This is what I know and love. But there have been times when I have had to move out....' She paused, and we waited for her to continue.

An activist amongst us broke the silence, 'Why did you have to go?'

'Some times are hard.' Shashi's forehead puckered in annoyed lines. Then she lapsed into silence again. Unease hung in the air. The indistinct mumble of workers at lunchtime wafted in to fill the small, empty space left by Shashi's suspended story. As a team, we had a hunch about her gender identity. Also, we were well aware of the various rumours that floated around about sexual relationships between men. Shashi figured in them prominently. But these were open collective secrets, impregnable at the individual level. In our conversations and meetings that had happened earlier, we had often brought up the subject, mostly in the context of sexual health and protection. But Shashi rarely spoke or when she did, she preferred to plunge into mundane, everyday details, deflecting the subject of gender identity and sexual preference at the slightest possibility of its revelation with regard to her. This time too, when Shashi spoke again, her tone was flat; turning to the others in the group, to seek their affirmation, she rattled on hurriedly, 'Most of us have lands, big or small, and we are all farmers. My forefathers worked on the fields and so do my father and my mother. So does everyone else here. We do not get other kinds of work, though some of us can grow enough food for the year. But the trouble is that we do not find work, and everyone needs work to earn money, right? We need the money to buy what our land cannot give. Here, the work that we can get is in the factories. That's where I am working too, but it does not pay well. It is not even a regular income. Sometimes when you show up for work, they just ask you to come back another day. One cannot live with this kind of uncertainty. Most families migrate for work outside the village in October or November. They go to Kathiwad for work and return around February/March during the Holi festival to till the land, and so on, year after year. People leave the village to earn a living, and then return. Some, however, continue to stay back and work in the factories here. Others, like me, have tried both kinds of employment.' Then suddenly interrupting her train of thought, she brought the meeting to an end, 'And now it is time to go back to work.'

And so it was; we could hear the workers returning to work. We were accustomed to abrupt ends to our meetings. But this time I was sure that I had heard a ring of relief in Shashi's voice as she got up and dusted the sand off her *lungi* and turned away with a wave of her hand, '*Aavajo*'.

'*Aavajo*,' the three of us from Vikalp replied in chorus.

We were pleasantly surprised the next day. Shashi walked into Vikalp's office with another worker from a different factory unit who had opened up about her gender identity and sexual preference. Shashi said, 'I was oscillating between telling and not telling you all, but when I met Sanu she told me that she knew you all. I asked her if she could bring me here and introduce me properly. I'd clearly begun to see the risks involved (in my lifestyle); my own health was ample evidence of the dangers I was in. I also learned about HIV/AIDS,' she explained, hesitantly and haltingly. 'I have been to *Badwa Buva* (traditional healer) but that medicine worked for only some time, then the itching and soreness reappeared. I did not really understand that the STI has a specific cycle, and that the absence of full treatment can bring it on again. The earlier treatment had already cost me quite a bit, and so I felt upset and cheated by the private doctor.'

In response, we followed up with counselling and accompanied her to the hospital, making sure that she adhered to the prescribed treatment. Shashi began to bring her partners for treatment and counselling to us. She said to us, 'In the beginning, most of them scoffed at my suggestions; I think their masculine egos got hurt. I did feel awkward myself, but when I shared with them my improved health status and explained all that I've learned, they agreed to come along.'

It was in this context that Shashi began to open up to us, but just as I had recorded the details of her early life, she vanished into thin air. I wondered if she was uncomfortable sharing more with us? What was it that drove her away, where did she go? There was no hint of anything in her narrative about what could have prompted her to up and leave.

At the beginning of our conversation, Shashi had said to me, 'It is nice to talk about my life. I like it. You can use my real name. People over here already speculate about my identity, but they do not really know. I am happy talking about my life, because I have never done that before, never. It is much nicer talking here than over there. Not everyone will understand. I can talk about my life freely and have it written out. I cannot think about writing it myself. I have only recently learnt how to write my name in English.' Then smiling, she added, 'And you know why? Even if I did know to write, I am not sure I would sit and write it all down. But talking, yes. This is a good arrangement. You write, and I will tell you. But write in English, will you? Yes. English is good. My people here do not know about me. They will not read English. But at least the others who know English should know about us.'

She began telling me about her family, 'You know my formal name. Rathwa Sanmathbhai Chintanbhai. This is how everyone is named here in our tribal way of life. You know that by now. The name first has our tribal identity, followed by the individual's name, and then the name of the father. For men, you add *bhai* and for women it is *ben,* but I like my other name, Shashi, without the addition of *bhai.*' We exchanged a smile of shared knowledge at this.

Shashi did not identify as male, so her choice of a name without the epithet *bhai* enabled her to distance herself from it. This decision made a vital difference to her self-perception. 'You know my formal name. But I never liked it from the start; from as far back as I can remember, I felt I was a girl. Though I was known as a son, male and all that, from deep within me, I knew that I was a woman. It just did not feel right to be known as a man. On the outside, I was born as a man, but inside I felt I am a woman. I did not feel right in my male body. I live in these two conflicting worlds. Earlier, I had not known of anyone who was like me, until I met Aju. Then she introduced me to Sanu. This is how I am in this office. I used to be diffident to come on my own over here in this office. There was no one like me in my world. At least, I did not know anyone until I met Aju and Sanu.

'Unlike other men, and that includes both my fathers, I had no problem doing household chores with my mother. On the contrary, I enjoyed doing the chores. Nor did I play the usual games boys played. I would often dream of wearing women's clothes, imagine myself adorned with powder, paint, jewels, and braided hair. Whenever I got a chance, I indulged myself secretly. Wearing a *bindi* or bangles gave me some solace, but it was a solace that dissipated sooner than the time it takes for dead leaves to fall off a tree. The occasions were so few and far between, while my longing and awareness of who I truly was so intense. It continues to press upon me. Sometimes I think my whole life will be over in this longing, caught in these two worlds: one, an unnatural make-believe world of being a man, and the other inhabited by who I really am. Now there is the pressure to get me married!

'Since I was no good at school, my stepfather sent me into the forest to graze animals. This decision turned out to be good for me. It helped me connect with other children, and it took me into a different world and offered opportunities for friendship. I, along with some others, used to take the animals into the forest. Families who sent their animals for grazing gave us money, so I started earning at an early age. When I used to wake up to take the animals out for grazing, the sky would still be filled with stars. I would gaze at them through sleep-smeared eyes, and there were times when I simply wanted to turn around and fall asleep again. But it was also a time of fun and frolic. I'd do the cooking with my mother, rolling the *roti* and chopping and peeling the *shak,* fetching water from the well, the two of us together quietly going about our work. It also meant that one set of chores for the day was over. Then, it was time for me to go along with the other boys and girls to the forest. We would set off into the forest with our herd of cattle, slow and clumsy. Rumbling past households that were just awakening to the day, we would run ahead, alongside and behind the animals to keep them together and moving at one pace, swinging our sticks even as the jingling bells around the necks of the cattle told us the herd was on the right track. In the forest, we chased one another, racing, falling, and catching up. We played *gilli-danda* and *lan-*

gadi. When I look back at that time, I feel perhaps it was the best time and place for me. Away from home, in the forest, I learnt a thing or two.

'I remember the moment clearly. Not as a particular day or month, but in the way the sun rose in the forest. It broke with a gentle light, and as I walked past the huge *mahuva* tree I saw a boy and girl together. I knew the girl. She was the older of the two. They were having sex right before my eyes out in the open under the sky. I stood rooted, staring, and yet not really seeing. They did not see me. They were too lost in each other, and I, with myself. Later, much later, after the day was done, in the night and the other days that followed, images of that day and odd remnants which I did not think I remembered came back to me in bits and pieces. Incidents, gestures, glances, and words exchanged between boys and girls, sudden disappearances and appearances of partners, voices suddenly sinking to ominous whispers when I chanced upon pairs—all of it began to make sense. But at that time nothing resonated within me. I had no sexual desire yet, so there was no thread to which I could relate. I did not know who I could ask questions. I knew it was something that could not be discussed. I knew that much.

'How I knew that, I cannot say...We...we just know. Some of us, amongst my close group of friends, talked about it, but none of us really knew anything in detail, barring that children are the outcome of the act. It is difficult for me to pinpoint the exact moment when I came to know about sexual relationships. But if I were to name it, perhaps that was the moment, when I saw the boy and the girl in the forest.'

Ironically, it was the forest, considered the archetype of disorder and incoherence, that first brought home to Shashi an articulate awareness of sex. Even as the 'heritage' of secrecy around sex was passed down to yet another generation, that experience altered Shashi's understanding of human relationships inexplicably.

'Though the incident in the forest bothered me at first, I soon forgot about it. I was weighed down by my own preoccupations. My sense of self came through female identification, but the rest of the world denied me that experience. No matter what I did to fit into the role assigned to me as a male, I failed. I just could not turn away from my feeling of being a woman. Following the animals around as they gingerly roamed about and picked their way through the pathways to grass and shrubs, I found my way here in these forests. Separated from my friends, I was often left to myself with my thoughts. I talked to myself a lot those days. Not daring to talk aloud to anyone, I preferred my own company. As I grew older, I had to take on work that paid more. I was a fully-grown lad, I was told. I must have been 16 years old, maybe a year or two older, I do not know the exact age, when I began to work at construction sites and mines. In those days, we got 11 rupees daily as wages. I did the work of carrying stones and emptying them out onto the trucks. Or carrying water and sprinkling it to keep the cemented walls wet. Unlike our cattle-grazing days in the forest, most of us here were grown boys and girls of around 18 to 20 years. The others were far older. There was openness amongst us. Or maybe we were all at that young age when we were raring to explore and experience intimacies. Whatever the reasons, here I saw a far greater propensity to be open. Boys and girls mixed with one another freely.

'I had changed and now I understood what I saw. I was older now. I was taller, my voice had changed, and though I did not have a thick growth of hair like most boys, I nonetheless faced the prospect of facial hair appearing every morning. I resented that possibility and all those other imposed associations that made me a man over and over again. Often anger welled up inside me and I cried out against god for subjecting me to this duality in my life.

'It was while working at the construction site that I finally found myself in more ways than one. The openness amongst all of us brought me the recognition of my own sexual desire. I experienced intense stirrings, a longing for intimacy that I had not known previously. It was during this time that I saw very clearly that I was interested in boys. Though I connected with women easily, and till today I enjoy a real friendship with them, there was no electric current within me for them; it was the boys/men who moved me. Ever since I can remember, I felt I was different from the others around me, and now my attraction for people of the same sex reinforced that feeling—of being there and still of not being a part. ...There I was, unlike those boys who happily paired themselves off with girls, I could only look at the boys with longing, pain, and my tension of desire that found no sanction and yet it was there right inside me all the time. Then I met the boy with whom I had my first sexual experience. He was from my own village, but it had taken us that long to find each other. Just like me, he too felt drawn to men. It was an indefinable feeling of togetherness. We connected instantly and recognised our desire for one another. My fantasies and longing for a man found fulfilment. Our sexual relationship bonded us more, and I felt my isolation recede. Soon after, our newly found confidence led us both to respond positively to the overtures made by a man a little older than us. Now, the three of us were seeking pleasure and solace from each other's company. However, the furtive behaviour that we had to ensure was something I thoroughly disliked, but looking back, this relationship confirmed what I knew: the nature of my desire and the irreversibility of it. I was born this way.

'As I grew older, the pressure to marry increased. I have been putting it off but it keeps returning, and is ever stronger now. I do not know what to do. I love my mother and she insists I marry. My birth father wants to fulfil his obligation as a father as well. He too wants me to get married. Marriage is not for me, I know. After my experiences at the construction site, I knew that marriage was not possible for me. Not with a woman anyway. Did you know that in three villages in Chhotaudepur—Surkheda, Ambada, and Sanada—a woman marries a woman? She heads the wedding procession and garlands the bride, and all the marriage rituals are performed between them. In these villages, there were three *dev* (gods) who did not marry. As a result, no young man marries there. If anyone goes against this tradition, their marriage is ruined. In order to prevent that catastrophe, the intended bridegroom's sister goes in her brother's place, and marries the would-be-bride of her brother. That's what I mean when I say one woman marries another woman... Marriage is an all-important event in everyone's life. Even if there is a bar placed on it, people will come up with a solution. And what a solution this is! Generally, two women and two men cannot live together or marry one another. But here...for a while, it is allowed. Maybe these three deities were like me! Who knows? But how does one ward off this marriage pressure?'

I suggested to Shashi that we could talk to her mother and father. But she turned this offer down vehemently. 'They will not like an outsider telling them that their son is a woman.'

I persisted, 'This is not what we are going to tell them; we can tell them—'

Shashi interrupted me with, 'Whatever reason you give them, it will not be a good reason for them. We have lonely lives to lead. Except every now and then, when we find a partner....'

After these conversations, which continued over a fortnight, Shashi vanished. When she did not come to the office, we thought she had merely taken a break, but then we learnt that she had not reported for work at the factory either. We let a day or two go by. Unperturbed until then, we made perfunctory inquiries about her whereabouts with the workers whom we met. But we drew a blank. We asked Hanifbhai if Shashi had taken leave, but he shrugged and said, 'Only a few workers let us know that they would be absent; most simply do not turn up. There is an understanding that when they do not come for work, their wages are cut.' Besides, Shashi had started work with him only a few months back. All he could show us was an attendance sheet that had her name but no address. For a week, we waited for her to show up but there was no sign of her. We then went to the address she had written in our register. On our way there, we met her brother and mother. We needed no introduction to the two of them; the resemblance was unmistakable. Their bodies bore the tension that we carried in ours, searching for Shashi. As Shashi's friend introduced us, I saw how desperate they were for information about her whereabouts. They were suspicious of us, and yet hopeful that we would tell them where she was. The presence of Shashi's friend helped to ease the situation. We learnt from the family that generally, Shashi's absence did not extend beyond a day or two. 'This was the longest spell and there has not even been a phone call from her.'

Her mother had been to various people with whom Shashi was friends, but all of them had denied seeing her. Though Shashi's mother was convinced that 'a woman who bewitches all men here' would know...she said they were *langotiya yaars*, the woman apparently said she knew nothing. The mother kept saying though, 'I bet she knows, I am telling you she knows.'

After discussing all possibilities, we thought it was better to wait for a few days before approaching the police. Especially because Shashi's mother was so convinced that 'that woman would know'. Her son gently pulled her away, and as they walked away from us, we wondered who this woman was that Shashi's mother kept referring to. We were told she was a well-known sex worker in the area. Two weeks later, Shashi called one of our activists. She was calling from another number and spoke in a hurried, muffled tone; she wanted to meet two of us on a particular day and place. She did not want any of this to be told to her family. It was all getting more mysterious and this unsettled us. Is she safe? Where is she? Why can she not see us right now? But those questions remained unanswered. She had already disconnected the call. Clearly, she was under some pressure or someone's influence.

We had to wait for Tuesday afternoon, a full three days later. We met Shashi behind the tea shop, in the vegetable market. It was a quiet, slow-paced sunny day, with the lane almost bereft of people. Shashi had chosen the place and time well. She was dressed in a sari with long earrings, and bangles adorned her wrists. She told us she had joined Roshan *masi's* group of *hijras,* who live in shared households, and that was the reason none of us had seen her for so many days. She also informed us that her biological father knew about it. Since Shashi did not live with her father, it had not occurred to us to ask him about her whereabouts. She said she had joined the community of *masis* willingly. But now, she no longer wanted to stay amongst them and she wanted to know if something could be done to get her out. 'Is there a way out for me? If I stay there, I will commit suicide.'

The fact that Shashi had joined the community of *masis* took us completely by surprise. In our conversations, she had never hinted at it. However, rewinding our conversations, I heard and read the silences and signs in Shashi's narrative. They should have alerted me. I recalled the unease in the silence and an irritable puckered brow that Shashi wore when we had asked her why and when she had to move. She had kept quiet for a long time. She had even talked of marriage pressure. I realised that I had failed to listen closely and connect the dots. I had missed the opportunity to probe deeper and reach out to her. But would my listening more actively have helped in making a timely intervention? I was not sure. Now, however, Shashi was clearly seeking us out. We needed to respond.

We were aware that the community of *masis* was a closed group. They had rules and norms which were critical for a vulnerable group to have and live by. We respected their rules and this made our task more daunting and placed us squarely in a dilemma. Would it not be invasive if we were to intervene? How

could we make ourselves less offensive while asking them to allow Shashi to leave the community? It is well-known that once
one joins the *hijra* community one cannot leave it. A lot of money is spent by the *toli* on the new entrant. The primary person
in charge of this specific community was familiar to us. We decided that a bunch of activists, especially those from the local
area, would approach her and ask her to let Shashi leave on the
grounds that the family had sought us out and demanded her
return. We felt we should not mention that it was Shashi who
wanted to leave. We decided we would only bring that up as a
last recourse. But we needed to ascertain what Shashi thought of
this strategy.

We tried to contact the number from where she had called
earlier but were not able to get through. A week later, Shashi
called us. She told us she was aware that we had been trying to
call her. But the person whose number she used did not want
to be seen by Roshan *masi* to be supporting Shashi. These calls
had to be made surreptitiously, away from the gaze of Roshan
masi. The calls could not be long either. When we asked her if
we should say that her family wanted her back, she vehemently
opposed the suggestion, 'My father had to give them a signed
affidavit which said that he consented to my decision of joining
the *masis*.'

'What about your mother; she had not given her consent, we
can say she wants you back?'

'My father is the authority—his say is what matters.' We
could sense that she wanted the conversation to be brief. There
was no other possibility but to let the community know that
Shashi wanted to leave. Finally, we approached Roshan *masi* and
told her Shashi did not want to stay in the community. She did
not believe us. When we asked that Shashi be brought face to face
with us all, Roshan *masi* said she was presently not there. Roshan
masi also discouraged us from waiting until Shashi's return, saying she had to go out herself.

We went to Roshan *masi* for several days after that. But she argued, 'I have spent a lot of money on her coming here. Who will compensate me? Shashi? She does not have this kind of money, this will impact the community adversely, and I cannot let this happen to all my children here. Shashi made a commitment to the community.'

We were at a loss with regard to overcoming this impasse, but as luck would have it, one of our activists saw Roshan *masi* in the Taluka Court engaged with an advocate known to us as an ally of the organisation. The activist lost no time in sharing with the team her idea that we should seek the help of this advocate in negotiating with Roshan *masi*. The next day we went to meet the advocate. We had just mentioned Shashi when the advocate intervened, saying, 'That one who has joined the *masis*? I know Roshan *masi* and even Shashi. I was the one who wrote out the document of consent given by Shashi and her father.' He heard us out and agreed to intervene and negotiate as an advocate. The involvement of an advocate known to both parties helped in resolving the problem. It took a few weeks but by the end of it, we managed to get Shashi out.

When Shashi returned, she had a lot to share. 'Before I came here, I had been talking to Roshan *masi* about joining them. I bonded with her instantly; it relieved me of such a burden to simply talk aloud to someone who felt the same. I thought joining them would be like living with people like me. Being here means we cannot be ourselves; all the time we have to pretend. In mainstream society, as a person having a male body, my yearning to dress as a woman would simply be ridiculed. I thought being amongst the *hijra* community would enable me to be myself and actually wear women's clothes every day.

'A part of me admired and envied the *masis*. They lived the life they wanted. And as long as I lived within this "respectable society" with whom I could not relate, I could never hope to live and dress the way I wanted, except on rare occasions. I felt conflicted and finally approached the *masis* to allow me to join their group. They told me they would think about it and let me know. Then they did not respond for a long time. I felt rejected by the very women I thought were like me.

'While all this was going on, my relationship with all of you was beginning to grow. All the same, I did not dare tell you or anyone else that I had been talking to the *masis*; though I did try to tell you at the factory about how I felt. But somehow I could not tell you any specifics then, or later when I came to the organisation because Roshan *masi* had not said a definite yes to my joining them. I felt if I told you I was joining Roshan *masi* and then she refused, it would unnecessarily become the talk of the town. I did not want my family to know anything. But I did tell my brother. I knew my mother would never let me go. What if she stopped me? What if someone reported me to the police? Frankly, I was sceptical about everyone. At that time, I did not trust anyone. So, I simply dropped out of contact with a whole lot of people I knew and with you all also. I joined the *masis* from my own father's house, and that is how even my mother did not know what I had done. Though I felt I had to tell my mother. But how was I to do it? I knew the *masis* would not hear of it. I wanted to leave. That was certain. I told only my brother. But my mother, no, no. I did not tell her.'

Shashi lowered her voice, thinking about those difficult days and hard decisions. 'My father too, when I told him about my decision, refused to hear anything further. "Why? Why?" he kept asking me. But what could I tell him? He did not understand. He was disappointed in me, his son, the male heir.... The *masis* would not have me unless my father gave formal permission. An affidavit had to be signed by him, and my father would not give me permission or sign the document. So we continued like that for many days, a tense silence lying between us. The *masi* community was pressing for more assurance than just my oral commitment. I stopped going to work in the factory; I stopped coming to see all of you. All of my energy was spent on convincing my father to sign, but he refused.

'I went on a fast. I did not eat a morsel. I simply did nothing all day. I threatened to end my life. When my father saw me morose and sullen, and not eating or drinking, he finally signed the affidavit. But this was not the end of my troubles. Now we had to give the *masis* money. I had some money, but not enough to meet what they wanted. I had a supportive relationship with my stepbrother so he stepped in to help me.

'The *masis* took me from my real father's home with a big procession, a band playing along, *masis* singing and dancing, flowers strewn along the way. I was adorned like a bride. My stepsister whom my mother calls "that woman"—her name is Amtiben—I wore her red wedding sari, a lot of jewellery and henna on my hands and feet. My pictures were taken, a video was made, and I was brought into the community with rituals and great respect. I do not recall all those ceremonies now. I was in a daze, leaving my family and home. At the *masis*, I was assigned to be a wife to one of them, and so I had to act in accordance with what my husband instructed. As a wife I had to do the sweeping, cleaning, fetching water, readying the bath, and laying out the clothes. All that was fine with me, I did not mind it at all. I am a woman, and I did not mind doing these household jobs. Besides, the community had hired help to do the chores. But I missed going about freely wherever I wished without anyone stopping me. This felt strange. First to live inside all the time, and then to step out chaperoned. My mobility was in their control. I told myself perhaps this is just for the initial few days, and then it will change—this surveillance. It feels like you are being looked after but that's not it. I thought it would change, but it didn't. They would not let me out of their sight. They even took away my phone. I could not call anyone. In my other life, I could go where I pleased without any hindrance. I had not anticipated this; to tell you the truth, I had no idea that all these restrictions would be put on me. Though I must say, being a woman and wearing women's clothes was a relief. But that was not all I wanted.

'The other problem was that I had to beg. This upset me so much, to beg for money,' Shashi shook her head ruefully. 'I did not like to beg. It hurt my self-respect. Whatever money I got, I could not keep with me, not a penny. From morning till evening, we had to go begging. It was not that it was tiring; I can work all day if I have to—it's just that I did not like begging at all, not at all. I had to go and beg even in the villages where people from our tribal community lived. I had also not counted on being confined to one room for days on end. I was feeling so dissatisfied. I simply could not adapt to this kind of change. The dissatisfaction became greater as months sped by. I think I lived there for five months? More? Ok, I do not remember the exact months. I wished to leave, simply leave. But I was not allowed to do so. Finally, my sister in the community gave me her phone and I called you. It was a relief to talk about what I was feeling. The *masis* have a strong grip; they are a powerful community. Being part of a community had fulfilled a crucial need in my life, and though I had overcome many hurdles in joining Roshan *masi*, now I felt suffocated. I must tell you that Roshan *masi* was the first person who really and truly understood me. But I knew I could not continue to live with them. I began to miss the days in the factory, I was earning there—I had full autonomy and control over my own money. I missed my family too.

'I knew that my mother would be the most affected. My brother did not tell my mother that he knew where I had gone. He kept his word. But once he saw how upset she was, he also joined her and began to threaten Roshan *masi* that he would hang himself and commit suicide if I was not allowed to return. My mother went to my stepsister's house and asked where I had gone. Almost every day she would go there, and Amti's house is almost a whole day's walk away. When Amti said she did not know anything, my mother would hurl abuses at her.

'My mother knew we were close, so she guessed Amti would know, and indeed she did know. But it was I who had asked Amti not to tell anyone. I knew that my mother would go to her house, but I never thought that she would begin abusing her, or that she would go there every day. Then, someone in the village recognised me while I was out begging. This hurt me a lot, begging from those who knew me. I thought about my mother and how she would feel if she got to know that I was out begging. But this is how my mother learnt the truth about me. A fierce fight broke out between the *masis* and my family members. My family felt humiliated, they said that I had lowered the family respect and honour by begging and joining the *masis*.

'In the *hijra* community, the control they have over each individual is tremendous. Once someone enters the community, it is very difficult to get out. The *masis* follow strict codes and traditions. Plus, they had spent money on me. I could understand that. I was earning for them, so my leaving the community would add to their losses. When someone leaves the community, it affects everyone; each of us has a role and it is like a family and I…but I could not live there—that was also the truth.

'The entire team at Vikalp collected money for me to give to the *masis*; some we paid right away, and some we promised to pay at a later date. I will work hard and return that amount. I prayed to god Jesus and Babadev. I believe in both gods so I prayed to them, promising an offering of the same amount if I could be released from the *masis*. I continue to believe in Jesus. Whenever I am in trouble, I go to the *girjaghar* where there are always 100 to 200 people praying, and God listens. That is where I go when I need my wishes to be granted.

'The life I had fantasised about with the *masis* was very different in reality. When my wish to be set free came true, there were no words to adequately describe how I felt. You have seen how the hills and the fields here begin to smile after the rains; it was something like that, my happiness on being released. The abundance one sees after the rains. Our hills and trees here all glow green. I was like them, glowing with happiness, all clean and new, back to my life as I knew it.'

After her return from the community of *masis*, Shashi decided to go to Kathiawad. 'I do not like the idea of staying here after all the fuss I've created. Besides, I am not sure if my return home would mean a renewal of the pressure to marry. Perhaps they think I have overcome my gender problem and I will now settle down with a woman. They do not understand. They think I am simply being pig-headed when I say I will not marry, but why should I ruin another woman's life? I have seen my stepsister, Amti, when she was married to a man like me…she was unhappy, and I'm sure he felt burdened too. Then there is the pressure to have children. And where do children come from? Marrying is self-entrapment. But many like me marry because they worry who will give them *roti* and take care of them in their old age. And so they pass as "regular men"; only the insiders know the entire truth. But I could not live like that—one look at me and anybody can guess there's a woman inside! It is written all over me. Yet, I could still be forced to marry a woman, and that is something I want to avoid. Plus I'd rather not face the neighbours and my community now having returned from the *masis*. I can do without their comments and censure. The best option for me is to simply go away. I have been in Kathiawad before. We stay and work there, earn and go back.'

When she returned from Kathiawad in March just before Holi, she came to meet us. 'The good thing over there was that work kept me occupied, and I was happy to be out in the open and away from everything over here. We worked in the fields picking cotton from six in the morning until six in the evening with an hour's break for lunch. It does get tiring, bending over the plants for so long in the sun. At least it is the winter sun, so it is hot but not as hot as in the summer. For me, after living in the *hijra* community, working out in the open meant freedom, and I did not have to face them or anyone else.'

We asked her if she had found someone there. Shashi confessed to having had short-term relationships but nothing more than that. 'It gets lonely. Of course, we find men to "hook up" with. These relationships might span a few months; when it is time to leave, it's also time for the relationship to end. Besides I had to earn enough to repay Roshan *masi*. Looking back I think she was kind to let me go. What if she had put her foot down? We did not have the money to go to court. What would I have done? I will try to meet Roshan *masi* and try to make up with her before I return to Kathiawad.'

Shashi stayed for another seven months in Chhotaudepur and then returned to Kathiawad. The next time she visited, she was excited. 'I have found someone. When I got back this time, newer people arrived. I knew only two workers from the previous time, but after working such long shifts together, friendships sprout quickly amongst workers. But the man I fell in love with is called Devesh. He arrived 15 days after my arrival there. He is younger than me and more educated, so my accounts were well looked after by him. He had a diary, and he made a note in that diary every day of our work, his and mine. We were given 100 rupees for our living expenses each week, and we lived in a room on the farm belonging to the *Seth* so we didn't have any rent to pay. We were supposed to receive 80 rupees every day in cash, though it was not given at the end of each day. Instead, we received our full payment only when it was time to return. If people had to leave before this date, then the *Seth* settled the accounts as per the number of days they had worked. Some of us, such as me, kept accounts by making vertical lines with charcoal on the walls of our room, so we could count the number of days we had worked. Of course, there are many instances in which workers are taken for a ride, especially since many of us cannot read and write. You see, workers like me do not really have any autonomy, or choice of work; to get our wages we have to work till the time of our return.

'Devesh and I lived in the same room and did our household chores together. I used to peel the vegetables and he would cook them; I rolled the *rotis* and washed our clothes, he washed the utensils. During the day we were busy, but the nights were good. We could sleep together and nobody had anything to say. Of course, people had a sense about us, but when you are not in your own community and neighbourhood there is a different kind of freedom. There was no voice inside me telling me to be careful. No fear of being caught. After a month over here, I will go to his house and see him in his district. In the village, we would not have been able to live like this, so close under one roof, but working on the farm had given us both an avenue to experience love in a way I have not done before. Going away was the best way out for me. There are many others like me, who need to get away. So yes, it is hard work, but it is also enjoyable. Sometimes money is not the only driving force for migration. I know two women who are living with one another; though they are from our village, they practically spend all their time in Kutch because they go out to work on the farms there.'

Two months later when we met Shashi, she looked under the weather. We learnt that she had gone to see her lover and live with his family. 'Over there we were seen as friends—"special friends". It felt strange after having lived as lovers. Somehow, I did not think of all this before going there. It was disappointing. His mother would talk with me and ask me to explain to him the importance of settling down with a woman. I would only nod. How could I tell her I was his woman? Most men like him succumb to marriage eventually. While I was there, marriage proposals came for him. Of course, I knew that ultimately he would marry, but so soon...when one stands face to face with reality, it is entirely different. All this changed our relationship entirely. Earlier he would try to pacify me, hug and hold me if I got angry or felt bad.' Shashi dropped her gaze and refused to look up as she said this, 'This time his behaviour was different. I know it has ended; this relationship of mine has ended. Maybe he will marry. I do not know, I do not want to know either. He will come to work this year also, so I don't know if I should go this year. It will be hard...I did not tell you earlier, but I have been through this before. Men leave us after making promises.

'Earlier also, I was pressured to marry. My biological father, who did not usually contact me, began getting in touch with me frequently. He was bound by duty, he said, to get his son married. And so he called me and sent messages with people who knew both families. My mother came under pressure as well. She also began to push me to go to my father. This was the first time that I had returned to my father's house after my parents separated. I had no clear idea what I would tell him, or how I would explain my refusal to marry. The prospect was daunting. Since I did not live with my father, he had no idea about me. But did my mother have some idea about me? I guess she may have had her suspicions. She was, anyway, aware of my fondness for feminine clothing and ornaments, but about my preference for men in the sense of sexual relationship with them, I don't know if she really knew, at least at that time.

'At my father's house when he began to talk of women and marriage, the reality of it all weighed down on me. I struggled to speak and I could not open my mouth. I could not muster the courage to tell him outright. On the other hand, I could no longer live that lie. One day and two nights after I reached there, I went up to my father and told him I could not marry a woman because I considered myself a woman. I loved men. My father could not understand me. I remember his puzzled face and the frown. His eyes filled with tears as he turned away from me to hide his pain and disappointment.

'I did not feel like staying there. But I could not return immediately to my mother's house either. What would I tell them?

The only place I could think of going was to my maternal uncle's house. I went there and started working with them. He ran a hotel, and I took up work there. The space provided me some measure of independence away from family and the pressure to be like them. Also, I did not want my mother worrying about me. She would be fine if she knew I was staying with people she knew. I let her know that I had spoken to my father and he was fine with me not marrying. But I could tell that she was not happy with that decision. But she loved me. I can tell you she loves me, really loves me. It was her love that helped her to reconcile with my decision.

'The hotel was located on a relatively busy intersection and had a certain anonymity about it. I liked this part the most, for I would not be recognised here. Over the years Chhotaudepur has changed. The quarries here have led to the opening of factories, and mining has increased. The construction of roads has made the area accessible. People working in the transport industry, and recently other migrant workers like Bengalis, have started to come here. Almost all of them come to the hotel to have tea, dinner, or lunch. Not everyone who came there was known to us.

'When I was in the second year of work at the hotel, a truck driver came by often for tea. Then I noticed he began to come on a more regular basis. He interested me, and he too seemed interested in me. When he came to the restaurant, I made it a point to serve him tea myself. Gradually, he began to come daily and especially ask for tea made by me. We both felt drawn to one another. Then he started talking to me, and one day we met each other alone in a secluded corner of a field for the first time. As the days passed, we confessed our love for one another.'

Shashi's face lit up as she thought about those days, recalling her lover. 'From that day onwards, we could not let a day pass without seeing each other. When he arrived, we would sit, talk, and then walk away together on our special trip. We came together as one in the dark of the night, under the sky, behind a tree or some quiet spot; we loved one another. But as time went by, we began to meet in the room that my uncle had given me. I would unlock the room and return to finish my work until 9 p.m. In the meantime, my friend would come in and wait there for me, bringing his cycle into the room to prevent people from knowing that he was inside. At around four in the morning, my aunt would come to the hotel to begin the day. Since my room was in the premises of the hotel, I'd wake my friend before my aunt arrived. Though he often complained about it, he nevertheless got up every day at that odd hour. Both of us were afraid of letting my aunt and uncle know about our relationship. It was hard, but when there is no acceptance of relationships like ours, we have to strategise carefully. We have to put up with indignities as well. We lived like a couple, as husband and wife, for four years. Time flew so fast. Those were the most memorable days for me. I miss those days. Later, I stopped waking up my friend that early. He told me that people were starting to wonder where he had been the whole night after seeing him return home at such early hours. I felt bad for him to have people pass comments about him, so I let him wait a while longer in the mornings until it was safe for him to go.

'But then suddenly, something happened to my partner. I did not sense any change in him to forewarn me of the events that followed. He told me he needed money. This was nothing new as it happened all the time in our relationship, and I had already given him some money previously. This time too, I gave him the money he asked for, but what I did not know was that he had a plan. He had been working on it quietly, and so smartly. He took that money and never returned it. It has been years now. I do not know what happened. Until this day I have no idea. I tried to find out from his friends, and they told me he was now married and had a son. He lives in Baroda and continues to work as a driver in the city. I felt like going there, seeing him once, asking him… but I did not go.

'It was such a blow. Suddenly life became so meaningless. I needed to get out of the hotel and that room, and I began to work in the factory. As time passed, I recovered. I developed several relationships with truck and jeep drivers, and workers from in and around the nearby village. I began to have multiple partnerships. I supported people with whom I had relationships with money, time, and other resources. I had fun and I enjoyed myself. Sometimes I got money, at other times I gave some to those whom I liked and chose for myself. I stopped bothering about the future or saving up for some unknown need that may not even arise, telling myself "what future should I worry about?" I have myself. These temporary relationships were easier to deal with. I did not wish to engage with a particular partner. Breaking up really hurts, and now I am in the same place again—feeling let down. I must say, this time it is different. I can talk about it. I have the support of so many others like me. But at the end of the day, everyone has to deal with their share of pain alone.

'All my options to find work seem closed. I do not want to go to Kathiawad knowing that our relationship is at an end. I do not want to go to the factory either. I just do not feel like doing anything. But I have to pay back Roshan *masi*.'

After this meeting, once again we did not see Shashi in the weekly market, nor at the tea stall or in the organisation. It was disturbing to find her gone again. When we asked about her, we learnt she was at home, 'doing nothing'.

Some of us went to Shashi's house and asked her to come to the organisation several times. As days went by, Shashi responded to our visits and began to come to the organisation every now and then. Sitting quietly, carefully observing and coming up with questions, we did not realise how and when Shashi began to take on work at the office—from handing a glass of water, to putting away files, tidying the office and then participating in meetings, making interventions, leading group discussions, and presenting her point of view.

She began to open up more publicly, treading on subjects she had not talked about earlier. 'Those of us who do not marry, and feel uncomfortable as a "man" face all kinds of trouble. Men find us easy prey. Everywhere, markets to workplaces, or buses, no public place is quite the place for us as it is for you. People like me are often beaten up by families, partners, and some of us are forced to marry. I too have been beaten up, forced to have sex, and as you know already, we end up paying as well. Most of the trouble occurs when we go for a new partner, a short-term partner, and the older ones feel sidelined. No matter how hard we try to hide it, word gets around quickly. It is a small circle after all, so-and-so will tell so-and-so. To avoid any scenes, I try to meet my lover at a secluded spot, like a riverbank or a quiet corner in another village.

'There was another time when we just about escaped a whole gang of men. It was the second *navratra*. I noticed a man starting to follow me; he then started pestering me and pleading with me. On the third day, when I was with three others, somebody caught hold of me from behind. As I turned around, I saw it was that same man, and he had with him 10 to 15 others. They had been hiding behind a building. When I saw them, I began to grapple with him. My heart was thumping madly. I did not want to go with him because I foresaw my fate. My friends had quickened their pace and were calling back to me "run, run!" After a struggle, I escaped his grip as the group kept closing in. Fortunately, the *garba* ground was nearby and since it was a festival time, many people were there. We did not dare shout out, afraid that it was us who would be blamed. Who would believe us? No one. But when these *goondas* saw the people around after our scuffle, they had to abandon their chase.

'I remember once we were out and it was past eleven at night, the time when policemen are out and looking for anybody suspicious. I was with a few friends; some policemen spotted us next to an ex-government building which is now abandoned. The big rooms are locked, but since it is close to the school grounds, a lot of students used to climb up the stairs for quiet, private moments with their partners. When the policemen saw us near that building, they grew suspicious.

"'Halt!" They shouted so loudly that it pierced through the night. These *khaki*-dressed men think the public is their father's property, especially us tribals. This is how they treat us. We have had many brushes with the police, but that day they let us go. It was such a relief!

'This is the best part of living in your own place and amongst the people you know. It feels safer than it would be in an unfamiliar place. We have a community here and I can seek their help if anything goes awry in a strange place. Of course, it can happen anywhere, but one can hope for help and reach out for it here. The thing is I love this place; I've lived here all my life.'

Shashi slowly grew on us like leaves on treetops, unfurling and blooming without notice. We missed her on the days when she remained absent to represent her community at various protests and meetings. Though excited and enthusiastic to share what she had seen and learnt, I think she missed us as much. 'But this is where I belong, here in Chhotaudepur amongst you all,' she would tell us. 'No matter what the city, even if it is in Gujarat, like Baroda, Ahmedabad, Surat, I like it best in Chhotaudepur and more than the meetings, I enjoy talking about the protests—those are fun,' she would say, her eyes sparkling. 'In the meetings, one has to sit, and I am no good sitting the whole day long. I remember the year we organised a protest here, against proposed amendments in the law for sex work. The news about our protest came out in the papers. It was July 2009—I remember the month because it poured so heavily. Our posters and we were dripping wet; we ended up losing our camera but I remember the year, because two years previously I had just started to come to the organisation more often.'

Shashi's protest in Delhi was the one she recounted with great relish, for the many firsts she had experienced there, and it was a treat to listen to her. 'After I left Gujarat for the first time for Delhi, imagine sleeping on the train and waking up in Delhi! And what a city it is! People from all over the country had come. It was a very big rally. All of us gathered to protest amendments that the government was going to bring in which would worsen the sex workers' situation. No, no, I do not remember the dates and the year of the protest in Delhi. There were many, so many of us from everywhere in the country, at that time I could never have imagined! And all of us wearing what we wanted, singing and dancing. Of course, people on the streets who were watching the rally laughed at us, but it did not matter to us because we were so many. Now, I have travelled outside of Gujarat and know there are so, so many of us, so how can we be wrong? I tell myself, if it were so, then perhaps all the men who love women are wrong…Who is to say what is right and what is wrong? There is no right or wrong. Not in love. This needs no telling.

'I liked the rally and what we stood up to, because as "female sex workers", I also feel like our choice of work means we are viewed in the same way as transgender people or homosexuals— people who have "other" kinds of relationships, and thus sacrificing our respect and rights in society. I know that meeting and interacting with the people outside our village and city has taught me many things. My life has changed in many ways. But the trouble in going to another city is that the language, food, everything becomes different. Besides, in no other town would I be able to afford a house of my own. Not me or others like me. I have this dream. A dream that has only been partially built.'

When asked to share it, she snuggled tight and warm into herself, her feet under her, her arms crossed over her chest and eyes closed as if she was imagining it, and she said, 'I have a dream to build my own house, but for now it is a room, my very own room. I am working hard to make it come true with my family and my money. I wanted a space of my own. Not entirely separate, and yet a space that is mine. Recently I have begun to build that dream brick by brick: a small two-room space within the family home, where I can live on my own and keep myself alive, different as I am from the rest. I dream of having a loving and caring partner. I can live with him here in my house, and we can in some measure live in a world that is of our reckoning and choice.'

A few months later, Shashi invited us to see what she had built. We walked along with her. Sighing deeply, Shashi spread her arms wide to show the bare earth. 'There used to be thick trees here, but as the mining spreads, the trees have disappeared and the forests have depleted. Those of us who used to collect gum, flowers, and fruits in the forests can no longer survive on that work. Now, to collect firewood we have to go miles,' Shashi explained. 'And even then we return with almost nothing because many times the guards steal upon us and stop us.'

The tar road ended as we turned towards Shashi's village, picking our way through the *kaccha* pathway. I swallowed hard the painful pang that rose inside me hearing the rumble of blasts in the distance. The picture replaying in my mind was that of a piece of earth I had seen earlier, ruthlessly ripped apart, the sand and stones dug out of its bosom. An entire sky in a bowl of water, spotless and tasting like childhood, dried up and lost—like the art of the bow and arrow, or the *pithora* paintings that once adorned the dwellings here, now absent from Shashi's house and several other houses.

'Yes, we used to have these paintings for prosperity and good fortune, but not anymore. There are few who know how to make them. It has become expensive to get them done: all the rituals that have to be performed beforehand. Those who make them have begun to work in the mines, they get paid better there.'

Silence filled the intensely white blazing day. The houses here were surrounded by spaces that boasted a few *tad* and *mauva* trees without a trace of boundaries between them. Just spaces and cupped voices floating over the neighbourly interiors, an occasional twitter overhead and the cots laid under the languorous shade of trees. Far into the distance, watched over by the dark hills, one could see the upturned black soil ready to receive the rains and grow into fulsome fields. 'This is it,' Shashi points out, her pride and pleasure irrepressible in her smile. We follow her gaze. Without a grain of doubt, the woman who was just about to leave the house as we entered was Shashi's mother, though much older than when we had last met her. The resemblance between the two was still astonishing. Especially when she smiled so warmly and let us in. Shashi's stepbrother too looked just like her, barring the moustache and tobacco-stained teeth. Children from different fathers, and yet the mother shone through them both, bonding the two strongly. We stepped back into the *verandah* and walked straight up to Shashi's room. Transparent curtains tied in the doorway ballooned outwards and gave off gentle gleams of light. But you could see through the curtains—privacy was simply a flimsy curtain. We stepped into the first room, almost empty, and into the adjoining next room: these were the two rooms Shashi had dreamed of. The inner room had a ceiling and a table fan. A small television lay on the triangular shelf between two walls, but nothing worked because there was no electricity. On the opposite side, tucked deeper inside the room, away from the entrance and the direct gaze of anyone walking in, was a single bed. 'Now my dream of a partner waits to come alive, then the bed will be a size bigger,' she said. 'Right now, I am happy to simply own this space.' Her brother's wife, lean and dark, comes in followed by her two sons and hands us glasses of water which I notice are not filled to the brim. When she takes away the glasses, Shashi tells us that water has to be fetched from a well outside, 'Not really far, about 10 to 15 minutes away, so we use our water carefully, but do you want more?' She smiled mischievously, 'I am the only woman in the family, and we welcome girls here.'

Shashi's exposure and her own maturity allowed her to embrace her gender identity more openly, a lock on her forehead, bangles on her wrist and attire that had the feminine touch. It was clear she was only a hair's breadth away from expressing her sexual preference aloud. 'Marriage pressure has ceased altogether, and my mother is happy to have me back. Though not entirely indifferent, my stepfather does not interfere in my life. Grounded in the day-to-day responsibility of providing for the family, he is happy to have me work with him on his fields; plus there is my contribution to the family income. My father often tells me, "I am a content man."'

In 2010, Shashi's father passed away. We learnt that the quiet, old man ran a fever for three days. When Shashi and her mother proposed taking him to a doctor, he said, 'A visit there will cost ten rupees now because I can walk, but how will you get me back? That could cost 500 rupees.' With a simple shake of his hand, he turned down their suggestions and simply lay down quietly as was his habit. On the morning of the third day, his premonition came true.

Our next visit to Shashi's house in 2015 was prompted by the tragic loss of her younger brother. 'We showed him to a doctor but he said nothing. For quite some time now, blood had stopped forming in his body. He smoked a lot, he was addicted to...' Rubbing her palms together, Shashi indicated her brother's addiction to tobacco without mentioning it. I remembered her brother's stained teeth the first time I had seen him; he was a copy of Shashi except for those teeth. I remembered his wife—then she was carrying what would be their third child. In her sigh, I now heard the weight of responsibility that had fallen on Shashi's shoulders. I wondered how she would cope. Though she seemed burdened with these new responsibilities, she was keen to know 'If that judgment of the Supreme Court—well yes NALSA Judgment—would it really lead to the government recognising us?' The ring of uncertainty and disbelief was painful to hear in Shashi's voice.

'It has been a year and nothing seems to change, what do you think, will we ever get that recognition you were talking about?'

'We are trying to get it implemented,' I tried to reassure her.

She wanted some confirmation. 'That will take another few years, no? I am getting old, how long am I supposed to live this kind of double life. It makes me angry because I see that there is something for us but it is so far out...'

A year later, while on a field visit near Shashi's village, we dropped by to see her. She was not there. Her brother's wife told us that she now lives most days in the hut on the fields, like her father had done before her. We waited for her. We noticed that in the outer room of the house, there were pictures of Shashi clustered together on the wall, all of them in female clothes— she wore makeup and stood bejewelled smiling into the studio camera. Above them was her brother's picture with his moustache. When Shashi arrived, she was sweating and tired. 'It is a long walk,' she explained, wiping her dripping forehead. 'But look!' She pointed to her clothes, her broad smile infecting us. She was dressed in feminine clothes, a tucked T-shirt stained in a dark patch of sweat, like a blouse over the *chaniya*, and a red *odhni* to boot. Her hair, though short, was cut in a feminine style. We settled in for a cosy chat. 'When my father and my brother both passed away, I had to take charge. That meant I had to live in our community and face society, my neighbours, and my father's family. I thought—how long would I have to live a double life? My time was running out. Especially after all those representations to the Collector and other lawyers, telling them about us and all what the judgment had said about us all, I told myself, it has to be changed. Everything cannot be left to the government, and even if the government does make changes, nothing can change overnight in my daily life. Can the government come and tell my family "she is a woman"? No. For them to see what I am I will have to make some changes here and now and face up to whatever happens then. So, I did that; I mean I made changes. Yes, I did that. Slowly, every day, bit by bit, people came to know, just as I grew to learn how to look people in the eye and say who I was. I know that I am not alone in my liking for men, I know that now. My most exciting trip, going to Delhi this time in a balloon (aeroplane) to stop the Transgender Bill, was shorter than it had been by train; I sat in the seat and the next minute, we had arrived. I went there to protest. You see, the government tries to pass wrong laws like the Transgender Bill and here we are, trying to get that judgement implemented which is more in favour of us. There are people like me the world over. Once you learn this from inside your head, heart, and all your bones in your body, there is no fear. The fear is only from the state. But once we cross out that "other fear" inside us, we can live our lives, and only be occasionally interrupted by the state. People around me, all of them, they all know me. Ask them, and they will tell you or smile away your question. Look at the way I am dressed like a woman, I dress like this all the time and no one says anything. People in my community invite me for festivals, for births, deaths, and marriages. No one is ashamed of inviting me. I have people over too: my father's family, my brothers, sisters and their children, and my mother's side of the family. They all come here, or we all go there. I am neither an outcaste nor an isolated enigma.' With a nod and an infectious smile she says, '*Ab main anand mein hoon.*' (I am happy now.)

There are no roads to Shashi's house yet; electricity is random and candle light and kerosene lamps fill the evenings. Shashi and her family pull up buckets of water from the well. Nowadays a lot of responsibility rests on her. She works in the field by day, and in the night, she is at the dolomite crushing units. Is there something else besides roads, electricity, and readily available water that makes for happiness?

'My employer is a kind *seth*,' explained Shashi, 'Muslim, yes, and I, a Hindu, but we have no problem here. No problem.

Everyone knows it is our leaders who divide us. Of course, I have my other interests and attractions. So my life goes on…and you? What about you?' I tell Shashi about myself and a warmth fills me. As we bid each other goodbye, I pass by two trees that have grown together like siblings. I notice that one of them strangely cradles a sapling of another tree on its lap, its leaves rounded and tender unlike the scaly trunk it is sprouting on. As I walk past them, the setting summer sun fills me with peace, and for one brief moment I can say in all honesty, '*Mein anand mein hoon*.'

4

Of a Different Mettle

Often, the general public and the state make the wrong assumption that 'sex work' and 'trafficking' are always connected; sometimes, they incorrectly use the terms interchangeably, much the same way some might do with 'trans' and 'intersex'. According to the National Crime Records Bureau, 21.5% of the rescued victims of trafficking had been trafficked for the purposes of prostitution, the second-highest reason after forced labour (45.5%). Not all sex workers are in the profession as a result of trafficking; in fact, many are not, yet a bill proposed in 2018 to investigate, rescue, protect, and rehabilitate victims of trafficking actually has the potential to negatively affect sex workers.

The idea behind the Trafficking of Persons (Prevention, Protection and Rehabilitation) Bill is that it will require state governments to set up 'Protection Homes' that will provide shelter, food, counselling, and medical services to victims. Of course, this sounds good on paper, but after hearing stories of community members' experiences in shelter homes, (one such story is included in this book) one cannot help but be sceptical. The critiques, though, are only regurgitations of those that already exist, surrounding previous laws concerning sex work. The bill has in no way been informed by research or analysis, and is completely blind to the negative health and social development outcomes it could produce. This bill has not yet been passed, but it bears similarities to the Transgender Persons (Protection of Rights) Bill that did get passed in 2018; the premise of both bills is to offer 'protection', but they are underpinned with a tone of policing, saying, 'you yourself do not know what is good/best for you'; an untruth which I only realised after mistakenly believing it at first.

In the early 1990s, I found myself working in resettlement colonies in Delhi as part of a women's group. This was when I engaged with sex workers for the first time. I was a part of a group of activists who rushed in to 'rescue' these women. As we worked round the clock in our rescue attempt, we soon learnt that our efforts came from our reading of the prefabricated script of heteronormativity, the text of which existed only in our heads. It was a paradox that surfaced only when we saw the lived reality of the women we were trying to 'rescue' from men; this is these women's choice of work, and what they chose to do with their bodies. I carried the chaos home with me. I recognised my own judgemental attitude and how it bore similarities to those who judged me. The complex knot created by patriarchy, and the ideals of 'good' and 'bad' women, slowly unravelled over time.

I soon found that the oppression and ousting of sex workers mirrored that of the queer community, and with the same factors as drivers of this trajectory. In precolonial times, many prostitutes were close to elites and high courts, and these were spaces in which they were respected. They were not just viewed as sex objects, but also as charming and intelligent people, with their conversations and company being just as prized as their looks. The 'common' prostitutes, who were not rubbing shoulders with the powerful and wealthy, were regarded as a means of purifying towns, necessary outlets for men's sexual drives, and for maintaining the moral order. Although hierarchies existed within the occupation, as they do in all fields of work, sex workers in general were accepted and allowed to participate in mainstream life.

It was post 1857 that they started to be seen as a threat to the British order, that their position in society became sullied. Prostitutes were increasingly pushed into a strictly defined and narrow space, stripped of all emotional and intellectual functions.[26] The occupation became entirely physical. At the same time, jobs in other sectors became scarce, leading to many other women from the oppressed castes and classes turning to sex work; the profession thus became more competitive and wages decreased. Concurrently, ideals on marriage, monogamy, and the wife as the 'true multifaceted companion' became popular; the prostitute was now dirty and immoral. Sex workers found themselves ousted, and their presence in public spaces was no longer tolerated. An open condemnation of prostitutes now ensures respectability for those condemning them. While other stories in the book have direct and oblique references to sex work, I wanted to also include the personal story of a sex worker, both as part of our organisational journey and in grateful acknowledgment of my learning through them, in the hope that many others will also be as enriched as I was in listening and narrating these stories.

It was through Shashi that we met Amtiben. We knew all about her long before we met her in person, and even before we had set foot in her town. Every now and then, her name and fame would come up in conversations; 'when she walks down the road, men in this town go crazy'; 'this *dhandeywali* ensnares the youth, the middle-aged, and the older men—all of the men here', but Shashi, who was unfazed by her reputation, had another opinion on her. 'I know Amtiben. She is of a different mettle. I remember her striding down the banks of the Orsang River every day as the morning melted away. She was as fierce as the midday sun that beat down on us as she made her way to the fields. The colours of her *choli–ghagra* (blouse and skirt) seemed to match the rage she carried inside her. She walked with her arms pulled firmly behind, her fingers gripping the wooden handle of an axe.' Amtiben's reputation, and the image that Shashi painted of her, filled us with an insatiable desire to meet her.

---

26 Gupta, Charu. *Sexuality, Obscenity and Community Women, Muslims, and the Hindu Public in Colonial India*. Permanent Black, 2001, p. 111.

5

No Walls, No Roof, Nothing but the Earth under the Open Sky—My Birthplace

In 2006, we met Amtiben for the first time at her home that was situated on the road that curved around her village. The house rose gently from the bosom of the earth, spanning a long way from its boundary. The filigree gate delicately glimmered in the sun as the teak and *mahua* branches trembled beside it. When we neared the end of the road, Amtiben came out to greet us with an open countenance and smiling eyes. I am sure those eyes had read our surprise in the way our steps had suddenly faltered on seeing the house. Before the introductions were finished, she plunged into the history of her house and their possession of it. 'My father came here from a nearby village at the age of fourteen. There was a poly-technic here, which was run by a trust. He got a job as a caretaker and was given a house. It is a big house, you'll see, but we live in a limited space. It's not in the best state… My father lived here before I was born. Then the polytechnic closed and an *Ashramshala* was started, and my father continued to work here.

'I also used to fill water for the school, going down the river, carrying the *matlu* (earthen vessel) over my head, and putting them in their respective stands. When I was this small,' she said, gesturing two feet above the ground, 'I would get paid 10 rupees for that. But soon, the school closed. Before that, there was a glass factory here. People say that rupee notes were printed here, and there was an underground tunnel leading all the way up to the Santhali hill, look, over there, until there was a raid and the tunnel was closed off. I believe the tunnel is still here, in this house, but now it is all closed up. People have said they found treasure here. Sometimes I wonder if there is treasure still hidden underneath…exciting, isn't it? I love to imagine that there is treasure and I will discover it,' she said, her eyes twinkling mischievously, 'I'll become rich and use the money to repair the house and use it for people like me. When it rains, the roof leaks; the walls and the floors are cracked, and you can see that the paint is peeling off. The house is big and old. It would cost a lot to get it done. But then I ask myself, who will take care of it after I am gone? I do not have children…people like us may want them but cannot have them. Well, I cannot think like that, nor can I plan like others do.' I wondered if that note of wistfulness hid a desire for children.

'So, we carry on somehow in this dilapidated house. My father is weak and ailing; he cannot do anything and just sits on the cot the whole day. I am the one who runs this household and even then, he puts his decrepit old feet up all the time, exercising his authority over me! I wonder, what's the point of trying to control me now? Just an old habit? There is little we can do about our future, mine or his. He probably never thought he would be in such a state.'

So that was Amtiben. A dreamy-eyed and eternal romantic who looked out beyond the mundane, and still remained grounded. That day, like most others, Amtiben's curls were unruly. Amtiben's big black eyes were always gleaming with mischief, darting up and down as she sized up people and situations. Welcoming us with a nod of her head and her hands spread wide, she urged us to follow her. I noticed her colourful bangles as they tinkled down from her wrists to her elbows; her nails were brightly polished and light kept bouncing off her nose pin every now and then. As we

followed her, the rhythm of her anklet's tinkling matched her footsteps as she called out to us; 'Come, come this way,' she said, her
voice infectiously cheerful. 'This house was donated by the king
to my father. A house like this is a treasure, with all this land and
the river over there. Look out from this window here, come here,
closer, up here.' Pointing, she showed us the river, saying, 'All this
has been a boon for our family.' We looked out and saw the Orsang River skirt around the house, brimming with the monsoon
rains, singing of songs, trysts, and secret treasures it had witnessed
over the generations. After cups of tea, formal introductions to her
parents, and a walk around the sprawling house, we parted on a
promise that Amti would share her story soon, and that she would
explain why she had always carried an axe with her.

   We met again a few months later. 'When my father came here,
there were hardly any units, but if you look around now, they're
everywhere. Once known as the land of rivers, forests, and hills,
it is now covered in dust and piles of stones from the mines. But
these are the very units that put money in our hands when we
had none. These units have shaped and altered many lives here.
The story of my axe, well, that too is connected to these units, in
more ways than one.

   'I carried an axe everywhere with me. I carried it from my
house to the fields, to the factory units, and everywhere else.
I carried it with me every day for a long, long time. We tribals
are known for our bows and arrows, and for our zeal for justice. My elder brother was killed and I was blamed for it. People
would pass snide remarks, and my blood would boil listening to
those stories, and I would become so enraged.' She paused for a
moment. 'Well, in one way you could say I was responsi...' She
stopped abruptly. She sat there reflecting, her face resting between her forefinger and middle finger. After a while, she began again. 'Well, not really, if you consider all what happened.
I would carry the axe around with me just so I would be able to
retaliate and scare people off if they commented on my brother's

death. It's not that I did not care about him, I did. Perhaps that was what angered me. I liked him and I think of him often… All these years, he could have been with us.

'There was this one man, Bhavsingh, he would say, "It is on account of this sister that the eldest brother died, she has brought dishonour to the family." It is a long story, but I'll tell you. My sister and I were born from my mother's womb and all my brothers are from my father's first wife. I had four brothers, and now of course, I have two. One of them died, supposedly because of me, and the other one fell sick and died young. There was a time when we all lived together, brothers, sisters and parents, all together. Now, my brothers live separately and my elder sister is married with a family of her own. I am the only one who lives with my parents. Time has changed us all. I carried the axe every day for months. There wasn't a single day during that time when I did not have it with me. But as people stopped calling me names, and my anger cooled, I stopped carrying the axe.

'The story of the axe begins with Nathu Kaka. He lived right across the road from us. In our villages, we address our neighbours in kinship terms, even when they are not related to us. So, we called him Kaka. He had two daughters, Sejal and Naina, and we were also two sisters, Daksha and I. Naina would ask me to carry messages from her to her lover and keep a lookout when she met with him. My house was near the dolomite factory where men and women worked together. Men do the work of blasting, digging the pit, and breaking the stones, and also working as drivers. Women clear the sand, fill it, and carry it to the tractors. Naina worked there, and her "friend" was a driver. They would meet at the mining site. Since the site was close to our houses, my job was to warn her if anyone came near the location of their rendezvous. If I saw somebody approaching, I would signal by clearing my throat, throwing a stone, or calling out loudly to my sister. In return for all of this, Naina would pay me five rupees.

'Winter had just ended, and there were only a few months left of my fifth class in school when my brother figured out what I was doing for Naina. He came up to me,

"What were you talking to him about?"

"Me? With whom?" I asked, pretending not to understand what he was talking about.

"Khan Sahab's son, Aslam. What were you talking to him about?"

"Me? No, I do not know him."

"I do not know him!" He mocked me. "Don't we all know that? We all know him! I know what you are doing; pimping for Naina, that is what you are doing. He is not the kind of person you should be talking to, and Naina too. You think I don't know what's going on? I will tell our father, just wait and see. He will set you right!"

'That day however, I escaped. Maybe my brother decided not to report it to my father. In any case, I continued watching out for Naina. She was kind to me, continuing to hand over five rupees every time I kept watch. With that money, I was able to buy things that I wanted—hair clips, bangles, trinkets, cream—all secretly stored away into a small trunk.' Amtiben smiled mischievously as she recalled the trunk, 'It was all broken. The back was almost gone, and the bottom too had nearly completely rusted. But from the front, the trunk looked whole, and it had a latch. I bought a lock worth five rupees and put it on the latch, creating the illusion that it was secure!' She burst out laughing. 'It served my purpose well, hiding my things from my sister who would have taken them all away. Neither she nor anyone else guessed that the back of the trunk was completely open. I would store away my goodies by simply pulling the trunk away from the wall, and then pushing it back. Watching out for Naina had proven to be beneficial for me.'

When recalling these incidents, Amtiben would imitate each person's tone and facial expression, plunging straight into the next dialogue without pausing to name the speaker, but her gestures and body language allowed the listener to identify which character she was playing. She talked of her life in a way that evoked drama and suspense. 'Whenever my brother yelled at me, I would tell Naina, and to comfort me, she would take me to the market and buy me things. Once, she bought me a *chaniya* and *choli*. But that day I was unlucky, very unlucky. My brother spotted me upon my return, and I'm sure he told my father. "What did you get from the bazaar?"' she said, imitating her brother in a gruff, authoritative tone. 'Nothing,' she said meekly, imitating her monosyllabic reply with her eyes down and arms glued to her sides.

"I am going now but I will come home and I will take your remand in the evening."

And again, her voice took on a gruff tone to indicate this was her brother she was imitating. Then, returning to her normal pitch she looked at us and continued conversationally, 'As the evening drew closer, so did my father's return. I thought about running away, and I almost did, before my brother called out, "Where are you sneaking off to?" He pulled my arm, and dragged me along with him, and with me standing next to my father, he showed him the trunk. He brought a *datali* (sickle) to force the lock open, that piddle of a lock!' Demonstrating the size with two fingers, she smiled, 'It was the size of the *datali*, that lock which was worth only five rupees; if you saw the contrast between its size and the three of us crowded around the trunk, it would make you laugh. I tried to tell him about its broken and open back, but I thought it might anger him more. The lock opened without so much as a twinge, and he pulled out all of my treasures that were stowed away—clothes, threads…you know, those coloured threads, with tiny, tiny bells (*ghunghrus*) on their ends. I often used them to tie my hair in a ponytail, and then those and all of the other things were pulled out and thrown about as evidence of my waywardness. My father slapped me hard, twice across my face.

'Who got you all these?' Amtiben glared at us, with her fore-head puckered and an expression as fierce as the voice she used to enact her father. 'I told him it was Naina, and before I finished re-plying, he was demanding to know why. "I did not have the money so she paid for me; after a week, when I water and manure the fields and tend to the watermelons," I told him, "I will earn enough to repay her." I had to lie to save myself.

'"Don't you dare meet with this woman again, I forbid you!" he warned me. I nodded obediently. My brother watched me like a hawk and did everything possible to prevent me from meeting Naina. For two days, I could not escape his watchful eye. Then, on the third day when I slipped out, my nephew reported it to my brother. I was beaten up again. Yes, yes, we were frequently beaten up. Especially me, I was always in trouble for something or the other. But in those days, Naina was the one who was living out of bounds. When we were yelled at for spending time with Naina, she was called "that woman". Later, I learned the reason why we were told to avoid her.

'Close to the factory, there is a shack that sells the local brew. Generally, men in the village gather there to drink and talk about events and people from the village. Bragging about their con-quests, they would learn of one another's love affairs, forced mar-riages, likely elopements, abortions, and pregnancies. My brother learned about Naina's pregnancy this way. I don't know whether this story was true or not, but as days and months passed, I found that my brother got stricter and more abusive. Sometimes he only made slight digs at "that woman's character", and at other times, he yelled at us openly while giving reasons for why I should stay away from her.

'It is hard to tell you how old I was then. The school-leaving certificate says I was born in 1979. I recently learned this myself, when the activists from Vikalp helped me get my election card. To get the election card, we had to show the school-leaving certifi-cate.' We asked Amtiben how the school knew her date and year of birth. 'Of course they do not know. No one knows. What happens in our village is this: an elderly person from our families attends the school admission, and the people over there look at us and write it all down for us.

'No one remembers the month or the year of my birth; usually, most people remember birthdays through some incident or the other. In my case, it was a little different. My father often beat up my mother and they would fight. On the day I was about to be born, my father had thrown my mother out of the house. Soon after that, my mother went into labour. That was how I came to be born outside in the open. No walls, no roof, nothing but the earth under the open sky. Fortunately, Bachubhai Soni saw my mother and helped her. That was how I survived. He called my *dadi* and mediated with my father on my mother's behalf. He gave my mother food and shelter. He saw to it that she and I both had a bath, clothes, and other things. That was how the famous Amtiben of this town arrived in this world! You write it all down. People should know how I came into this world, free as a bird. And I continue to be a free bird.

'My brother kept trying to control me. I did not like it. Calculating by the school-leaving certificate, I must have been fourteen or fifteen then. I had failed the fifth class for the second time, and after that, I stopped going to school. My father tried very hard to persuade me to continue going, as did my brother. They thought that if I continued school, it would deter me from spending time with Naina, but I'm stubborn, and refused to go back. Perhaps my father relented because…I seem to keep coming back to this incident from school; the more I avoid it, the more it comes up. It is hard to talk about it, and also hard to not talk of it, especially since I am telling you my story. Disputes and tension continued to build up around this incident from school, and that led to my brother's sudden and untimely death.

'When I stopped going to school, I started working in our fields with my father. He insisted I work with him. He wanted to keep watch over me. If I expressed reluctance, he would hit me and shout at me. So, I went along, scared that if I did not, it would invite more trouble. We have five acres of agricultural land. During the day, after working for some time, my father would often disappear to go and meet with the other woman he loved. She was Shashi's mother.' She turned to look at Shashi, and they exchanged a smile, the warmth of their bond enveloping all of us. 'I did all kinds of work. Sowing, watering, laying the manure, I even ploughed the field. Yes, I ploughed the field, and I was good at it. I was able to manage the two jobs at the same time. You have to follow the track carefully, prod the oxen to make them go forward and turn them round at the end of the field. I would merely tell them to do so, and they would turn around and walk back. You have to take control. While prodding the animal, I also had to keep an eye on the bag of seeds tied to the plough so that the seeds were strewn along the track in the overturned soil. Yes, yes, in our parts, there are women like me who plough their fields, because the men migrate, and if they do not return by the time the fields have to be ploughed, women start the work.

'After doing our work, I would return home with my father in the evening. Usually, he would return by five or six and then we would head home together, but that day, he did not. I wandered over to the river while waiting for him. I liked to go to the riverside and fish there. The river never dries up entirely. Where we live, there are small water bodies in the river, and fishes abound. I waited there for some time, but my father did not come. Finally, I began to walk back alone; by the time I reached home, I was quite hungry and quickly sat down to eat my food and then went to fetch the cows back home.

'While I was away, my brother returned, and when he did not find me at home, he became very angry. "Where is she? Has she gone to that woman again? Where is she?" he demanded of my mother. Though my mother told him that I had gone to get the cows home, he did not believe her. He was angry with me and suspicious of my movements in any case, and now he had an outburst of rage. He was convinced that Naina would influence me and get me into the same kind of trouble. He walked away, blinded by anger, headed straight to Naina's house, and shouted out for me at the top of his lungs, demanding to know my whereabouts. Naina heard him, and equally angry at the insinuation, retorted with an abuse, "Why do you ask me? You come around asking me as if your own sisters are (sahukars) such good women..."

'I can only infer what must have happened to him. He had decided that Naina's company was a negative influence on me. Her response must only have angered him more. He strode towards Naina and, without thinking, he began to hit her. When Naina's mother saw him approaching, she ran out and called to her husband. Naina's mother returned with her husband, who carried a wooden rod in his hand. Raising it high above him, he brought it down on my brother's head. My brother fell, his body crumpling to the ground. Our house was nearby, and my father, who had finally come from the fields by then, was standing outside. When he saw my brother fall, he thought he would get up and fight back. He was strong and always fought back. Only this time, he did not get up...

'People blame me, but like I said, one thing happened after the other, and then my brother was killed. He was a good brother. He used to beat and shout at us, but he was a good man. When my father's first wife died, that is, my brother's mother, he used to cook and take good care of us. He had always been very fond of us...so fond of us all. He wanted us to be good women, my sister and me. He cooked, cleaned, and did much more. He did a lot of the housework. We were quite a handful. My father's family is Bhakats. This means that the family does not drink alcohol or eat meat, eggs, or anything that is non-vegetarian. My mother was his second wife. She belongs to the Nugra sect, and they eat eggs, meat, etc. The Bhakats cannot eat food prepared by Nugras, so my brother cooked for the family. He was young and he had to go to school, but he would only go to school after he had done all the cooking. I feel sad that he passed away like that. Then my mother began to do the cooking.

'The community guru came to our *chacha's* house, and my mother was given the *tulsi mala* by the guru. This meant that my mother had become a Bhakat. From then on, food cooked by my mother could be eaten by the whole family. But it is not true that all Bhakats do not drink or eat non-vegetarian food. Everyone does everything, it's just that some do it openly and others do it furtively. Some get caught and others get away with it. Daksha, my older sister, gets away with it.

'And this one here,' she said, pointing to herself, 'sitting before you, belongs to the group that gets caught.

'There never was a pair of sisters so different. And yet, I would say that Daksha did everything that I did. The difference was that she rarely got caught and I was always in trouble. I have always been open about everything. Talking, yes, talking, that's what does it. That's how I get caught. I cannot hide anything and when I do, I feel suffocated. It's just the way I am. I like what I like and I do what I like, it's that simple. No matter what people may say or do to dissuade me… Perhaps I am not as adamant now, but still, if I want to do something, I will find a way to do it.

'It's not that Daksha doesn't go after what she wants, she does, she breaks norms. But she tends to do things in a more subtle way, so even when she does break them, it doesn't draw attention. Daksha prayed every day and went about her routine dutifully. Just like her, I too had no other option but to do all the household chores. I got up early to fetch water, sweep, and clean before I went to school. But every now and then, I would avoid doing all my chores. I would play around, and my father would say menacingly, "You…you, what are you doing jumping around like a monkey? Where do you think you are going?"

'Sometimes, I simply ran away to swim in the river you saw behind our house, or to ride a donkey. We had donkeys on our farm; they carried watermelons to the markets. We cultivated these in the dry riverbed. Not any more... The government does not allow people like us to do that anymore. The people with the big trucks carry away the sand from our rivers. There is no restriction on them. The rules only apply to us, to the poor people. We do not dig sand and cut trees in such large quantities, but we are the ones who get punished.

'You understand what I am trying to explain about my sister and I? I mean, in the ways that we are different? People are like that, different from one another. My sister has trouble articulating what she wants. Most women have this problem. She always worries about what people will say and think of her. For example, my sister would only spend money if it was given to her. She used her slippers until they were worn so thin that thorns and pebbles pricked through the soles. And even when there was a gaping hole, she would get them mended. But given the opportunity, she would steal from my trunk; that's why I had to lock it. I am different. I didn't like to wait to be given money. I somehow managed to get myself a new pair of shoes to wear to school.

'Did I tell you that my father wanted his daughters, I mean us, Daksha and me, to study until we got a secondary education? He was adamant about it. He said that it could change our futures. I wonder how much our futures would have changed by continuing to study... I am barely able to read and write, except in Gujarati... If you ask me, I changed the course of my future, and it was not because I attended school. I have learned more outside of school than in the classroom.' Amtiben laughed out loud as she recalled the dress she had to wear to school. 'White shoes, socks, and a white frock with a brown belt. That's what we had to wear, and we rarely did. Shoes were unaffordable, and a white dress...for us...we never had such clothes at home.

'I did not like school for many different reasons. I told my father all that, but he did not listen. We sat there in the classroom, the teachers came in one after another, and we would have to listen to them. All they did was ask us questions. And when we did not answer, we had to hold our ears and stand up and squat, stand up and squat, over and over again. Sometimes they would hit us. The only class I liked was when Jagrutiben taught us Gujarati. I could understand it, and she was a good teacher. My friends in school named me *Jhajuru* master!' She was equally amused and embarrassed when I asked her why. 'Because I would go to the toilet frequently, or run away from school. Often, my sister had to carry my schoolbag back home. Since I used to leave the school just like that, she would catch up with me and beat me. The more I was beaten up, the less I wanted to go. What could I tell this sister of mine? That school made no sense to me? That I was embarrassed and unable to follow? I said nothing to her.

'My sister would make *khichadi* and carry it in the tiffin to school. I resisted carrying lunch. Since they insisted, I did, but I always longed to eat other things. On the way to school, I saw a shop filled with things that I wanted to eat and could not. We did not have much, not enough for food other than the *dhal-bhat* I ate every day. We didn't have enough to even occasionally taste the delicacies in the shops that were on display before us each day. The school was a good half hour away from our house, and every day, when I passed by the shops, I longed to eat something. But it was impossible. Then one day, I had an idea. While on my way to school, I started to call out to the people who passed by and those whom I knew, "Tai, Kaki, or Chacha," I would say, "Can you give me four annas, eight annas?" and so on. People would give it to me. I was able to collect a little money. I was young then, and with that money, I would go up to the shopkeeper and ask for what I wanted.

'Once, a neighbour from our village saw me begging on the way to school. He called out to me, and when I ran up to him, he tied me to a tree and told me to open my mouth wide enough for the amount of money I wanted. I did that, and he began to put four-anna, eight-anna, and one-rupee coins into my mouth. I was already choking; my jaws ached and my mouth dribbled. I realised that the more the money he poured in my mouth, the more was the danger of it going down my stomach. After that, I did not ask for money anymore, but I still wanted to buy snacks, sweets, bangles, and earrings. Not having money did not change wanting things. I learned that early on.

'I often reached school late and was punished by the teacher. I had to run around the school compound twice. After all the work at home and the long walk to school, who wanted to run around like that? Once I made sure that the teacher was gone, I would climb up the tamarind tree. Then, just before five, which was when school got over, I would come down and hide behind the buses. When other children who came in the buses were ready to leave, I would slip out quietly and walk back home.'

Amtiben's father thought of education as something that would benefit his children, and he insisted that they attend school regularly. However, school failed the expectations of many parents and children. It was an education that alienated girls like Amti. The school did not take into account the day-to-day world of tribal communities, especially tribal girls. Living on the periphery, both of their villages and of society at large, these girls may require different arrangements of learning, including different methods and syllabi that are anchored in their lived realities. Levelling all people down to one structure continues to create 'outsiders' in many different forms. The onus of assimilation is thrust upon the less privileged without a mutual exchange of welcoming their worlds into school curricula. This creates an erasure or conceals cultural diversity. Ultimately, such an approach deprives everyone of a critical learning opportunity. It makes our learning impoverished, for, in the process, we fail to learn about other worlds, lives, and struggles. The way Amti described the school uniform and the laughter that the recollection provoked in her are all indications of the deep divide between the inherited system of the colonisers and the lives of communities in the rural tribal areas.

'I was the kind of child who invited trouble, even at school. I have more than my share of those kinds of memories, most of which I don't care to relive. There was this one time—sometimes I think, if we had buses to take us to school this incident might never have happened—there was a boy called Arun who would often ask my sister to sit on his cycle when we were on our way to school. She would pick up a stone, throw it at him, and continue walking ahead on her own. But I guess I was the foolish one. When he would ask me, I would gladly sit on the seat behind him. My sister would try to dissuade me but I would not let her interfere. And so, it went on like this for many days—he would give me rides and money too. One day, he tricked me into coming to his house. "Amti, come to my uncle's house to have a delicious meal." He had planned it all and I had no idea. Instead of asking him what the occasion was, I wanted to know, "What are the dishes they are making?"

'"*Puri, ladwa, dhebra* and *shak*," he replied. These are delicacies and are cooked very rarely in most of our households. When I heard the names of those dishes, I was tempted. I thought I must go. I didn't say yes or no. But we were friends, and he knew I liked good food. He took my silence for a yes. When he came looking for me at school, I couldn't say no. I went off without telling my sister. I left my schoolbag because I was in a hurry to get out of school and eat. Arun took me on his cycle to his uncle's house. His aunt was sitting on the cot outside the house, looking relaxed. It occurred to me that she did not look very busy, as she was likely to if there was so much food to be prepared. I thought she had finished all the cooking. "Come, beta," she called me. I promptly asked for food, "Give me whatever it is that you have cooked."

"'Wash your hands and feet. I will get the food.' She ushered us in and returned soon with the plate of rice and *dhal*. My face fell when I saw the usual food. "Give me *ladwa* and *dhebra*. I eat rice and *dhal* every day. What is so new about that? I do not want to eat this."

"Who told you that I have made *ladwa* and *dhebra*?"

"Arun told me, that is why I have come here to eat." Coaxing me to eat what she had brought, she said, "This is what I have now. Maybe next time you come…" After a while, Arun's aunt went away to the fields to work. Arun pulled my hand and took me inside a room. He told me to sit on the cot. I sat down. He sat next to me and he asked me if I could sing. "Yes, I can sing."

"Do you know how to jump?"

"Yes."

"How come you do not know how to write?"

"I know how to write, but I do not know how to read. I can write by looking at the letters. If you write them down now, I can copy them and write them all down as well…"

"Yeah, yeah, you can write…Can you? Sure you can." He put his fingers in mine and came close, very close. He pressed his head to mine as we sat side by side. I could hear him breathe. I liked him; I did not know what to say or do—nothing at all, nothing. I was in awe of him—he was much older, taller, and stronger than I was. I could not say a word. He unbuttoned my blouse and asked me to let down my hair and lie down. I could hear my heart beating. He pushed me down by the shoulder onto the bed, straightened my legs, and began to undo my hair.

"'Did you know, you can improve your mind by eating *maga-jtari?*" I did not reply; I couldn't find the words. I was both scared and excited all at the same time. I don't remember exactly what happened. I don't remember when and how he tied both my legs and I…I still get a lump in my throat when I think about it, about how nervous and afraid I was. I began to sweat profusely. I tried hard to throw him off but I could not move my legs. A searing pain

shot through my body and then I began to scream; I screamed and
screamed, as if my throat was bursting. My clothes were stained
with blood, so I threw them under the cot; there was my underwear
and a top. I wept a lot. I could not walk or sit. I felt like going to the
bathroom again and again. I wondered what had happened to me. I
just could not understand. I don't remember if Arun was there after
that, I have no memory at all. I kept crying to myself until Arun's
aunt returned. I told her how Arun had got on top of me...that I
was in this state because of him, I told her. She pressed me close to
her and consoled me, but I could not stop crying. Now, I cannot
cry, ever. No matter what happens, no tears will come to my eyes.

'Arun's aunt heated some water and gave me a bath. She
bought me new clothes and gave me some money. It was a while
before I left the house. It hurt so much I could not even walk. I
was studying in the fifth class at the time. It was after this incident
that I left school. I hardly remember how I walked back...was I
alone, or did that fellow come, or did his aunt walk with me? I
remember nothing, nothing but the pain and the shock of it all.

'I liked him, Arun. I thought he was a good man but I did not
think...I mean, I had no idea, no idea at all of what he would do.
I had no idea what it could come to, no idea... He was so gentle.
He would call out to me, and we would meet up, and I would go
with him. He had all the freedom to roam around. I liked that,
being able to move around freely. So, when he asked me to join,
I would go along. I did not like school anyway, so I would skip
school and go with him. All I was interested in was playing with
tikdi, eating plums, bangles, *kajal*. When he called me that day, I
went without thinking. How are we to know when no one tells us
or warns us? All I did was simply go along with him, one part of
me willing, and one part of me unaware and believing that there
would be good food. My sister would tell me not to go there, or
not to do this or not to do that, but there were so many things we
were not allowed to do, and I did all of them. And in most cases, nothing happened. When my sister saw me, she stood there

shocked, "What happened to you, why do you look so pale? Why have you changed your clothes? What happened?" She kept asking me what was wrong, "Where were you? Where did you go?" I told her everything. My father found out from my brother after my brother managed to extract what had happened from my sister. My father asked me, "Who did this?" I told my father the whole incident—how it had happened, how he had taken me, riding on the bicycle with a promise of good food and all, how he had taken me inside the house and the room, how he had tied me up, how his aunt had bathed me, the new clothes that she had got me, everything, I told him everything.

'My father did not say a word to me. He did not even hit me. "How could you go away from school the way you did? You did not even inform your sister." The next day, my father went to Arun's uncle's house. "Did my daughter come to your house?" They denied it. Then, he took me with him to their house. I said I had been there. Arun's aunt said that I must have come when she was away. I told my father she had been there. "In which room did this happen?" my father asked, and I showed him the room and the *chokdi* where I had had a bath. It still had bloodstains on the wall. My father called the elderly people of the community and put pressure on Arun's uncle and father to make them acknowledge and apologise. But Arun's father was a sarpanch, and a powerful man, so it was hard to resolve the problem.

'Arun, however, said that he would marry me, and wanted to live with me. So, the matter ended with us getting engaged. A year later, Arun's father killed somebody and my father said that he would not get his daughter married to a family of murderers. It was my father's reaction that surprised me the most. He had always been very violent with my mother, my sister, and me. He even used to hit Shashi's mother, even though they were not married. He used to hit her as if he owned her. But he did not even hit me once, not even once when he found out what had happened. I think he realised that it was not my fault.

'I sensed that Shashi, who was known as Mukesh back then, was my half-brother, because her mother would come with her to our house. I remember my mother making a face and remarking, "This woman is your father's keep." My father used to give her wood, and other things, like wheat, grain, *masalas,* all to help her. Since my mother did not like them coming to our house, or giving anything to them, my father would send these things through me. We also worked in Shashi's fields, my father and I. As Shashi and I became close, I learnt that her mother had attempted to jump in the well when her marriage was fixed because she was so in love with my father. Their relationship continued after her marriage. She often went to her brother's house so that she could meet my father, but neither she nor Shashi was welcome there, so my father would smuggle food and other necessities from our house and keep them near a bush for her. Though he does not acknowledge Shashi openly, it's like everyone knows and no one knows; let's say everyone pretends not to know. It is something like an open secret that she is my father's child. My father did help raise Shashi. If we were to sit and count how many siblings we are and how many children my father has had, there would be so many of us, brothers and sisters spread all over these villages.

'My brothers, whom I grew up with, do not support our old father. Even when the old man was sick, I went knocking on their doors for help, but no, they turned me away. I am like my father in many ways. Hot-headed and stubborn. After that, I no longer went to them. When I'm in trouble, sick or ailing, Shashi comes to help. She cooks and does odd jobs around the house. We get along well. When she said that she would be happier with the *hijras* than in her family, I thought, why not? Every person deserves to be happy in the way they want to live their life, so I went along with her wishes.

'The whole thing is like a wedding. So, I gave her my red wedding sari, put *mehendi* on her hands, arms, and feet; I painted her nails, lips, helped her with jewellery, and ensured that everything she wore was matching, from her head to her toes, her look complete with styled hair. I promised her I would not tell her mother. She is very close to her mother. She did not have the heart to tell her. I kept my word. Two days later, when her mother came looking, I did not open my mouth. Her mother would come every day and abuse me, holding me responsible for her disappearance. Generally, she and her family thought that I would know the whereabouts of Shashi. Yes, it was true, I did know. But I had given my word not to say anything. Finally, it was the others who told her. When she came out to beg with the other *hijras*, people in the village noticed her in a red saree and told her mother. That was how she found out about Shashi. She cried and wailed "I have lost my son to the *hijras*!"

'Shashi and I are alike in many ways. We have learnt to turn a deaf ear to what the world has to say against us. It is with Shashi that I share an affinity; even though my sister Daksha and I are born of the same father and mother, have eaten the same food, lived under the same roof, I am still closer to Shashi. Daksha's husband is a good-for-nothing drunk. I've had to shout at him several times to keep him in line and have settled their domestic disputes on more than one occasion. He beats her and does not give her any money. The last time he turned my sister out, I went out with a thick log of wood to hunt him down. I had to slap him hard to set him right. I am forced to adopt this method with him because nothing else works. When they run out of all resources, he throws my sister out. "Tell your father to give you something," he demands. He has the guts to make demands! What can our father give him now? He is old and sick. But, of course, he will mention only my father and not me, because I am only a woman, a daughter at that. This is a male-dominated society. I do not count. My father does. Mentioning me as the head of the family would hurt his manhood. What manhood is this, I ask? No matter how self-sufficient and independent I am, and irrespective of the fact that I am the one who supports the family, my name cannot precede my father's name. That is how it is. A woman's place is in her husband's house. A woman like me, who has returned home from her husband's house, is seen as a usurper and a bad woman. I had to marry, as all women have to, but it turned out that my husband was like Shashi, so I returned soon after. Since then, I have been single, though I have had several love affairs.

'Looking back, if I were to pick a time or an incident that changed my life, it would be the time when I failed fifth class for the second time. That whole incident with Arun was the point at which a succession of changes started to follow, thick and fast one after another—from the innocent fun and frolic we had in school, to beginning work on our farm, then in the factory because the farm could not provide the cash we needed, to the beginning of my involvement with a man, then my marriage, and before I knew it, I was back home again.

'I found factory work taxing. Lifting and carrying stones...it was hard, very hard. And it paid very little. What can one hope to do with this kind of money? Just survive? Are we to work so hard and just live and not afford even a little bit of fun? As a child in school, in my adulthood, and all through my marriage, all I knew was scarcity and violence. I suppose at some point, I will want children; everyone wants to have children and give them the good things of life. It is a simple truth.

'In the factory, after all the hard work we did, payments were not made daily. And on top of that, they could fire anyone at will. So, one day, just like that, you could find yourself without work and wages,' she said as she snapped her fingers for emphasis. 'I worked there for six months or so, then gave it up. I told myself that kind of work was not for me.

'Why do you think women like us prefer sex work? What are the other jobs that would give us security and decent money, where we would be paid on time, we didn't have to work as hard or be so servile to our employers, and where we could have the things we want, the dreams we dream? Surely, that cannot be a crime? Tell me, what other good livelihoods are available to us? Should we steal? Break open a safe? What should we do? We are known, well known, all of us in our profession. You got to know me because of my *dhandha,* right? People say men go crazy when I walk through the town. I am popular. I am proud to be known and equally proud of my work. We have the freedom to express ourselves; there is a difference between doing sex as "work" and being with someone you love. Maybe for the world outside, we are bad women, but we exist and our work exists because people want our services. But this pretence still exists, these ideas about one man being with one woman. It existed inside me as well.

'While working at the factory, I was attracted to a man from a minority community. He reciprocated my love and I was happy. But then came the question about marriage. My father and mother wanted me to get married; I did not. I told my father how I felt but he refused to listen. I was in love with this fellow, so I proposed marriage to him. I knew that marrying him would be difficult, but I was ready to face it all, the opposition and the hostility. What was there to fear? I told him, "You know the others who oppose and shame us—after all, what do they give us?" But he did not agree. He said our communities would not allow it and they would come after us. He told me to marry the man my parents had chosen and said we could continue to meet like before, or think about marriage at a later date. I believed him. I was naïve. I must have been no more than twenty years old. I had to get married, and soon I found that the man I married was like Shashi, which further pushed me towards my lover. I would come frequently to my father's village and we would meet; in fact, I would stay over with him. And so, our relationship continued.

'When my other brother noticed the frequency of my visits home, he got angry. He came to my in-laws' house and talked about my relationship with the other fellow. He beat me so badly in front of my in-laws that my little finger is crooked to this day. Though I was disgraced, I felt relieved of the burden of maintaining this farce of a marriage. Since nobody wanted me at my marital home, I stopped going there. For many years, I did not get a divorce, because my in-laws demanded money. According to them and our traditional practices, I was the one who had deserted my husband, so I owed them the bride price money and some compensation.

'With Vikalp's intervention, I finally got a divorce and a bit of money. After my return, there was no money at home, nothing at all. As my father got older and I was married off, all our agricultural land went into the hands of my brothers. They were the ones who tilled the land, and once they got full control, we got nothing. To this day, we have nothing from them. My partner at the time stood by me and shared some of my responsibilities. My parents were older by then. They did not have much and depended upon me for many things. My father does not know that I am divorced and that I received some compensation. He is too old, and I feel there is no need for him to be involved in all my affairs. I am on my own, and always have been.

'I struggled to make ends meet. Meanwhile, my relationship with my partner began to deteriorate. He would get drunk and beat me up. I tried my best to cope and continue with the relationship. This was my first love as an adult, but living daily with a drunkard pulled me down, too far down... It became impossible for me. After enduring a lot of pain, I was able to sever my ties with him. From then on, I found a different way to exist. This is how and why I came to be known as the most wanted woman in our town.

'After that, I got into a series of relationships, some with married men. One of them left his wife and began to live with me on the outskirts of the village. When the community learnt of our relationship, they tracked us down to the place where we often met. While I managed to escape, he was beaten up. Of course, my name and fame reached everywhere, right up to the police stations here, and beyond.

'This man was suspicious beyond belief. He was the one who was married, with a wife, and had children; I should have been the one who felt insecure in the relationship. But it was he who felt insecure. He would drink and beat me, calling me a prostitute. It is not a word anyone would like to hear from someone you think is decent. I am one, fine; call me what you will, but it is used as an abusive term against us. When it is thrown in your face to demean you… Well, I have never experienced such sadness and rage as I did when I was with him. I felt trapped. I tried to commit suicide. But the man's friend took me to the hospital and saved me.

'This gesture his friend did enraged my partner and gave him grounds to allege a deeper involvement between us that did not exist then. But maybe his suggestion worked on us.' She laughed out loud, winked at us, and continued, 'At that time, this allegation was entirely false, but then, it wasn't. But after that one involvement with a married man, I was wary since I had experienced the trouble that married men bring. The second time around, I insisted that the other guy take his wife's permission to have a relationship with me. He did that, and his wife gave permission. But this relationship too fell through.

'Until then, I had been trying to stay on a long-term basis with one man. Generally, the understanding was that the person would take care of me and all my needs, in good and bad times. But after a series of these relationships failed, a basic truth dawned on me. Not one, not a single one of the men whom I lived with, really cared; my thinking alone could not make the relationship work for long, and it would not involve care or love. They came to me to satisfy their needs. I used to think my relationships were different, but now, I feel they were no different from those of sex workers, who meet with different men on different days. Just because I believed that my relationships were based on loving one man at a time, it did not make that true. I had foolishly created this dream world which fell apart when

I began to live in it. So now you see why I make this difference between sex as work and sex while in love. When we are at work, a customer's touch does not feel like a violation. It is work, not sex. It may be hard for you to understand. We are being paid. It is something like somebody cooking for wages and then also cooking at home for family. The physical act is the same, but the attitude and the emotions are different. We are not wives. When I was living with men, these lines often got blurred.

'Carried away by this delusional world, which was non-existent beyond my imagination, I got pregnant twice. This created more trouble than I had bargained for. I wanted to keep the child both times, but I had to let it go. Children are so tied to marriages that men do not want the women they have affairs with to have a child. It was impossible to reason with them. When I talked to you earlier, it was not such a strong desire, but now, over the years I do wish to have a child without the compulsion of marriage. Anyway, for whatever time those relationships lasted, it felt like I was a "regular" woman. By regular, I mean "good, a good woman." In a way, it makes you feel good, until you realise that in this male-dominated world, no woman can be good enough.

'And so, I came to understand that everyone was selfish and had different motives of their own. When I had been involved with that man before my marriage, and he told me we could get married later, I believed him. They seek you out for their own benefit. I was so upset, but then I told myself—we all do it. Everyone does, right? You do it, I do it, everyone does it. We all play our part to mould situations and people to meet our needs. We please those people who we know can fulfil our needs.

'It is similar to us pleasing one of our customers. Our work is to keep our customers pleased, and in return, they give us money. If a customer is very pleased, they will listen to us and indulge us, give us whatever we ask for. It is a relationship driven by needs; you see what I am saying?' She scanned my expression to see if I had understood what she was saying.

'Short or long, it is a relationship, and we know it will end, but for the time it lasts, it is a relationship. And then, there are others who do not give us anything; they come to have sex, and the payment is simply money; sometimes not paid, at other times, deferred. Often, we have the same, regular customers. Customers with their regular demands, like people coming to the same hotel over and over to order their favourite dish. We have to know how to read our customers right. Some of them are from the police department. It's ironic—we are not defined as criminals or do something illegal, but they do make those associated with us into criminals, so we do not stand far from that insult either. But we are not criminals and neither are our customers. Our services are needed. Why can't the government see this?

'If you ask me, no one wants to be caught or do the catch-ing—the police, for example, no, they don't want to do it. And the customer? All he wants is a quiet entrance and exit, no undue attention. And us? We don't want to be seen or arrested either. We have families to feed and clothe, children to educate; our lives depend on the work we do. Getting arrested would mean that our people, old and young, will suffer. And those who run the hotels? They don't want to be raided either. You see, none of the parties want to play this game of cat and mouse. But sex is deeply mor-al; the state and the society have laid it down in the law and in norms. We are seen as loose women with excessive sexual desire. I ask those who come to us, are they "sexless, without desire?"'

Amti laughed at herself as much as she laughed at and with others. She made each moment or interaction a sheer joy, un-tainted by cynicism, even as she recounted with pride and ironic humour her job of providing satisfaction to customers and how it requires skills that improve with age. 'Of course, customers prefer young women, but older women have something that the young lack on both sides of this business. Many young customers learn from us before they settle into marriage. There is more to our work than mere gratification. How should I put it? We have to be out of the "ordinary". Some people come looking for magic, and we make magic happen. These are the customers with whom I rarely settle for less than 500 to 1,000 rupees.'

Amtiben reads her customers with uncanny accuracy. One of her customers always sought Amti's help for sending him the 'right woman, but a different one each time'. Amti, however, sent him the same woman each time, just with a different name. 'She needed money to pay her debts and get her child married, and I knew that he would never find out.'

'How?' I asked.

'Well, he never looks higher up than the breasts. If he did, then he would know!'

When Amtiben's parents passed away several years later, her brothers wanted to claim the house she had lived in. I went with Amtiben to visit the house that she loved and lived in. It stood forlorn without its occupant, and the boundary wall that surrounded its large space was all but gone. Perhaps it had deliberately been broken down and its stones carried away to make another protection in another name, place, and time. Just like Amtiben herself, who had moved away to another life to follow her heart. 'Getting older, I wanted a child before it was too late.'

I knew that Amtiben had stoically borne the pregnancy and the care needed to bring life into the world. 'I am happy to raise this boy while I have the strength to do so. I have found someone who can be a father to my child, and however long it lasts, it is good enough for me. I have fulfilled most of my desires and dreams. I wanted a child and now I have him. And I have the money to see him through his infancy to his adulthood.

'You saw the house. It is falling apart now. When I lived there, I took care of it. It was I who took care of my parents in their old age; I even spent money on the upkeep of the land. Now that my parents have passed, my brother is staking a claim to it. I have filed a case. My father had left it in my name in his will. I come here for the hearings, to meet old friends, and to just be here...

this is where I belong; I return to it every now and then, and I will keep coming here as long as I can.'

We looked at one another and smiled. We shared a love for this place, for the times that we had spent here and the stories that we told one another. 'Yes, me too,' I said, 'I too will keep coming here.' We continue to meet occasionally. Her child has started to walk. 'In another year or two, he will go to an English-medium private school,' Amtiben shares.

6

Post Box-31, GPO, Raopura

In 2002, as work on HIV/AIDS developed across the country, Vikalp partnered with the Gujarat State Aids Control Society, giving the organisation a kind of legitimacy and personal shield to work under whilst engaging with queer issues. Although this project did not include lesbian and bisexual women or trans men, we were able to discover that there were much higher numbers of people within that bracket than we had previously anticipated. We soon realised the limitation of our reach, as well as the constraints of many women being unable to fully disclose their sexual preference, a problem we ourselves and many other groups had experienced. We wanted to connect with these people, so we set up a telephone helpline and got ourselves a post-box number which we named 'Parma'.

'Single Women's Forum. PARMA is an informal group working for the rights of Single Women. Those interested in joining this forum may contact at: PARMA, Post Box-31, GPO, Raopura, Vadodara.' (Times of India. 20 November 2003.)

The usage of the term 'Single Women' was not our choice but a compromise we had to make, since the previous advertisement that was made mentioning the word 'lesbian' was not accepted in the regional newspapers. This made us aware that we would have to resort to different strategies and be 'open' only at selected times and places. 'Single women' was not exactly the right word-choice for women who loved women, but using it meant that the *Times of India* finally agreed to publish it in the English edition of its newspaper; however, this also minimised the scope of its reach, since most of the people we were trying to reach would have been Gujarati readers, not English. It was a reality test. Society was not going to concede that easily.

There are two names, Vikalp and Parma. The two names are symptomatic of our journey. 'Parma' is the post box of the initial years when we began to work in 2003. Some of these stories, like this letter and then Ankit's story, reflect this part of our journey.

It was not an easy decision to bring the letter which follows into the public eye. A few months after we received the letter, we went looking for the address that was given on the envelope, but it was not traceable. The idea then was simply to meet the person, but we were not successful. For a long time after that, the letter stayed, and continues to do so, in our files in its Gujarati original, just like a lot of other paraphernalia that we have collected over the years. But as the years went by, like the clippings that we keep flipping over, we debated if this letter could be put out in the public space. The writer himself says that he has changed the names and, in fact, adds, 'If you put this letter before society, men like me will have been given a voice.'

We really had no answers to the contradiction between the untraceable address on the one hand and the letter itself saying that it being put out in society would help men like him. We wondered if this meant that, while the writer wanted to stay anonymous, he wanted the world to know his dilemmas and conflicts. Though this reason is the most imperative one, and gave us ethical grounds to go ahead, there were several other reasons which made us reflect and debate. The relationship was between biologically different genders, so would this relationship not be heterosexual? It was based on changed interplay of gender roles, so would that be within the ambit of queer sexuality? What is queer sexuality? Is it not constituted of gender roles? Or is that alone what accounts for what we call queer sexuality? What is the measure of that composite whole we are seeking to define with the term 'queer sexuality'? Did not the writer identify as the gender opposite to his/her biologically assigned sex? The writer identified as a woman. We wondered if her relationship with a woman facilitated him or her to identify as lesbian. How do we answer or understand the question he/she raises? Were we ethically right to question the identity he chooses or even arrogate ourselves to the position of settling his second thoughts on that identity?

In all these discussions, the one important aspect that we had touched upon but did not dwell on was the wish of the writer, who wanted us to put out the letter. Were we too wrapped up in the boundaries of identities that we believed defined us truly— were we making boxes that we had argued had to be undone to let us in? Finally, as an organisation which champions gender and sexual choice, we felt that the letter needed to be in the public space.

7

Leefafey Mein Bandh Kuch Baate: Some Conversations Sealed in Envelopes

Respected…

I wished to write this letter after I read an article on lesbians under the title 'Vaacha' in *Chitralekha*, dated 19/7/04.

Firstly, I congratulate you for the efforts you are making to free women from guilt. I, personally, thank you very much.

My case is similar to the one shown in the movie *Dayra*. Biologically, I am male, but at a very young age, one of my close relatives had homosexual relationships with me, which in turn made me a passive homo. It took me years to escape that feeling. I got married, I have a son, but now my wife and I are separated. We didn't get a divorce, but we have been staying apart for years. Mentally, I have become feminine. I like to be a woman. I feel very relaxed and happy when I wear dresses made for women. But I don't like men; I hate them. I was in search of a woman who would become my husband. It is not possible that only a man can become a husband! It is possible that in the future a woman could become the President of India—what is wrong with that? A husband is a person who possesses the qualities of a lord, who demonstrates ownership, who is possessive, who rules over a wife.

Fortunately, I did find a woman who accepted me as a wife. Our married life was exactly like the movie *Dayra*. Her name is

Mukta. She really released me from my masculinity. I spoke to her frankly about my effeminate feelings, my inner feelings. Initially, she laughed a lot. Then, she said that she would think about it and answer me. It took her a month, but finally, she agreed. She accepted me just out of sympathy. I had nothing with which I could have sex with a woman. I used to get pleasure just out of oral sex. If I were to tell you in a little detail, I felt content by licking her vagina. And she also got pleasure in it. In fact, she was well-satisfied with her husband sexually. She used to come to me only two days a week.

All of this is no more. As soon as her son got married and her daughter-in-law arrived, she left all this behind. And now, I will be left to my fate, to live alone.

Twice a year, once on her birthday and also on Diwali, I send her a sari and other gifts.

Today I am 70 years old. My body is good and healthy. Though biologically I am male, psychologically I am totally like a female. I have not been able to put Mukta out of my mind. What name can be given to the relationship between us? Can this be called a lesbian relationship? Perhaps not. But what is your opinion about what happens to people like us? Within society, I live like a man, respectable, honoured, a family man. But I have to hide other things.

Is there an organisation for people like us? From what I have observed of society, many women have a male personality and many men possess feminine qualities like me. Human beings are complex and full of inconsistencies, yet they are divided only as male and female, and only on the basis of biological sex. The word *manushya* (human being) is derived from the word *manas* (mind). Shouldn't we take into consideration the mind of a person while designating them as male or female?

When I was young, I thought many times about changing my sex using medical facilities. But I didn't have that much money, and even doctors refused to do it. Now, at this age, I don't think about it. All I wish for is a friendship with a woman who would respect my femininity. Only women can help such men. The next age will be a women's age.

The issue of feminine men is not new; it has existed for ages, and some have found a few solutions. During the festival of Navratri, many men wore female clothes and let go of their masculinity. I would go to female spaces known as *sakhi sampradaya*, live out my long-time desire to be a woman, and return rejuvenated. Today, our society is in need of such therapeutic spaces where these feminine men can stay for some time and get rid of their masculinity.

I am indebted to Mukta. She provided me with such relief. She is totally uneducated and yet she accepted me as a wife. We stayed together for twelve years. During the initial two years, she felt uncomfortable, but after that, she played her role very well. In a true sense, she became my owner, lord, and husband. She commanded me. She was a maid, but whenever I used to go over there, she would have me do all the housework. I washed her clothes, swept, washed the utensils, cooked, and fed her. But she never liked my cooking, so I just had to help her in the kitchen. In the final years, she also beat me up. I have also put up with being beaten with a rolling pin. But I was happy.

I did not find women's clothes comfortable the whole time, but if I was dressed in male clothes, she would reprimand me like a strict teacher and order me to wear women's clothes. She used to give orders like 'stand up' and 'get ready,' and I had to follow them and get dressed in women's clothes. After this, she would order me to work. While I worked, she would relax and watch television the whole time. If I did not do something properly, she would scold me. But still, she filled my life with love. I miss her a lot. Now, I feel very lonely.

I used to pay her only a thousand rupees a month, but in turn, she gave me a lot…. I feel that only a woman who is from a village and is unlettered could have done everything that she did for me. She had a large heart, an understanding of the problem, and above all, she accepted me. I don't believe that she did all this just for money. It is indeed true that she needed the money, there is no denying it, but she did her duty with love, attachment, and geniality.

I have changed the names in this. If you put this before society, then men like me will have been given a voice. Personally, I just need one piece of information from you, which is, is there or is there not an organisation that exists for people like me?

Such problems do not have any permanent solutions. The human mind is like mercury, and that is why many solutions can create just as many new problems. There are myths in the *Puranas* where the person changes her/his sex by going into the river and emerges transformed, but such things do not happen in real life. Perhaps science may find a solution.

Sincerely,

8

Something This Name Lacks

'I am _____,[27] but I do not particularly like this name; writing it over and over again ever since I learnt to write, I should have gotten used to it, yet there is something that this name lacks.' I leaned towards him, about to intervene, when he stopped me, 'Wait!' he said, holding up his hand. 'Wait, first listen to my story, and then write it the way I am saying it. My official name, the name that appears in all my certificates, does not express who I am, but I do not want the reader to know everything right away.'

Our relationship spanned more than a decade and we had weathered storms worse than this. This was merely a gust of wind that ruffled us, a useful one that kept us apart as narrator and writer. We did not quite fit into the duality of a narrator/ writer relationship; we were more like willing co-parents in the unfolding of the story; we were in this together. 'So how should we begin, then?' I asked. He did not give me an answer immediately, but rose from his chair and pulled out his cell phone from his pocket. Ankit's most precious possession, then and now. He was inseparable from his phone, and for good reason. He set it down on the table between us, saying, 'In case she calls, I have to pick it up fast. I gave her the phone that she

---

[27] Ankit did not want to include a female name he was once called but has never related to.

calls from, and nobody knows about it.' Settling down again, he said, 'I was thinking, maybe we should start from the very beginning.'

'What beginning?' I asked.

'When we did not know one another, I mean, with the letters. Let's begin with the letters. You have them?' I moved across to him and Ankit and I sat side-by-side, going back in time as we reread the letters together.

24 July 2004

Dear friend,

I read your interview in Chitralekha, *and I felt a great sense of relief in my heart to know that at last, there is some-one who understands lesbian relationships. Yes, I am a lesbian too. I met my friend, whom I will call Komal, seven years ago. She lives a hundred kilometres away from where I live. That is why we cannot meet one another.*

We would write letters to each other and occasionally talk over the phone. We meet only during vacations. We both presumed that we would forget about one another after some time, but that has not happened. Every moment of every day, we can feel one another's presence. She loves me so much that I am unable to describe it, and I too cannot live without her. For the sake of her own happiness, I asked her to forget about me, but she was not at all willing to listen. Now, we have both com-pleted our education, and her father is in a great hurry to get her married. She is the only daughter. I tell her to marry, but she says, 'You can kill me instead. I will not marry anybody else.' I have asked her to promise me not to commit suicide, whatever the circumstances may be. She promised, and so I am confident that she will not do any such thing. She is not willing, and neither am I ready, to forget her. Our families do not know about our relationship. We both belong to the same caste. We do not want to separate, so what can we do? Give us

some suggestions, please. This is what I want, to live with her,
so tell us how. I will be so grateful. I have included my address
below and I enclose a self-addressed envelope.

Yours sincerely,

We began to reminisce about our first meeting. 'That was in
2004. The first time we met was in the jeep in which you came,
right? That was funny, each of us trying to play it safe. Did you
know I came with another friend of mine that day? I rode the
motorbike and she sat behind me. But when I saw three women
in the jeep, I felt safe, so I told her to get off quickly and I rode
over to where you had pulled over,' he said. We laughed at the
ridiculousness of the precautions we had both taken. But Ankit
was right—safety was important, both socially and physically. A
safe but simple way to meet was at a recognisable landmark in
the main market.

We parked our vehicles along the roadside and had our
first conversation right there. Words flowed seamlessly as we
shared the stories of our lives, the dim sounds from the market
buzzing in the background. We bonded instantly despite the
distance, age, and other differences between us. So, I was not
surprised when Ankit invited us to his house for lunch that
very day. But we held back a little, wary of what might follow,
'Will it be alright to have us over? What will you tell your family...about us?'

'I will deal with that.' I was struck by the beauty of his masculinity. He had long lashes over dark eyes that had been wet
with tears a while ago but were now alert, having since returned
from that space of emotion. He quelled our fears, asking us to
follow him on his motorbike as he rode ahead. Even then, I had
been curious to know exactly how he dealt with what he referred
to as 'that' when he said 'I will deal with "that"'. What did he tell
or not tell his family? Now more at ease with one another as we
reminisced about our times together, I could not resist asking,

'Remember when you took us to your house, the first day? What did you tell your sisters-in-law about who we were and how you knew us?'

'Curious, huh?'

'Well, I was wondering, but if you don't want to tell…'

'No, no, I don't mind. I told them you were my friends… or rather friends of friends who were on their way to Dwarka. Simple. Komal is a relative of my younger sister-in-law, and her family had suspicions about us. They did not like it when we met and talked to one another… She sort of knew about me, and God knows what she had told my brother. As for my elder *bhabhi*, I did not tell you this before, but she is actually my older brother's second wife and does not belong to our caste. My brother was involved with her while still married to his first wife, so his first wife left him as well as their two daughters. By that time, my mother had passed away, so there was no adult woman in the family to take care of the household and the two girls. My elder sister was married at fifteen, I was in the ninth class, and my younger sister needed to be taken care of. She had mental problems; she said she heard voices and was given some treatment for it. My brother took this opportunity to marry my *bhabhi* (his second wife). My elder *bhabhi* is different…having transgressed various norms set out for women, she is bolder than most, but subservient to my brother. She came into our family as a solver of crises. She has seen me through my crushes and heartaches. For different reasons, both my *bhabhis* were able to sense something about me, or maybe they know more than I think they do. But I have chosen not to find out. If I had told them anything more on that day, I don't know what they would have said to my brothers and what I might have had to face upon their return. You would have noticed that there were only women and children in the house when you visited; there were no men to cross-examine us. The timing was right. My brothers and my father used to come for lunch at two in the afternoon, so that was why I kept telling you to hurry. It is my older brother who basically disapproves of me. My father is somewhat tolerant. My other brother fumes at me, his disapproval coming from the fact that I was suspected of being involved with his wife's relative.

'In our community, women have to marry and live under the control of men. I am unmarried and suspected of being in love with a woman! Marriage to a man is a requirement for all girls. Even before they are married formally, girls are betrothed. No one asks the girl if she likes the boy or not, and later it does not matter what the boy has grown up to be, whether he is a man with or without a job, adequately educated or not, drunk-ard or not. It's the girl's destiny. Once engaged, both parties stand committed to it, and whoever calls it off has to pay the other party. In our community, there is a tradition of exchang-ing women. Take a woman and give a woman. In case such an exchange is not possible, 20-25 tolas of gold have to be given as compensation. Marriage is a very important event for the fami-ly, especially for girls.

'Girls can neither marry outside of the caste nor can they marry a boy of their choice. The family decides these things; this has been the case for generations. As soon as my youngest sister, the one who was unwell, had "improved enough" after seeing a psychiatrist and taking medications, she was married at 22. She could not marry the boy she liked, but my brother was able to choose his second wife from outside of the caste and marry her! And did you know that my brother is now involved with another woman? She is not a part of the family; she lives elsewhere in her own house, but everyone in town knows about this, including my *bhabhi*. But what can she do? Both women have sons that my brother has fathered.

'My sister is not particularly happy in her marriage, but she is unable to do anything like this. Once, she came to our house for the Janmashtami festival, and quietly slipped away with the boy she loved. But later, she was upset and guilt-ridden, so she went and told her husband what she had done. He was involved with another woman all the while, but as men, it is their prerogative, you see. He was so furious and beat her up so badly that her face got all blue and swollen. My father had to get involved. Do you see how the rules change? Men can take as many women as they like. My sister spent just one day with that other man and she had to face such violence. As for people like me, we are not allowed to love at all, not even one woman. We harm no one, and yet simple things like inviting friends home can become a problem. It is hard to predict how my brothers would have reacted. The best thing to do was to avoid confrontation with them and that is what I did.' Our timing was just right. Ankit and his family, like many others we know, found solace in this familiar tactic of the 'knowing and unknowing' space between zones of familial hierarchies and the ambiguity of silences.

'I have also faced the pressure to get married. As I grew older, my relatives, *Bhabhi*, everyone around me started saying "Ankit should get married". But I kept refusing. "Will you not marry?" they asked me, surprised. A simple no for an answer evoked even more questions: "You will live alone? All your life? What will happen in your old age…" Relatives would look at me in disbelief, and say, "Everyone needs someone," with a hint of mockery in their voice at my apparent lack of understanding. "What will you do later in life?"

'But I stuck to my words. I told my father clearly very early on that I would never marry. Every time the subject came up, I would fly into uncontrollable fits of anger. I don't know why. I would hurl abuses, shout in protest, and tell my father I just wanted to stay the way I was. Finally, he relented, and even though he did not say it in many words, he let me be. Over time, the subject of my marriage somehow stopped coming up. My father was far more accommodating than my brother. My brother sent his son to an English medium school but not his daughter. He tells his daughter educating girls is not important, learning how to use computers is a waste of time, and that she will marry and not work.'

I remember the trip to Ankit's family home back in 2004. Ankit wound his way through the busy streets on his motorbike, and we followed him in our jeep. Not very tall, he wore a shirt that slightly ballooned up behind him as he looked over his shoulder now and then to guide us to his house. As we navigated through traffic, *chagdas* and carts, we gradually left the bazaar behind and entered a more residential area. The land dipped and curved, and on that slight bend stood Ankit's house. As we stood in the open doorway, a sudden breeze rushed in, carrying the sounds and smells of cows, calves, and musty hay. We had arrived during the languorous spell between the various chores of a household. Across the cowshed, beside the tap, on a platform was a stack of buckets, upside-down on top of one another. A pair of brooms rested in a corner, and a little ahead, a loaded clothesline split the courtyard into two. Ankit and his father both lived in the room upstairs as insider/outsiders to the family units of the two brothers, their wives, and their five children. We met them all except the men in the house; we were surrounded by warmth as we ate off the sparkling steel *thalis* and *katoris* that were filled to the brim. Recalling the food we had eaten that day, I said, 'It was a great feast! I remember the taste of that cool and fresh buttermilk with each morsel that we took; it was delicious. I guess it had to be. We were in a *Bharwad* household after all, with cows in the shed.'

'Yes, indeed you were in a *Bharwad* household, but there are no cows in the shed now. The year you came was the last time we kept cows. A lot has changed since your visit. Both my *bhabhis* found it difficult to take care of the animals, since animals need a lot of care. In a way, my mother was the last one to continue our traditional *Bharwad* work. I remember her going from door to door to sell milk. I was in the ninth class when she passed away. After my grandfather, she was the one who revived our traditional occupation of keeping and tending to cows. Our traditional job of keeping the cows changed with my father. He got into the business of printing and dyeing saris. The town we live in is known for dyeing. The entire town and the surrounding areas rely on this industry for their livelihood. On one hand, some farmers protest against these industries, and on the other hand is the government's inaction with regard to them. You see, the rivers and the underground water are contaminated with the chemicals used in the dyeing industry. You must have seen the coloured waters and the froth of the pollution; it's visible now, that's how bad it has become. This is because of the gum-like substance called silicate that is used to dye the material. The farmers demand action from the government to put a check on it. But nothing changes. In fact, now, my two brothers are also involved in this work.

'Earlier, the farmers and we, the cattle-keepers, could coexist. But not anymore. We all vie for the same things, like these industries. Both we and the farmers are having a hard time just trying to survive these days. Many people, my own uncle, for example, have rented their land to this industry. Washing *ghats* have been constructed on the farming land. When the dyeing and washing takes place in these spots, the chemical seeps into the soil, destroying the crops and vegetables. Then, of course, farmers also suffer when monsoons fail or when there is excess rain.

'But my father says the Machhu dam tragedy was the worst disaster that he ever saw in his lifetime. It was in 1979 that the dam burst in August; I had just turned three. I have a faint recollection of dark clouds, incessant rain, and a sense of panic that gripped our family as all of us shifted to the factory. The factory is on a higher ground and the elders felt that, if at all our homes were to get flooded, we would still be safe up there. My father said we were fortunate that we did not experience the floods in that way, but the stories of those who suffered sent a shiver down our spines. The farmers were badly hit in the tragedy, and our community was too. The water swept away thousands of our cattle, and animals and trees all vanished in seconds. People lost their children, families, homes, and livelihoods. All gone in a flash. The government did little to help. Komal and her family lived around that region. We heard that there were people who removed ornaments off the dead bodies. Some people even allege that Komal's family was involved…but there is no telling the truth from the rumours.

'If there is one thing that I can vouch for, it's that my father is different in many ways. Even in my case, he is more tolerant than Komal's father. After our first meeting with both of you in my house, he was reluctant, but he let me go to Baroda to meet you. Komal's mother does not keep well, so the men of the house control everything. Since Komal is the only daughter, and now that she has graduated and her engagement is over, she can get married anytime. Earlier we might have gone our respective ways, Komal and I, but after reading that interview article and meeting you all, everything changed. I began to think differently. After you left, I called Komal and told her about the possibility of us living together becoming a reality. But I knew little about how things would unfold. The inevitability of her engagement hung over us like a sword. Her parents were looking for a good match. We did not want to separate then. We feared her engagement would do just that, separate us. But I kept hoping, and look where we are now? Still planning our getaway, and still at the place we were so many years ago. Separate and apart from one another and yet, I am still hoping.'

Looking at his cell phone and then at me, Ankit said, 'Sometimes, I feel like I am the one keeping this relationship alive. Do you know why I came to Baroda the first time? To plan our exit from our family homes, yes, but most importantly, to see for myself what kind of place it was that Komal would be going to after leaving home. Komal insisted that she should come alone and that I was to follow later. I can tell you now that I was apprehensive about coming to Baroda. I know we had met you but

…you know how it is, it was the first time that I had travelled that far.'

Looking away from me, he continued, 'I had roped in my cousin to accompany me, remember?' I heard the tremor in Ankit's voice and saw his dark eyes tearing up. I nodded in affirmation while he stretched out his hand to hold his mobile, as if waiting for it to ring. But it did not ring that afternoon. I did not press him to continue. I could see his frustration as he looked at his silent phone.

When Ankit came to see us in Baroda, after our first meeting, it was already the end of 2004. We had sat with him for hours, weighing different options, mixing and matching different ways in which the couple could get away, from plan A to plan B; when the night had begun to fade, we were yet to arrive at a foolproof, secure plan. The fact that they were both adults meant they stood a good chance of being able to defend themselves against any legal action, but this did nothing to ease their worries regarding caste and family relations, or of Section 377 being applied to them. All Ankit could bring himself to reveal at that time was Komal's real name and a photo of her that he carried in his wallet.

About four months later, we got a chance to meet Komal. She came with Ankit for a day. Petite, with large eyes and lustrous long hair, she wondered and whispered to Ankit how an organisation that did such good work could have no pictures of any gods or goddesses. Nonetheless, when she was around us, she felt free to snuggle close to Ankit and to tell us, 'There is always so much to say to one another, even though we talk every day.' Ankit added happily, 'We had not seen each other in quite a long time.' This trip was special for both of them, particularly so for Komal, because it gave her freedom from the daily grind. As a young woman with two brothers, the responsibilities of doing a lot of housework as well as keeping up the family's honour fell on her shoulders. With Ankit, she saw another possibility in her life. 'There will be far less control when I live with him.' She intertwined her fingers with his and looked at him. 'Right?' Since her absence would affect the family in more ways than one, she had planned the trip carefully over time. She had told her parents that she was going on a trip with friends from school. When her father came to drop her off, she boarded the bus that headed for the town she had mentioned. On the way, she got off and joined Ankit.

It was on this visit that we concretely planned Komal's getaway. We did all the planning, from boarding the bus to drafting the letters she would write and drop off to her parents in case an FIR was filed under missing person or kidnapping charges, or even theft. Parents have often done this to put pressure on their children and force them to return home. We cautioned them both that they would have to bear the consequences; no matter which one of them walked away from their families first, the other would be implicated for sure.

There was no way around that. Their friendship was known in both families, and each could be questioned about the other. Moreover, the fact they both belonged to the same caste impacted both families. Since there were marriage alliances between these two families, it was unlikely that her parents would relent, since 'family honour' was at stake. Even if it were a boy-meets-girl story, it could still have stood a remote chance, but their elopement was too scandalous for the families and community. Reality had created a sordid world around us. And yet, that day, we parted on a high. The magic of love and human hope often surpasses the mundane. Promises of staying together, now and forever, are as real as reaching the sky.

After their return, within six months, somewhere around the end of 2005, Ankit called. 'Komal's formally engaged, and soon her marriage dates will be fixed.' For Ankit, this did not amount to Komal going back on her commitment. 'It gives us more time and silences any suspicions about us being involved with one another,' he said on the phone. Komal had found out that the man she was due to marry was in love with another girl, which had given the couple hope. Komal felt encouraged, and so she told her future husband that she was also in love with someone else, though she withheld that her lover was a trans man. 'She was not in the least dismayed by the engagement, and she told me to not worry either. Even though her mobility was becoming more restricted, she felt certain she would be able to get away before she was married. She did not worry about the urgency with which her parents pursued her marriage plans.' Komal continued to plot her getaway with Ankit, and Ankit with us.

The intersection of Komal's engagement and their plans to elope brought us closer to Ankit. Initially, Komal's engagement did not dampen Ankit's spirits, but as the months wore on, the foreboding shadow of Komal's marriage grew darker and affected his optimism. 'Now I worry more because she has been engaged and we are still apart. She keeps telling me to wait, wait…but how long is one to wait? When will that right time come? She tells me that I must trust her. I do that but…' His voice faltered and then lapsed into silence. During this period, we exchanged many letters and had longer conversations. While at these meetings, Ankit continued to share the story of his life.

'Looking back, I can tell that my mother's death fundamentally changed our home from the inside.

'When she died, my father was away, in Mumbai. He could not come for her cremation. She complained of severe chest pain, so my brothers took her to Rajkot, but it did not help. I was the one who received the news of my mother's death. I did not cry. A strange kind of courage or numbness came over me. I did what had to be done, mechanically. But when they picked her up and carried her away, I cried.

'With my mother gone, the order in the household was completely disrupted. Her absence on my return from school was quite hard on me. From food, clothes, a sense of security, care …everything seemed to simply have been blown away or turned upside down. And then, my brother remarried. We had a new woman in the house. I experienced these changes intensely, and more so at a personal level. My body was changing. I was in the ninth class and these changes completely disrupted my sense of self. I was at a loss, unable to understand myself or the world around me. This filled me with anxiety. As I grew up, I experienced a lot of difficulty around my breasts. I hated that they "gave me away", so I started to eat less to keep my body fat down, and now it has become a habit. I remember, once there was a man who looked at me; I was waiting outside the school and suddenly he said, "Look at your breasts!"

'I can still hear the taunt in his voice. I stood silently, shocked, unable to find the words to retort. I hated this part of my body. It drew attention that I so desperately warded off. I did not like all these changes that were happening to my body. Especially the breasts—I wanted to cut them with a blade or a knife. But I could not do anything. I used to feel like taking a cloth and tying them both so that they did not show from the outside; I tried it once and then gave up. In the beginning, I used to wear a vest—it was a warm one but I wore it nonetheless and continued to do so for three years until it was completely worn out. I would wash it every day and then wear it again, waiting for it to dry. Girls would ask me, puzzled, "You are wearing a sweater in this heat?"

"No, it is not a sweater, not a sweater."

'I would brush aside their curiosity. What could one say? Then, I began to wear male undergarments. My undershirt was very tight-fitting, and this gave me some relief. My *bhabhi,* the elder one, would buy them for me; she still does.' As an explanation, Ankit added, 'We generally do not talk about these matters, but I have to ask her. If I go to the shopkeeper, he will wonder why a woman is asking for male undergarments. So, I had to tell her to do the buying. I have never worn girls' underwear. I do not like it. I did not know anything—I did not know why and how periods happened. I was around 13 or 14 years old. My older

sister told me how to use a cloth. She warned me that the same
thing would happen every month. It bothered me so much that
I would go up on the *agasi* (terrace) and sit for hours, just thinking. I would go up to be with myself to think.'

'What did you think about?'

'I do not know exactly, but it was something like "why am
I like this?" You know what I mean, the way I am, dressed as a
boy, feeling like a boy, but a girl, breasts, and periods and all…
At that time, I had no idea why, why it was me, of all people. I
was not like my sister, and I wondered why. My sister said that
she did not know either. At school, the compulsion of wearing a skirt and blouse had started. People like us face all kinds
of difficulties; many women ask me, "Are you a woman?" They
look at me closely for confirmation. "Do you get periods?" It's
like I am always up for scrutiny. I hate to be in these situations
where the most pressing concern is to fit me into a category.
In photographs from my childhood, I am wearing pants and
a shirt and my hair is short, exactly like a boy. My father was
doing well those days so he went to Mumbai often for work.
He would buy us new clothes, watches, shoes; I remember the
fights I would have with my brothers. I would never wear the
clothes that my father bought for me; instead, I would wear my
brothers' clothes.'

'Why?' I asked.

'I liked their clothes more.'

'Because their clothes were designed for men?' I wanted to
know.

'The clothes my father bought for me were also clothes meant
for men. I just liked my brothers' clothes better. Their clothes assured me those were male clothes. My parents had accepted the
way I dressed. Since they had accepted it, no one else could say
anything. Everything about me was boyish from the very beginning. I do not remember experiencing any compulsion to wear
female clothes at home.

'It was my mobility that was under threat, not the way I dressed. I was restrained from going around with male friends and returning late, especially once I reached the tenth class. My brother beat me with a belt to stop me from hanging out with boys. If only he knew! Everything about me—my habits, the way I walked, talked, ate, and dressed—was that of a boy. If you ask me to name a period or a time when I began to dress or behave like a boy, I can't, because I was always like this. No one could tell I was born a girl. People would look at me and would venture bets to know if I was a boy or a girl. Those who would bet that I was a girl would win since this was the truth, in one way. But those who bet I was a boy—they recognised who I was. So, in fact, they should have won the bet. I agreed wholeheartedly with them.

'I remember once, when I was a child, I went with my father to get a haircut. At the barber's, there was a group of men sitting around. They looked up and down at me and wondered about my gender. They placed a bet, and right there and then, they opened my pants. As they looked, all of them began to laugh. I stood there crying. Later, they gave me chocolates and biscuits.'

'Why?'

'To appease me, I guess, so that I would stop crying.'

'How old were you?'

'I was a child. I do not remember exactly how old but I do remember the whole incident.'

'Did your father intervene?'

'All I recall is that the atmosphere was full of fun and laughter. It was in this spirit that they verified my sex.'

Clearly, the incident had left an imprint on Ankit. As I write about the incident, it makes me think of the many levels of violence suffered by Ankit. At one level, Ankit's inability to recall his age when this incident occurred, or his father's response, is telling. Events, whether forgotten or remembered, sometimes act as mechanisms of self-defence. Perhaps Ankit's loss of memory about his father's reaction allowed him to continue viewing him as his protector, rather than question that role. He remembers the fact that he cried and that sweets were offered. He even knows why the sweets were offered. He registered the atmosphere of fun and laughter. Though painful, these memories do not threaten his familial relationship with his father. It is easier to go back and confront the humiliation faced when it is pinned down on strangers rather than family.

The abuse springs from socially sanctioned 'masculinity' that accorded this group of men the liberty to peep into the genitals of a child with impunity. Since the child does not identify as female, the projection of being a male is integrally linked to his sense of self. And this was mocked and completely demolished in the very space—a male hair salon—which he had visited to build and strengthen that identity. The compounding nature of violence the child faced is covert as gender variance is brutally put down.

The group of men grappling with their anxiety to fit Ankit into a binary, and in turn inflicting violence, is a familiar narrative. In his male persona, Ankit dangerously challenged the exclusivity of power and privileges men enjoyed. He had to be checked, and men, in their self-righteous prerogative to masculinity, did precisely that.

'You know, this thing about verifying my sex to know if I was a boy or a girl, it came up again and again. When I was studying in the fifth class, or maybe later, my teacher would come up close and try to look inside my shirt. I knew she wanted to verify if I was a girl or a boy. The compulsion of wearing a skirt and blouse was very hard on me. I liked to wear male clothes and I always wore my hair short, but when I came to the eighth class, we could no longer wear male clothes. We had to wear blue ribbons in our hair and oil them so that not a single strand fell out. I had to stick almost a dozen pins in my short hair to comply. It was an ordeal that I suffered every day. It still keeps happening. People look you up and down all the time, wondering.

'My parents also took me to a doctor for various tests. They had taken me for some minor ailment, and the doctor advised them to show me to a specialist from Mumbai, and so they took me to the specialist. He asked me to open my shirt and show him my breasts. I hated it but I had to do it. He examined me and my blood was taken for tests. I do not know what these tests were, nor know what they were looking for. What I know is that the report showed pairs of XX, Y, and all that.'

'And then?'

'The report came. It said I was a normal girl. After all the tests, funny they found I was a normal girl, with all the X's correctly paired. As if all the right pairing can explain it all. All I can say is perhaps it relieved my parents that I was normal. Or maybe the doctor told them more than they let me know,' he said, shrugging his shoulders, 'Who knows?'

Throughout our relationship, Ankit slowly divulged more of his childhood to me. 'In the evenings, I used to go out with my friend. He had been affected by polio. We got along well. Together, we went to the market to watch the girls and women come and go. It used to be fun. When a woman's bra strap showed, we would both get a thrill. We would nudge one another and show the other person the sight. My friends never talked of my sex or said that I was a girl. We were friends and that was it. I used to roam around with boys and I enjoyed it. I have always liked girls. I used to watch the models walk the ramp on TV and, during the song sequences of Bollywood films, I would watch the women, just for enjoyment. It was the English films that always "showed more" than the Indian films—lip kisses, tight hugs, and more.

'Weddings in our town were fun too. When I went for weddings, my eyes would follow the women closely; observing them, I would look for the most beautiful amongst them. As soon as I found the prettiest one, I would hover around her, looking at the way she styled her hair, the clothes that she wore, and all her feminine ways. I used to think that one day, I too would get married. That I would have a wife and that she would love me immensely. I used to think about the *barat* (bridegroom's party) I would have at my wedding, and how I would go as a bridegroom with the rest of my family to get my bride. I did not know that it was not meant to be. It was only after I reached adolescence that my family made me realise that I was a girl; girls become brides, not bridegrooms.

'For a long time, I did not know that I was different. Now, when we have to go for weddings and I have to choose the side to eat or sit, I often wonder which side I should go to, the ladies or the gents section? I hate that look when I am being assessed, stared at with curiosity, and commented upon. Exactly the same thing happens when it comes to using the toilets—I try to avoid going to such separate male and female spaces. People who are like me generally choose a school where boys and girls study together. But I chose to stay in the girls' school. I was already in love with a girl named Dipta. I told my mother that if those tests found that I was a boy, then I would marry Dipta. My mother agreed.

'Dipta was the first girl with whom I fell in love. She stood out from the others. She was beautiful, with her hair styled in what we called the "Diana cut". She stayed in touch with me even after she got married, but I felt that it was best for us to stay apart. In school, we studied in separate sections of the same class.

'If she was late, I used to save her a spot next to me at prayer time. Prayer time became our first meeting point. When I think back, Dipta grew up with a lot of freedom, unlike many of us. Her mother had gone to America and returned because she didn't like it. I felt that her mother knew about us and did nothing to stop us. Initially, Dipta did not understand that girls could love girls. I tried hard to get her attention. I bought a notebook and I wrote in it, from cover to cover in red ink, "I love you". I presented it to her the next day. She was moved. "I love you too," she said.

'Since we were in the same class, I began going to her house to study together. When I could not go to her house, I would cycle and hang out near her house and wait and watch. I knew that she would come out to the swing in the evening. Once I had seen her, I would return home. The next day, I would tell her the colour of the frock she was wearing the previous evening. She used to be surprised. I loved that. Then she would ask me how I knew. But of course, you never disclose all these things.

'Her house was small and pretty. She lived there with her mother. Her parents had separated. Her mother was a schoolteacher. I used to plan my visits so that they would coincide with the time that her mother went to school. I would bring her chocolates and we would watch the TV in the sitting room. Then she would come up close; our bodies would touch. I felt awkward and shy. Even though I loved her, I didn't know what to do. She was very sexy. She kissed me first, and then I felt encouraged. I too returned the kiss. My first sexual experience was good and intense. The trouble was that she was basically interested in boys. She had four boyfriends. Our relationship did not last.

'After things ended with Dipta, I found out that another girl was interested in me. I will call her Aruna. I wrote her a love letter, but she did not like it and complained to our principal. The principal called me into the office. When I saw her standing there, I knew why I had been summoned. The principal picked up my letter and asked me if I had written it. I said "yes". Ankit laughed as he recalled the incident. 'He looked at me so sternly and demanded an answer from me as to why I had done such a thing. Now, what does one say to that? It is such an absurd question, especially at our age. For five days, I was not allowed to sit in class. I was told to stand outside. The school was teeming with rumours about me. The principal sent a written complaint to my father and told him to watch me.

'The upshot of it all was that the whole school got to know that I had written a love letter to a girl! It created such a stir, and all of a sudden, my fortune changed. At recess time, girls would flock to me. One girl in particular would come up, kiss me, and then run away, even before I could draw a breath. Veena was another friend of mine, just a friend, we have been friends since class five. I think Veena was also interested in me, but she never acknowledged it openly. She would tell me, "I do not know how to kiss, teach me how to do it?" So, I taught her, and we would occasionally kiss.

'A girl that I really got involved with was Kamini. My suspicion is that Aruna showed my love letter to Kamini. I would often meet her during break time. I'd sit on the wall, and she would come up close enough for our knees to touch. Kamini and I attended the same tuition class after school. She constantly stared at me. When I looked up and caught her eye, she would look away, and when she saw me, I also looked away. We did not say anything about our love for one another. But I wrote her a letter. She responded and acknowledged that she loved me; then, our relationship changed. A religious function (*jagran*) in her house gave us an opportunity to meet. The adults were busy. That night, we were up till four in the morning. We slept together. She lived in a huge bungalow. She had a separate room and we slept there, just the two of us. It was the first time for us, being together in bed. It was a memorable night. I am sure she will remember me.

'So much happened between us. She would cry out in pleasure and want more sex even after; it was exciting to be with her, refreshingly exhausting. During the exams, I would go to study with her. We studied until 12 and sometimes until much later. After everyone had gone to sleep, we would have sex. In the morning, she would get up early, make breakfast and bring the tray to me. She really fed me—she enjoyed food and made me enjoy it too. Not only food, we also enjoyed watching movies. I saw many films with her. We would make out in the theatre, snuggling close in the dark. What better place than in a theatre?

With all the romantic songs and dancing, the environment added to our love.

'Then Dipta…you know, the first girl whom I had left? She wrote me a letter saying that she still loved me. I began seeing her as well. She would meet her boyfriend and me. We both had our partners. No, of course I did not tell her about Kamini. Nor did she tell me about her boyfriend.

'It was around this time that Komal came into my life. Our community marries within our caste, so Komal and I have a host of common relatives, and through them, gossip, information, news, and tensions between families are all passed down. It was via this network that Komal heard about me. We, as *Bharwad* people, have a practice of community weddings. The boys' and girls' families congregate to have their children's marriages together so that they can share the expenses of the wedding. Komal came to our town for one of these collective weddings. These events are like fairs—full of colours, people, food, songs, and loudspeakers for days. I did not know it then, but she told me she had come especially to see me.

'I was not interested in who came into our house, and I went about my business as usual. One morning, when I was having my morning cup of milk in the kitchen, I saw her at the sink, brushing her teeth. I told myself, "Well, well! This one is good-looking…" I saw that she spotted me. The next minute, she walked into the kitchen and began talking to me. Then we really got going, asking one another about the classes we were in, the subjects we took, our teachers, schools, and marks. She told me she would have to take the tenth class exam again because she failed the first time. I told her I was in the second year of my undergraduate course. All innocent stuff.

'She invited me to her house. I said yes and then I forgot all about it. I was involved with Dipta and Kamini then. She called me many times, and each time I said I would come, but I didn't. She did not stop calling me. Then one day, my brother and *bhabhi* were going to Komal's house. Colleges were closed and there was nothing to do, so I went with them to pass the time. My younger *bhabhi*, I told you, is related to Komal's family. She and my brother stayed there for a day or two and then returned. But since I was on my summer break, I ended up staying for 15 days. Komal and I slept on one settee in the sitting room. One night, Komal had period cramps and she was in a lot of pain. She turned to me and held me, wincing in pain. I tried to pacify her by saying that it would pass. I wrapped my arms around her, holding her gently and close. I ran my hands over her back and head. The warm exciting touch of our bodies changed our relationship. That night, we slept holding one another. What can I say, it had to happen, it was waiting to happen, our attraction to one another. Ironically, the biggest opposer of our relationship—her father—was the same person who gave us more opportunities to be together! He told us that it was too hot to sleep inside and suggested we sleep on the terrace. We did. There, we had no fear of anyone coming up and walking in on us. So that was how it started. I mean, physically. Komal's interest in me was quite evident before I made the first move. We did what we did, but we never took off our clothes. Not for another five years. When she started initiating—like opening my shirt buttons—I would tell her, "Fine, go ahead. I will take my turn later, just you wait".

'What I said was almost prophetic, because we really did have to wait. We had just confessed our love for one another when tensions between our families prevented us from seeing each other. For almost three years, we were only able to exchange letters. We managed to survive that period. Then came the mobiles; these became our lifelines and completely changed the way we communicated. We could now talk to one another for hours on end at night. We still do.

'Then we met again under the strangest of circumstances. It was just before I met you and Indira. I think that was the first time we made love without clothes. She fell sick and her parents wanted me to come and visit her. Komal's younger cousin had drowned in the underground water tank. When she saw her cousin, she was so shocked that she fell unconscious. She did not talk or eat anything for days. And worse, she did not even recognise anyone. Her father asked me to talk with her about earlier times, to revive her memory. Of course, now things are different, he wants to throw me out. But at that time, he called me for help. When I arrived, she was sleeping. I sat down quietly beside her. When she woke up, I asked her if she recognised me; she nodded yes. It was during this visit that she asked me to take off my clothes. I used to be reluctant to do it, but this time she insisted, "Before I die, I want to love you and hold you. I may not live, who knows?" Together, we overcame many hurdles. I used to feel awkward to show myself, but that has changed; we have managed to stay together even through those difficult times.

'Komal was not like the rest, she was different. Of all the girls I knew, she was the only one who said that she wanted to live with me. Though my relationship continued with Kamini, I often found myself thinking of Komal while talking to her. I even shared this with Kamini, and she was very upset. So, I had to deny the extent of my feelings for Komal. Once, I went to see Komal; knowing that Kamini would call me on the home phone, I told my elder *bhabhi* to tell her that I had gone to Rajkot in case she called. Unfortunately, when she called, instead of my elder *bhabhi,* the younger one picked up. She told her that I had gone to see Komal. That really hurt Kamini. She called me there and asked me to come immediately. But I told her it was not possible to come right away. Later, when I met Kamini, she asked me who I wanted to be in a relationship with. I had to tell her. It was Komal that I chose. It was not easy to break away from Kamini; I loved her too. But so far, it was only Komal who had talked about spending a lifetime with me. The rest, I knew would get married and leave me someday. I met Komal in 1998 when I was 22.

'I don't know how much Komal's parents know about our relationship. Our relationship never really stared them in the face. Letters, phone calls in the night… We meet so rarely, and they hardly
know anything about those meetings. All of it has been silent and
unobtrusive. Once, the secret phone that I had given Komal, the
one we used, was left unattended, and her brother handed it to her
and said nothing. We were worried for quite a while. Certainly,
they suspect something; they have advised her to sever all contact
with me. Not once, but several times, both directly and indirectly.

'We call and fix our meeting time. Then, I travel to her place
which is about 50 km away and we meet near the temple. We are
meeting the day after tomorrow. I will leave soon. She has asked
me to come. She says it's important, but refuses to tell me what it
is. Perhaps this time, she is ready to make our escape plan. I wish
she were ready to leave now, but there is always something that
comes up, and our plan gets postponed. Maybe this time, she will
decide that she's ready.'

Ankit left that evening with a promise to return soon and
continue with the rest of his story. We kept in touch through telephone and letters. After their meeting near the temple, Ankit had
escaped Komal's father by seconds. He and Komal had just parted when Ankit saw her father striding towards him, only to then
suddenly walk past without a word or a glance. Perhaps he chose
to ignore Ankit. But it was a grim foreboding of what would happen after their elopement. The reason Komal had called Ankit to
the temple was to tell him that she had manoeuvred a two-day
visit to a friend. During that time, Komal would come for a day
to Baroda with Ankit to celebrate the New Year with the group.
He sounded excited. It seemed that Komal's planned visit to
Baroda was a clear indication of her promise to leave and be with
Ankit very soon, though some people from within the group often asked Ankit what was holding Komal back from coming right
away. If not now, then when would she come? A few weeks later
we got the following letter.

Dear friends,

I am responding late to your letter, I am sorry. When you called, my father was around so I could not talk properly, and that is why I am writing to you. Right now, the situation is that Komal's mother is scheduled to have an operation. Her marriage is now being postponed until after Diwali.

I shared everything with my father, and his response has been far from encouraging. He asked me 'Where will you live? What will you eat? And what will you do? One cannot do such a thing. If you persist, I do not have any money to give you. You will have to do everything on your own.'

The other thing, as we had discussed, the plan is that only one of us will come away initially. Komal feels that she should go first. She continues to insist that I should follow her later, so that my name does not get linked with hers, and our relationship does not come under scrutiny. No one will like it if we are found out. For this reason, we cannot live together in Baroda. You have come to my house, so my family recognises you and knows your names. And my father knows that I came to meet you. Because of this, we will have to think of another place where we can live. We may have to hide for at least six months or one year, who knows. My father loves me a lot. I trust him. I know that no matter what, he will eventually come around.

I am more worried about Komal's father. He is a 'goonda' type of a guy and will stop at nothing. A total of 70 tolas of gold have come to Komal, so if the marriage does not happen, then all of this gold will have to be returned. I doubt her parents will be happy with this. But Komal is least interested in gold and wealth. We will live together no matter what happens, and whatever others may think.   Once her mother's operation is complete, then Komal can come away. She is fed up of hearing people pass comments, asking her questions about her marriage and putting pressure on her to marry. She does not talk

to her fiancé, and her mother gets angry that she does not talk
to him. She is in such a difficult situation. Sometimes, I suc-
ceed in convincing her that all this will pass and that the future
will be good. We are both tired of living separately. Right now,
all we have is hope from you. We trust you, and know that you
will know what's best.

If you courier the letter, it is generally delivered in the
morning. The postman delivers letters that are sent by post in
the afternoon. That's when my father returns home from the
factory for his afternoon nap. Please courier your letters.

As promised, Komal came with Ankit that new year. As the clock
struck twelve, and everyone raised a loud cheer, Komal's phone
rang out distinctly. Her fiancé was calling to wish her a happy
new year. Ankit was taken aback. She had saved his number as a
dot. The conversation alerted Ankit to the identity of the caller.
Ankit demanded, 'Why is he calling you if you claim you are
not in contact?' Komal countered that this kind of wishing was
merely a formality. Tension gripped the group as Ankit argued
that the call was not a mere formality, and that 'midnight calls
are made between people who are familiar with one another!'
Suddenly, someone shouted, 'Komal!'

Komal was slumped on the sofa, with her eyes shut, unmoving. Ankit was beside her, calling out her name. Others
lifted her feet up and made her lie down straight. Someone
brought water, others shook her, but she remained inert and
stiff. We rushed her to a hospital nearby. The doctors examined
her, and, finding her pulse and pressure normal, they asked us
not to worry since everything seemed normal. They said that
she should come to soon, and in the meantime, we should let
her rest. While Komal rested with Ankit beside her, the agitated
group wondered why Ankit was not being able to read the writing on the wall, but each time someone said that, Ankit would
become angry, saying that he knew Komal well. Some preferred

to remain silent while others continued to argue. The next day, Ankit and Komal left.

Back at home, the couple continued to find ways to talk. After her visit to Baroda, Komal came to Ankit's house. Being in the same community both helped and hindered. Though the relationship between the families had become tense, there was also a social pressure to maintain it. Taking advantage of these blurred lines, Komal had been able to visit. The older brother's daughter knew of Ankit's relationship with Komal, and she supported them. It was during this visit that the two were married before the deities in Ankit's house. Ankit, who was beginning to lose faith in Komal ever joining him, now believed Komal when she said that her contact with her fiancé was more of a perfunctory obligation. 'Why else would she bother to come and marry me?'

However, when Komal's marriage seemed to perpetually be getting postponed, Ankit grew despondent. Except for the commitment Komal had made, Ankit had no definite date from her as to when she planned to leave her home. Ankit had nobody in his family with whom to talk about all of this. Ever since he completed his LLB in 2003, Ankit had never applied for a job outside of town and had lived his life in anticipation of the moment when Komal would finally come and everything would fall into place. Years went by, and he continued to live in this town where he lacked good employment opportunities. Ankit did not find a job. Now, there was even more reason to not leave the town. Though the day of Komal's departure from her home remained vague and indefinite, Ankit was sure it was more imminent than ever before. For Ankit, it was imperative to be there to avoid suspicion of his involvement. Ankit was in a state of ennui, where any action seemed flawed and therefore futile.

Ankit sat, waiting for phone calls, brooding and sad, often worried over the future outcome but unable to do anything about it. Caught between hope and disappointment, his mood swings were taking a toll on his well-being. It took a lot of prodding and persuasion to get Ankit out of this mood. We somehow managed to get him to travel from his town to a nearby city, where we had him meet another trans person who had expressed a wish to meet 'people like me'. It was after this meeting that we asked Ankit to come and work within our growing queer community so that he could learn new skills and experience life more. Bit by bit, we succeeded in persuading him to come to Baroda. Living away from home for the first time and taking responsibility for his own needs helped to distract his mind from his problems. It also allowed for Ankit to see life within a much larger frame. A new challenge he now faced was this: how were the two of them to survive if there was going to be neither support nor resources from the family?

Ankit talked about this period saying, 'Those months that I spent here were critical for me, and now when I think about it, I wonder, how could I not have a bank account of my own? Or be unable to take care of my own needs myself? When I look back, I always smile when I think about Chandresh, the guy from Jamnagar we met before I came to Baroda. When I met him again, I heard him talk about himself and his partner in the traditional roles of a man and a woman. I said to him, "When you go there, you will forget all these ideas about roles of men and women, just the way I did". Then suddenly, Ankit turned to me, 'I wrote you a letter after I left from here. Do you have that? At least it will not be all about Komal. At that time, I had so many things on my mind. Let's see it.'

'Yes, let us see it. I have it. But there is something I wanted to ask you, the address on your letters reads "Chaprajni Bari". I know *bari* means window but this word *"chapraj"*, what does it—'

'This is the name of the king. It is a long story, but I like it because it speaks for people like us from oppressed castes.' Ankit narrated the story and I am rewriting it here as it was told to me, with Ankit's observations as well as my understanding and interpretation.

The story goes like this: A mochi (cobbler) hears of the beauty of the daughter of the Sultan of Delhi and yearns to see her. He meditates and prays for his wish to come true. The deities are pleased with his prayers, he is granted his wish, and the daughter pays him nocturnal visits, borne by the air. The mochi simply looks at her beauty in rapt admiration. But the daily ritual changes the colour of her skin; she looks darker and starts to smell of leather. When her father asks his daughter the reason for these changes, she is equally puzzled, except to say that every night she is uplifted with her bed and taken somewhere and returned before the day breaks. The father then tells her to ask the name of the place where she is being taken and with whom she meets. The daughter dutifully asks these questions and reports back to her father.

When the Sultan hears this, he is furious and mounts an attack on the king of Jetpur. In the meantime, when the Jetpur king and the people learn that the mochi was the reason for this attack, the people want to immediately kill/slice the mochi in two for having brought this trouble upon them. But the king restrains the people from resorting to such a violent action and goes into the battle. He dies fighting, defending his people, but not before a sweeper bravely attempts to save the king but dies in the process.

'Chaprajni Bari', where Ankit lives, is mostly inhabited by oppressed caste people. This story, handed down through the generations, is woven in the daily lives of people who live there. It looks at them through the high ramparts of the fort built long ago by the benign king known as Veer Chaprajwada. A statue of him riding a horse with a dagger in hand adorns the main crossroad of Jetpur. A temple in his name stands tall amidst the thick of the crowds that once was a quiet, lonely area. Every victory in election, any gains in life and other auspicious occa-

sion calls for a reverential bow of thanks at this temple. Not far
is the temple that commemorates the supreme sacrifice of the
sweeper named Jogda who died defending the king. A temple
that was built during those times being dedicated to someone
whose identity rests on the last rungs of the caste hierarchy is incredible, even now in our current democratic times, when people
from oppressed castes are denied entry into temples. But here in
Jetpur, though a story spun on some traditional ideas of women's
helplessness and some on predictions by angels, we have a story
that empowers the marginal community; it recognises the sacrifice made by them in the form of a temple built in the name of
Jogda Dada from the sweeper caste and the king who did his duty
of protecting his people without discrimination.

Ankit shared that he likes the story because it also shows the
prejudices that the powerful, dominant-caste and dominant-class
people hold about the oppressed castes, evident in the Sultan's
query about his daughter, who appears to look darker and smells
of leather. 'You tell me, which member of our caste will talk of
dark complexion and body odour? My community can be said to
smell of the herds we raise. This is not the way people should be
labelled; our TG (transgender) community is also labelled like
this. We do not like it.'

Having shared our ideas about the story, we read the letter
together. On rereading it, I said, 'You had asked for confidentiality when you wrote it. Do you want to put it out there?'

'Yeah, at that point, I did not want anyone to know about my
desire to undergo sex change. A lot has transpired since. So, we
can share the letter now. I do not want to have the sex change
intervention yet. I mean, I still do feel that I am not a woman,
and just saying that I am a man is not good enough. But being
a man has its drawbacks. Access to woman-centred spaces gets
limited. So, for now, I will not undergo surgery just yet. It is a
difficult situation, but I can cope. I don't know, I may stay the
way I am now.'

2007

Dear Friends,

Before I begin, I ask that this letter be kept confidential. That is why I called specifically to tell you this before you had the letter in your hand. This time last year, I was in Baroda, trying to learn new things and adjust to a new city and a new life, so different from what I was used to.

I remember my time there vividly, as if it was yesterday. I would go to the field during the day and return in the evening. I was so tired in the evenings that I was not able to talk to Komal. Those days, I used to feel so much anger brewing inside me. Komal was not coming to join me, I was in a new environment, I was not sure if I was doing the right thing. With or without reason, my anger would spill out from my eyes in tears. I could not tolerate anyone telling me anything, especially when you and others in the group told me that Komal may not come.

It used to feel as if everyone was finding fault with me. I had no work experience, I knew that, but I did try to do my best. Then, when I had to make the shift from living with you to the hostel, sadness overtook me. Somehow, I managed to adjust there, though I did not like it at first. Then I made friends, some of whom I still keep in touch with. Then life changed suddenly, and it became more enjoyable. I began to understand much more about life. I learnt a lot.

I did not want to open a bank account because I did not think it was important. Perhaps it was because I had never earned my own money before. Now that I have the account, I see its value. Neither did I see the necessity of bringing my motorcycle; I was not used to driving on such busy streets in a city. But when I did that, I was able to experience the city in a new way—I got to know the streets and my confidence grew.

In retrospect, I can say that my stay was good, even though there were moments of pain. Especially the time I worked at the superstore. I wanted to learn about different kinds of jobs and earn more, and there, I got a placement immediately. What a job it was! It turned out to be the worst period of my life working there, under that Hitler-like sethani's watchfulness. All of us worked so hard for so little money. We could not sit while working, except for the one-hour lunch break. I had never thought about the people who do this kind of work, until I was in the very same position. It was the most tiring work I ever did. When night fell, my feet ached so much that I could not go to sleep. Komal used to get angry, and then she would cry and ask me why I needed to go through all that.

All that, and more, has changed me. Being part of a group has taught me a lot about people and how there can be a different way to think: for example, about men and women, about carrying out my own routine, like folding, and washing clothes, leaving the bathroom in order, and managing money, booking railway tickets and travelling on my own. Most importantly, meeting someone who had actually done what we dreamed of...changing his gender. After meeting him, I am now thinking seriously about getting my gender changed. I do not like my body. I also want to be like him. I have discussed this with Komal, and she is agreeable to it. I do not know how to tell my father. Will you help me? I experience a lot of conflict. You people will understand my conflict, it is meaningless to talk about this with anyone else. This was one of the reasons that I called to request you to keep this letter to yourself.

Today, if someone tells me that Komal will not come or that I have to separate from her, I do not like it. I am telling you she will come. I am convinced. She cannot be without me.

The letter ends with usual queries about our health before signing off.

'In retrospect, the most valuable thing I learnt here was that I needed to earn. I remember it was around this time we had discussed the property and resources that I have. It was in this context that I asked you to talk to my father.'

Ankit's words helped me recollect that meeting with his father. At our request, Ankit's father had agreed to a very short stopover in Baroda. As queer activists, this was our first parental meet. Affable and soft-spoken, he had greying hair and a forehead furrowed with deep horizontal lines that revealed little of what went on in his mind. He listened intently as we spoke to him. Ankit would never marry in a traditional way, we reasoned with him, but the absence of marriage should not deprive him of his rightful share in the family resources and property. By birth, he was the unmarried daughter who had a share in the father's property. I remembered that we had a long discussion on deprivation of property or inheritance rights if a woman changes her gender.

While Ankit's father fully agreed with us, he said he had little in his name and in his bank account. The small piece of land he owned would fetch a negligible amount if sold now. Nonetheless, he promised to make sure that Ankit would be secure for the future. For him, this meeting was special. He was meeting people 'like his child' for the first time. He wanted to know if there were many more people like Ankit. He went on to ask in a whisper, 'Since childhood, she has been like this…' and with much hesitation, he asked, 'And those who are here, were they also like Ankit right from childhood?' We nodded in agreement. As we parted, a smiling goodbye and a warm handshake told us we were sending off a relieved parent.

Though Ankit's father did not mention it, Ankit surmised, 'If my name is included in the property settlement, my brothers will resist it and there will be tension in the family. Otherwise, he is well-meaning. In his own way, he has understood me and supported me throughout. He will do something for me. I think he knows me better now, after meeting other people like me.

'It was almost two years after I left Baroda, February 2009. I was in the first year of my postgrad studies. This was the year when I found out about her marriage. Ironically, this was also the year that our love was decriminalised, and there was such a surge of hope. I had attended those Pride marches on the streets when I had shouted "Queer and proud" till my throat nearly burst. Those bright colours, such crowds in the face of shame that we lived through daily—this was a sight that I had never imagined. I cried with joy. We were so happy as we walked the streets with our posters; that freedom, like my love, did not materialise, but I will always remember the year 2009 as special, the beginning of many changes in my life, kindling hope and desire.

'She called me in the night saying that those people were getting her married the next Saturday. She was calling from inside the bathroom, and her father was screaming from outside. The next day, she called to tell me that everything was uncertain. She said, "Since the *kuldevi* is not sanctioning this marriage, my mother is crying, but my brothers are impatient and my father is venting his anger. Nothing is decided yet." She asked me not to worry, because the chances were that nothing would come of it. But I was worried. Then, we did not communicate for a few days, which was unusual in our case; we usually spoke every day. When I called, the phone rang on and on, unanswered. I did not have her home number. I called her friend whose home we had met at in 2008, but she didn't pick up either. Desperate, I decided to go to her town to try and meet her. I thought of the computer centre where Komal had started going. I remembered her pointing it out to me. I went there, but it was closed. I went to the shop next door and asked for the computer teacher's home address and went there. She was wearing pants and a shirt. I think she is like us, but she does not say so. I told her that I was Komal's friend and I wanted her address.

'Perhaps she saw through me, or maybe Komal had told her about me, or she had somehow recognised me. It's hard to guess how exactly, but I am sure she recognised me—my gender and sexual preference, I mean. She told me obligingly that Komal was getting married soon, and that she would be coming in the evening to give her the invite. She suggested that I could meet her then. Shocked, I blurted out, "But she does not want to get married! We have plans to live together!" Somewhat rudely, as if waking me up, she looked harshly at me, bringing her face close to mine and said, almost menacingly, "Do you realise that Komal's marriage is fixed, and it is happening tomorrow? Tomorrow," she repeated, trying to drill it into me, "She is getting married." She even questioned if I was capable of taking care of Komal. I pleaded with her to give me Komal's number, or at the very least to give me a chance to talk with her. She dialled her landline number. Her mother picked up the phone and said that Komal had gone to get *henna* on her hands, that she would be coming in the evening. Suddenly hope sprang up in me. I asked the teacher if I could stay in her house until Komal arrived but she refused. Her refusal and my own persistence with Komal suddenly made me wonder what I was doing there. I was rushing from town to town, from shop to shop to see Komal, while she was happily getting her hands adorned with *henna*.

'It occurred to me it was not worth my while to wait for someone who could not make that call, that one call, to tell me the truth about her marriage. We talked for hours every day for so many years, and now when it was critical, she could not call and tell me straight out. It was all over, I told myself. But it was not to be. Not yet. I took a bus back to the hostel. The bus was very full, and there was one vacant seat next to a woman right at the back. When I reached the seat after wading through the throngs of people, this woman put her hand on it, craned her neck to call out to another woman, and asked her to sit beside her. I stood defeated, with my hands up, holding the horizontal rod that ran under the rickety roof through the bus. I stood in the bus, swaying for a full two hours, my hands aching with pain from clutching that rod. The music system in the bus played such sad songs. After a few hours, the bus halted and I called you and Indira. I did not have enough balance in my phone so I gave you all missed calls. Then you called back, and if you had not insisted that I come over right away, I might have done something to myself...'

After a long pause, he continued: 'To be let down after all those years of struggle...It is different now, but back then... while on the bus, I could not let it go. I simply could not come to terms with it. I needed to do something, have some contact with Komal. I had her husband's number. I still cared for her and I still hoped she would come, and calling her husband would publicise our relationship. It was after a lot of conflict that I called Ramesh. I introduced myself simply as Komal's friend, and then I asked him if he was getting married to her on Saturday. When he said yes, I began to torment him.

"Did Komal ever tell you that she loved you?"

"No. What's your name?"

"Do you not see that Komal is not interested in you? She is in love with someone else."

"Who...?"

'Then I cut the line. I assumed that he gave my number to Komal. Or perhaps it was Komal who asked her brother to call me. Barely a few minutes later, Komal's younger brother called me—twice, thrice—he did not stop. My phone kept ringing and I kept cutting the call. Pressing hard on that red button gave me some relief. Finally, I took his call, and he was shouting.

"You may have seen more Diwalis than me, but I have burst more crackers... Though I'm younger than you, I am more experienced in the ways of the world. Do you not know that girls always belong to boys? Since you are just a woman, I have refrained from putting your garlanded picture on the wall." He threatened and abused me. But I was insistent. "I want to talk to Komal," I kept repeating. I questioned why both he and his brother could have girlfriends who were not from the same caste, but Komal was not allowed to have even one friend. Reasserting his aggression, he said, "I can stop this marriage so long as it's a man that Komal chooses. Not you, a woman." Cursing me, he added, "Look at the way you live and behave, that is why." He refused to let me speak to Komal.

'While all this was going on, Komal's husband, Ramesh, kept calling me. I could hear the beep. I picked up the phone. He wanted to continue our conversation, asking me who I was once more. He acknowledged that Komal did tell him she loved another person. So, I told him that I was the other person, and that I was not a man but a woman. I heard the silence at the other end before I cut the line. It gave me some relief, but a short-lived one. It only lasted until I reached Baroda.'

When we saw Ankit that day, he was drained of all colour and cheer as he stood clutching his mobile. We held him close and brought him home. At that time, he told us only of the telephone calls he had made, his mad rush to Komal's town, the computer teacher's attitude, and the bus ride back to the hostel, but nothing about the absence of calls from Komal. He didn't share any of that then. He spoke to us, but it was difficult to follow the thread of his conversation, and he appeared lost. He kept coming back to one point—he wanted to hear from Komal, just one word from her. Sensing the persistence of his mood, my colleague intervened and called Komal's brother. We stressed the necessity of letting them talk whilst also mentioning that we belonged to an organisation that supports women in difficulties. This was one of those times. If anything were to happen to Ankit, the matter would be spread all over town and they would be held responsible.

Finally, Ankit got to speak briefly with Komal, and they agreed to talk more later that night. Komal had a way with Ankit. She convinced him that letting the marriage take place was good for them as a community, for both their families, and in the long run, good for them as a couple. She even recommitted herself to the promise of joining him very soon. Ten to fifteen days after the wedding, the bride returns ceremoniously from her in-laws' house to her parents. At that time, she would come to Ankit. She asked him to wait, just a little while longer, and she would come to him.

And so Komal got married and Ankit continued with his studies, his days interspersed with Komal's calls as he remained hopeful of her return. She told Ankit that she was not in her right senses in the days leading up to her marriage. She had been in hospital and returned only the night before her wedding, when her brother had allowed her to speak to him. Her mother and everyone else had lied to people who came by looking for her or had called asking to speak with her. They would tell them that Komal had gone to the beauty parlour, or that she was getting *mehendi* on her hands and feet. It was a cover-up, Komal said. An unwilling bride is not the best of stories for a wedding.

Ankit was beginning to seek answers. He told Komal that she had let him down by agreeing to get married, and Komal then blurted out she had consumed medicine to kill herself—she survived because her family rushed her to the hospital. Ankit continued to hover between uncertainty and the promise of her return. Komal came to him after ten days of marriage. She came for three days and stayed with Ankit, after telling her aunt that she was going to her parents' place. Now that she was married, everyone was convinced that there was nothing going on between Komal and Ankit. This visit restored Ankit's trust in Komal. Her husband did not attempt to consummate their relationship with her; he was dealing with his own break-up. Ruminating aloud, Ankit whispered, 'Sometimes, I think I should have talked to this man. It would have brought the situation to a head, and maybe he would even have called off the wedding...'

Komal returned again after a few months. 'Every time she returned, my hopes soared. I saw how she had crafted out the space and time, against so many odds, to come to me. All her efforts were a sign. The marriage, I thought, was just a temporary disruption. This second time, she dropped by on the way to her parents' house from her husband's village. She came with two distant cousins of hers. We sat in a restaurant for three hours, the four of us having cold drinks and snacks. I was ecstatic to have her sitting in front of me. We managed to take out a little time to spend together. We went to my hostel room to fetch my jeans. Komal's cousins wanted to wear jeans and have their pictures taken in them as jeans were forbidden for grown-up girls. I rode the bike with her sitting behind me. Komal took my toothbrush, bed sheet, and a pair of my jeans.

'See the kind of things she did? She would pick up my clothes and smell them, keep them close when she missed me. But there were also those other conversations which should have alerted me, but I was just too blind to even suspect it. After getting married, Komal asked me not to talk about our sexual relationship to anyone, especially her husband. I agreed because we did not talk about our sexual relationship to anyone else, and we rarely talked about it even between ourselves. In fact, that was the first time we spoke about it so openly. And I kept my word until Komal started avoiding me. Normally, we spoke three times a day, even after she got married. Then, suddenly, days went by without a call from her. She would say her phone ran out of charge or was sent for repair to a shop that had shut down because there was a death in their family. I began to call her landline, though our conversations had to be short and covert.

'For his part, Ramesh yearned for his lost love in this arranged marriage with Komal. Each nursing their pain, the married couple lay in their bed with their backs turned to each other. But while talking on the landline, it sounded like Komal was settling into becoming part of his family. Someone would ask her for the keys while she was on the phone, and I would hear them jingle. Or there were times when I would be asked to call back later because she was busy in the kitchen. A few times, I was told to hold the line as she had just seen Ramesh off to work. These brief glimpses and conversations were all trying to tell me something. I began to feel an indescribable sense of unease, as if a weight pressed down upon me. But I did not want to know where it came from.'

It was 2011, and Ankit was now awakening to a realisation, though he continued the ritual of talking to Komal on the phone. 'I could not stop myself. Prompted by habit and a fear of emptiness, I continued to call her to keep away the crushing weight of all those years of hoping and waiting. I could not let go even when I wanted to. I would have continued with the calls if it wasn't for that meeting with Komal's brother.

'He called and we met. I took one of my colleagues with me. The meeting started out peacefully as we settled in a quiet corner of the garden. But then, he began showering me with abuses, saying that I was ruining his sister's life. When I asked him how, he got louder and angrier, and, pointing his forefinger at me, said that I should know better, and asked me how I even dared to ask him that. Spewing more abuse, he said that people like me were the definition of shamelessness. Then, coming up menacingly close, he told me to stop calling his sister and disturbing her. I asked who had told him that I was ruining his sister's life. When he said it was Komal who felt this way, I sought proof. Komal's brother dialled her number from his phone. When she came on the line and said it was true, I was shocked. I sat with his phone, shaken and numb. He grabbed the phone from my hands and gave me one of those "I told you so" expressions. My colleague who, until then, had been so quiet, shouted him down and asked him to watch his language. Having his masculinity challenged, he made sure to assert it by turning around and hitting him hard, saying it would teach him a lesson or two. When I intervened, he swung out at me. I ducked in time. His rage lay in the empty fingers curled in hard on his palm.

'I stopped calling Komal after that. But one thing that ran-kled me the most was that I had no recourse left, nowhere to go to register my complaint, as it were. One day, I called Ramesh, without a strategy, and just like that, I told him that our relation-ship was sexual. I told him how many years we had been involved for, the promises we had made, our meetings even after their marriage, and our dream to live together. Everything, I told him everything. He didn't believe it. I offered to produce evidence and asked him to meet me away from our homes.'

After Ankit had set up this meeting, he asked us to accom-pany him. We met Ramesh in a garden across from a busy in-tersection, where an endless stream of people rushed home from work. We went as supporters, as witnesses to their years of love, as sources of information to authenticate the existence of such relationships. Ankit also staked his claim with written documents as evidence. On an appointed day, Ramesh came to his hostel to see them. Ankit showed him the letters Komal had written, the cards with red hearts and roses, sunsets, twitter-ing birds, and sailing boats under blue skies. He read them all month-by-month and year-by-year, in the same consecutive or-der that Ankit had kept them. 'I have been betrayed,' he moaned softly, and slumped down, forlorn. Before seeing him off at the bus stop, Ankit offered him a cold drink and then he returned to his hostel. Though Komal was lost and gone, a part of him was relieved in the assertion of his love.

Ankit was in college because he wanted to acquire a qualifi-cation that would fetch him a job so he could live with his part-ner. With Komal gone, there seemed no real reason for him to be there. But he carried on. He struggled on through those sleepless nights and the memories that haunted his days. He learnt to live with them. Sometimes he was blurry-eyed, ruminating, with-drawn, and depressed. In college, when people thought of him as an oddity and laughed at him, his anger came to his rescue. Openly claiming his love for women, he exposed their homophobia. His quiet daily presence calmed down the fear of the 'other' amongst his colleagues and even teachers. This exchange built a friendship that is alive even today. He began to engage with college in a way that he had never done before. He initiated steps to get his whole class to visit Vikalp for a training session on gender and sexuality. As part of practical course work, he got a bunch of students to take a trip to the rural tribal areas where he had gone a few years ago. He spoke with experiential knowledge which no books could match. Ankit had transformed right before our eyes. From the first time he met us accompanied by an escort, timid and shy, to acquiring confidence to move and hold his own.

'The year 2011 opened yet another chapter in my life. I had finished my postgrad and was looking for a job. The two years I spent in college had given me the confidence that I could handle the snide comments, abuses, and everything else that came with being who I was. Before I go for job interviews, I tell myself that I have been there before. But the truth is that each time it happens, I am back there, smarting. After facing one of these interview ordeals, I landed myself a job in the HR department of an auto company. It was a male-dominated space, which conflated my identity with that of *masis*, and it followed me in whispers behind my back. There is no way one can confront whispers. I quit the job within a week. At the interview for the job where I work now, one of them asked me, "You will work with women in villages and you will go dressed like this, in jeans? What if they all start wearing jeans?"

'By then, I had given several interviews and suffered several comments. A kind of fatigue overcame me. I did not care if they took me or not. I responded with a counter-comment that came straight from my heart and retorted, "They might even cite me as an example and educate their girls to make them independent. What they wear is their choice." The funny thing was that I was selected. Sometimes, the comments insult both our caste and gender. The struggle never ends, we know that. Every time these comments, questions, and stares come our way, it reopens a wound, and we are consumed by rage. There is no getting used to it. And we have to piece ourselves back together, again and yet again. How much do you think is left of us that is whole? It's the same in the case of loss, of promises and of partners.

'After college, the hunt for a job became an isolated and isolating terrain; uncertain and unfamiliar, it brought back a deep sadness that I had fought myself into hiding. This was when I met Neelam. I saw her through this haze, she was unhappy and so was I. She lived with her uncle and aunt, but living there, she felt restrained. Money was generally short. Her father used to gamble. He lost a lot of money, including his own house. When we met, her previous relationship was coming to an end. I would meet her in college and we would ride out together on my bike. I tried to help her out with money too. Having someone with whom I could talk openly about my kind of problems was such a relief. We both shared our grief. Each of us found a sympathetic listener in the other, and the next thing we knew, we had fallen in love. Within two months, we eloped.

'After eloping, the group suggested we first go to Raman and Damini, far away. We went there as they lived deep in a rural area, so no one would get to us. Sure enough, nothing happened the first few days. I know that Neelam's people came looking for us here in Baroda. When you people called my father to let us know that Neelam's relatives had come looking for us at the organisation, he called and told me to stay safe. Before going away, we signed on notarised affidavits and sent letters addressed to the police stations, etc., in case complaints were registered against her or me.

'While we were on the run, my father called to say that my sister (who had mental problems) had been hospitalised and was in a serious condition. Against all reason, I went to see her. Luckily, Neelam's family had not lodged a complaint, but still they were probably on the lookout for us. When I reached the hospital, I was

told that my sister had passed away due to burn injuries. I returned
to her house with the rest to complete the last rites. There we were,
all standing and mourning, but no one questioned her death. I was
especially told not to raise my voice when I went to pour those few
drops of water in her mouth as part of our ritual. "Nothing will
bring her back." It was the sheer indifference that hurt the most.
Her death rattles inside me, my silence and their silence. People
with mental conditions like hers should not have their lives end so
brutally. As it is, you know, her life was not easy, and her husband
did not make it any easier. She had to do hard work tending to
cows, household chores, raising children, all while fighting those
voices inside her head. If not neglected, she could have lived longer.

'After our elopement, we changed places frequently. Then,
Neelam and I began living with a woman whom I met whilst
studying computers. She lived alone, away from her family, and
was also a runaway of sorts. Another time, we lived as room-
mates in a house that specifically rented out their house to students. But that soon became difficult because neither of us was
actually a student. From there, we shifted to a house where the
landlord's wife was involved with a woman too. Often, we could
hear the couple fighting downstairs; it was not a particularly happy marriage. Often, she would use us as an excuse to go out or
return late, telling him that she was hanging out with us. She was
such a free woman, full of fun and laughter, but *Darbar* communities are known for their control over women. When they raised
the rent, we shifted from there too.

'With all of these shifts and increasing rent, my father
spoke with a friend of his and we were able to live in his flat.
Since the flat was far from the main city, it remained empty
and neglected. The owner was happy to have us live there and
pay a nominal rent as it meant that the property was taken care
of. But it was still a hand-to-mouth existence for us. When
we moved into the house, we had nothing. Slowly, we began

to acquire the necessities and settle down. I had left one job and got another, a contractual job that did not pay much. We had a hard time managing our finances, but we found ways to meet our expenses. When we fled, Neelam lost a year and her admission in the college. Having experienced the advantage of education, I was keen that she continue her studies or learn something that would provide her with better employment opportunities. The problem was that she had no certificates except a photocopy of her school-leaving certificate. While we worked around getting the documents, she took up work in a beauty parlour.

'The days turned to months, and Neelam's family began to show signs of coming to terms with their daughter's choice. Not out of acceptance or affection, but because of the realisation that their daughter would not return otherwise.

'Both families did not accept us. And when they did, it was in a way that excluded the other partner. Each of our families reached out to their own child, but together, as partners, we were not welcome in either family home. Every now and then, Neelam's family would attempt to persuade her to return. Her family reasoned that now that she was mature, she would understand the ways of the world better. As elders and as parents, they did not show the same maturity when Neelam asked them for her certificates.'

Even though the family's initial resistance against her living with Ankit was softening slightly, their refusal to hand over her birth and educational certificates showed that they were still far from compliance or acceptance. Neelam tried to keep them on agreeable terms by talking regularly on the phone, in the hope that she could eventually win them over. One day, Neelam grew concerned as to why she had not heard from her mother for a while. Unable to bear the uncertainty, she called her and was told that her father had just suffered a paralytic attack. Of course, he wanted to see his daughter for a few hours after such an ordeal, but Ankit warned her, 'It's a trap.' Others in our group also tried to dissuade her, but Neelam was convinced by the desperation in her mother's voice. Plus, her father had already had an attack like this a couple of years ago—it seemed legitimate, and most people in her situation would be worried for their parent's health. She persuaded Ankit to accompany her, and together, they caught a bus to the hospital.

As soon as they approached the hospital, they saw her uncle, aunt, and mother gathered in a worrisome knot around a car. Apprehensive and fearing the worst, Neelam asked what they were doing standing outside when her father was lying in the hospital. They pointed to the car, saying, 'He's in here.' Relieved, she rushed to open the car door and saw her father slump sideways, almost falling out. Her uncle came up behind and shut the door, saying, 'We must take him to the hospital. We were waiting for you.' In a flurry of haste, they propelled Neelam and Ankit inside the car. Soon it sped up, though on a route away from the hospital.

Neelam grew uneasy, and asked, 'Is this the way to the hospital?'

'We have to collect medical certificates from home.' The car stopped outside their house. 'We will be on our way soon, but come in for a while and have a cold drink or a cup of tea.'

Then, Neelam's father got out of the car, and she realised that it had all been a trap. Surrounded, there was little room for manoeuvre or escape. They stepped out of the car, followed closely by her uncle and her aunt. Now that the family had control over them, they made all possible efforts to block Neelam's gaze from Ankit. Certain that Ankit had cast a magical spell on her, they hoped that the less she looked at him, the more the spell would be weakened, and their daughter would be free. As cold drinks were served, Neelam quickly shot a look at Ankit from behind barricades of raised hands and backs, silently uttering a 'No'.

Neelam was ushered away into another room. Sitting Ankit down, Neelam's family aggressively told him to keep away from their daughter. They advised Ankit to forget her. When he threatened police action, they ridiculed and slapped him, almost pushing him out of the house. Seeing no other way, Ankit stepped out.

In the days that followed, Ankit tried to reach Neelam, but her parents had blocked all possible communication. Sensing that the family would not let her out, Neelam, after being captured, began to pretend that Ankit had forced her against her wishes to live with him. She even told them he had forcibly taken her signatures on the commitment bond and that he had locked her up. Ironically, it was her parents who had locked her up. She had no way to escape from there. Her mother and father believed her, but their relatives advised caution.

Neelam's performance was convincing enough to allow the family to slacken their watch over her. She waited for an opportunity. It came when her aunt forgot the phone in the room where Neelam was kept prisoner, and she stealthily grabbed it. Racing through her memories in search of Ankit's new number, she could not remember it, the panic making the task even harder. She slid into the bathroom so that she could call Ankit's father and ask him, all the while worried that the missing phone would give her away. Ankit's father sensed the urgency in her whispers and quickly gave her the number.

Before she crept out, she called Ankit and told him to stand outside her house around five in the evening the next day, as this gave her enough time to work on talking to her father. The next morning, she told him that she longed to eat *pani-puri,* but he insisted on accompanying her to the stall. Ankit was waiting outside Neelam's house when he saw the pair emerge, so Ankit followed them in a three-wheeler right to the shop. Whilst her father spoke to the shopkeeper, Neelam made her escape. She dashed towards the three-wheeler.

But her father was equally as quick and jumped into the auto with the two of them. Knowing the plan had gone awry, Neelam again played the 'victim', pretending to free herself from Ankit's grip. Her father was telling the auto driver to head towards his house whilst Ankit urged him to continue in the opposite direction. Completely flummoxed, the driver turned around to face the scene in the back seat. Now, others on the street were also stopping to stare. Neelam's father gathered a crowd, pleading with passers-by to stop Ankit from abducting his daughter. As viable options were becoming fewer by the second, Ankit took advantage of the crowd and attempted to turn the situation on its head. He cried out for help in finding the police station, saying 'it is in fact this man who is doing the abducting!'

This development stunned and outraged Neelam's father. But he agreed they should go to the police station, emboldened by the fact that one of his relatives had recently been inducted into the force. 'If that is what you want,' he shouted, 'then let's go. I will file a criminal charge against you. This will teach you a lesson. You will forget your spellbinding trickery!' Affronted at the injustice and the sheer audacity the man was displaying, Ankit shouted in agreement and passionate retaliation, 'Yes, let's go.' He gestured to the auto driver. 'Bejalpur station.'

Neelam chimed in, agreeing with her father, 'We'll see.' She feigned bravado and complete allegiance to her father, 'I will go there and tell them straight out that I do not want to go with him. We will put this matter to rest once and for all.' In the midst of a whirlwind of chaos and the crowds of a bustling market, it was ironic the warring parties had suddenly become diplomatic. As the auto weaved its way through the traffic, Neelam's father began calling around his brothers, including the recently recruited police officer.

As the three reached the police station, Neelam was whisked away into the Police Inspector's (PI) chambers. He asked her with whom she wanted to go, and she replied 'Ankit'. The police threatened her and told her she would not be allowed to leave until her statement was the contrary. When she repeated her first choice, the PI slapped her hard. She persisted, and gave the same answer again. He hit her again, twice on the same cheek, and it swelled up. Her head felt funny and there was a sharp pain in her ears. It took a long time for her to be able to chew food on that side afterwards.

The PI took off his belt and threatened her with it. He waved a rod before her, saying he would insert it inside her. 'If you are so keen, come and sleep with me. Your friend has only got a plaything. If you come with me, I will show you what real sex is.'

Neelam's mother and uncle arrived. With their presence, the PI ceased to abuse her. Her mother and uncle began to beat her. Neelam was exhausted; hours had slipped by. The uncertainty and the cruelty drove her to desperation. The police recorded what she said on the laptop. Relieved to be able to leave, she walked away, almost indifferent to what may happen next.

Ankit was summoned next. The PI played Neelam's recorded statement, telling Ankit to listen to it carefully. The PI said this established what Neelam's wishes were, but Ankit could hear the sobs in the recording. He demanded that Neelam's statement must be given in front of him otherwise he would not accept it.

'It is not my duty to bring you both face-to-face so that you may test the veracity of the girl's statement.' He threatened Ankit, 'I want to talk to your father, he should know what his daughter is up to.'

'I have done what I have done; my father is not responsible for what I do, do not involve him.'

'But,' the police officer insisted, 'he should know what you are up to.'

He demanded the phone number of Ankit's father and smugly typed it into the phone. He told him about Ankit wanting to live with a girl, and that she was in Ahmedabad with that same girl, who no longer wanted to live with him. Ankit's father, who tacitly supported his daughter and was already in the know, said, 'Send them both to court.'

After questioning and threatening Ankit, they made him sit outside and called Neelam back in. 'I realised that Neelam's relatives were conspiring together. I would need help from other sources to handle this situation. I called one of the community members who was part of our group and worked in the police department. It was hard getting through. While Neelam was alone with the PI, I kept trying to call. Finally, when I did get through, I shared the entire story. I gave the name of the police station and asked them to speak with the PI.'

Meanwhile, Neelam was asked what her friend did for a living. She told them that Ankit worked in the HR department of a company. The police continued to harass her, asking her for the full name of the company. When she said she didn't know, they laughed at her, scoffing at her ignorance and her inability to make the right choice. Then, the PI received a call.

Ankit waited outside, nervous about the outcome. Finally, they called him in, Neelam was sitting with her parents. In front of Ankit, they asked Neelam whom she wanted to stay with. When she answered that it was Ankit, her uncle and mother shouted at her. Her uncle blamed Neelam's parents and said that the dishonour that would fall upon their family as a result of all this would be because of them. Ankit was asked to write down his address and job. Ankit wrote something out. When they were eventually allowed to go, Neelam's uncle shouted, 'We will see how you get out of the city.'

Though afraid and shaken, they managed to get out of the city that night. Ankit's father did not show any animosity to Ankit's doings, and his willingness to go ahead with court proceedings prevented Neelam's parents from proceeding any further. They knew well enough that, legally, they had little to stand on. This whole episode distanced Neelam from her parents, and she lost any hope of ever retrieving her documents. And so, the couple embarked on the long, drawn-out process of procuring her school-leaving certificate.

Finally, in 2013, Neelam was admitted into the bachelor's programme in social work. Her relationship with her family was improving, and they were able to reconnect. 'What's funny is that when Section 377 was reimposed, our relationship met staggering difficulties. That is my memory of that black day. Just as I was beginning to believe that my love too had legitimacy, love and the law bypassed me.

'Honestly, our relationship had begun to show signs of strain in the first few weeks itself,' Ankit shared. 'When we first met, I shared my past and other things with her, things that one shares only with their intimate partner. Often, when we had differences, which grew into showdowns, she would threaten to expose me… to expose all of those things that I had confided in her about. When it happened the first time, I was taken aback. I had not expected this from her. I loved and trusted her. Then, she began to threaten me often, abusing me and insulting my family. She even beat me up. She would use derogatory words for my gender, my caste, and my physique…every inch of me came under her volley of abuses. I hate repeating them.

'I don't know when exactly or why, but violence erupted between us. Perhaps a year into our relationship, she would push me to get up and sit in the doorway of the bathroom while she washed clothes. I just had to sit there. It was almost compulsory. When it happened the first time, I let it go. But soon, it recurred, and a pattern set in. I would duck when she threw things at me, or turn away when she raised her hand. But when it became really hurtful, I had to stop her, if only to defend myself. I hit her back too. She wouldn't stop. From pinching to pulling my hair and mocking my identity, my gender, caste, everything that I stood for came under her vicious attack.

'I could no longer make love to her. Each crisis created a distance between us that was getting harder to cross over. Words sink deep and violence leaves a sting. We were drifting apart and yet, there was this pretence; somehow, I felt responsible for her. I was a lot older than her, and she had been studying when we eloped. I felt that she had to discontinue her studies because of our involvement, and I wanted her to graduate. I worked hard to get her admitted, and a private college is very expensive, but I did not mind. I have reaped the benefits of education and wanted her to enjoy the same too. I tried my best to make it work. People in our group who saw us could tell you how bad it was between us—it was visible to those around us. The abuse and ordering around happened even in the presence of others. She did not hit me in public, but still, the humiliation I suffered from the verbal abuse she hurled at me was as good as hitting.

'Do you remember when I came to you guys out of the blue? I had come to get away from her. I should have left her then, but she called me and I went back to her. We made up, each of us promising to change, but we had already fallen into a pattern. The last time I was with her, we were supposed to go and see my nephew who was recovering from a football injury, but at the last minute, Neelam called to say she didn't feel like coming. Later, she phoned to say she was at her mothers', but in the background, I could hear the movement of a vehicle, which made me think that she was going somewhere else that she didn't want to tell me. At this point, I was beyond caring. I was already well aware of her interest in others as she would cling onto her mobile late into the night. Sometimes, I would wake up to her on the phone. A male colleague even asked me if I was aware that Neelam had been calling him. In the beginning, this behaviour would upset me. I'd try to find out who she was talking to, but she'd bury the phone in her pocket or turn it off. Once, she even flung it onto the ground so that it broke. I bought her a new one.

'When we both returned, she from another city and I from seeing my nephew, we had a talk. She told me that she had gone to meet a trans man whom she had met through the group. She didn't deny sleeping with him. Actually, she even said it was her who had initiated it. I wasn't even surprised—another guy in the group had already warned me about her flirting with him.

'Neelam returned the next day because she realised that the relationship she was hoping to establish was not something that would work out for her. I noticed that she snuggled up close to me after that. But I told her not to expect love from me. It angered her, as it would do to anyone, naturally. Who would know better than me? It was the truth and had been so for a long time, but I had been avoiding telling her. She already knew it. I don't think she loved me either. She retaliated, of course, and said she would not like to stay with me if this was the case. I suggested she wait another two years to complete her studies and then we could both go our separate ways. She disagreed. At six the next morning, she was already packing her bag, pushing me to hurry so she would not miss her bus, nagging me, "*Chal, chal,* go, let's go, hurry." I suggested tea and breakfast, but she was in no mood to listen. I stopped at the ATM to withdraw some money and gave it to her. Some she took, the rest she threw in my face as she insulted me. The closer we got to the bus stop, the angrier she became. She probably assumed that this would be like other times, and we would reconcile. Sitting on the bike, she began hitting me, which was nothing new. Sitting behind me on the bike, she would keep hitting me, pulling my shirt, collar, belt, or hair, anything, just anything… I used to have a hard time driving. But this time, something had changed in me. I noticed people laughing as they caught sight of the two of us. My bike swerved as I took charge of it with trembling hands; people on the street were watching us. It got to a point that I was filled with rage, so much so that when she disembarked, I kicked my bike hard before getting back on. I heard a policeman shout after me. But I carried on. I have not seen her since.

'Do not ask me what led us there. I don't care to divulge—that chapter is closed. Perhaps in another lifetime, I will tell you. For now, I am single and happy, so happy. I want to remain single.'

9

Exposed

The World Social Forum (WSF) is an international meeting of NGOs, advocates, and a spectrum of social movements from all across the world. The WSF came to Mumbai in 2004, when queer law reform and visibility in many other countries were leaps and bounds ahead of India. The WSF benefited the Indian queer movement, as the inclusion of LGBTIQ+ at the event in Mumbai lead to an increase in visibility and awareness elsewhere in the country, though it was mostly confined to the metropolises.

During this time, we had planned to hold a workshop in conjunction with LABIA (Lesbians and Bisexuals in Action, based in Mumbai) to bring together the community to celebrate our similarities, but to also understand our differences across class and state lines. We wanted our event to reach as many people as possible, so of course, we agreed when a journalist asked to write a story on it.

The *Times of India* and the Vadodara edition of *Gujarat Samachar* published the story just prior to the workshop. It featured our individual names, and also that of the organisation (Parma at the time), described in the most unsavoury terms. And most shockingly, there was the word 'Lesbian'—it could have burned right through the pages. Though it was an attempt to personally belittle us, from an ideological sense you could say it was profitable to finally have the word 'lesbian' out there in black and white after years of tip-toeing around and hiding underneath ambiguities of 'single women'. From a practical sense, however, the repercussions were not favourable.

The communities and families with whom we worked had known us only as working with and for women, which was true, but there were no queer connotations. Our engagement with LBT was a recent occurrence and only known within our close, inner group. It was a tactical agreement not to disclose our own sexual and gender identities so that the organisation could continue its work uninterrupted. Silence was the common currency in exchange for some freedom of choice whilst still preserving family and community honour.

The identity of a 'women's group' was like a safety valve, and it worked well for us all. The news article had not only exposed the organisation as queer, but also all of those who might have spoken about attending the seminar. It shook a trust that we had nurtured carefully. The people who had expressed an eagerness to meet 'people like me' did not show up that day, nor the next. One of the families who knew us personally saw the newspaper article and soon expressed their disgust on the subject, completely shocked at the 'lies' we could tell. They forbade their daughter from attending the workshop. Most depleting was the feeling of letting down our community.

This was also the time when we were scheduled to meet with Virat. Virat had come forward to meet us following our dissent against the protests of the film *Girlfriend*. We did not have the gumption to invite him to the seminar, but we arranged a meeting in person.

10

A Man of Two Cities, West to South, Punjabi–Gujarati

'What will you do with my story?' Virat asked, and I tried to explain. But he rarely sat still. Making him sit in one place was like holding water in the palm of your hand—water runs out, and so did Virat. Barely a few minutes of conversation and he would get restless. On one occasion, he strode purposefully into the office. 'Write about me,' he said, pulling up a chair.

'I have never been as hurt as today, when she told me that she is a "normal girl". What does she mean? I felt that she was calling me abnormal. Then what about all the things that we did together? She and I, both of us did whatever we did out of our own will, and now she wants to get rid of me. I had to put the phone down because I was afraid I might say something that would hurt her.' He looked away, blinking hard.

'I want a sex change. She left me because I am a woman. Is sex change possible? I heard about it from a doctor when I applied for a job at the Suri hospital as a lab technician. It was there that I heard about sex change for the first time. But you tell me, is it possible? I mean, can it really happen?'

'Sure, yes.'

'Do you think I can... I mean, change mine?'

'Sure, yes.'

'Really?'

'Why not? Indeed, you can. But it is a long process requiring parental or family permissions, counselling, and getting various certificates...'

'Counselling, certificates...But you can help, can't you? Take me to a counsellor. Will you? When do you think you can...How much would such an operation cost?'

In so many ways, Virat was unstoppable. And that is the case even now, after more than a decade of knowing him. From when he was 20 years of age, to now, a 33-year-old. From a slim young person, to a strapping lad with a slight moustache and a voice that rings heavy and husky over the phone from a city in the south. It took me a while before I could tell myself, 'Oh! It is our Virat, the errant, the unpredictable Virat! Our own actor par excellence.'

Even before we met him in person, we had a taste of his indomitable will way back in June 2004 when he found his way into the office of the *Indian Express*. Having read about Parma's protest against the attacks on the film *Girlfriend* and its support for lesbians, Virat had tracked down the journalist who wrote the story. On the phone, when he was refused more information on the group, he arrived at the newspaper's office in person to convince the reporter. Anticipating hoax and abusive calls, we at Parma had expressly wished for confidentiality. But Virat's persistence wore the reporter down. We heard the note of impatience and weariness in her voice when she called us, 'Here is someone who wants to meet you, she identifies as lesbian...do I give her your number?'

So that was how we met Virat for the first time. It was neither in our office nor his, but in a cloak and dagger fashion, far outside both our turfs. We saw him as he walked towards us down the quiet nursery, full of flowers, colours, sunlight, and shadows. There was instant recognition on both sides. Lean and young, Virat was in his work uniform. He wore his hair short, had a confident look about him, and looked at the two of us directly with his smiling eyes. Drawing closer, we expressed our recognition in smiles, the uncertainty slowly dissipating, 'And I thought I was alone in feeling the way I did…'

After that first meeting, we began to meet in Vikalp. Occasionally, we'd meet him after his work at the K café, a mid-point for all of us, and have a chat before going our separate ways.

'How bad can it be for two people like us to love? Is it unlawful for two women to marry? What about living together? Is that illegal too?' The questions poured out one after the other. But he did not pause to listen to our responses, as if he was talking out loud to himself rather than to anyone else. But it was important that someone was there, listening to him. He'd come to us to talk about a fight with a customer. Or about a girl. At other times, it was because he was depressed and needed a listener. One day, he asked if I could get a dildo for him. I could not resist asking him why he needed it.

'*Aray yaar.* You ask such questions! As if you do not know that women get pleasure from it. That is why.'

Often, during our café times together, he would pull Indira's (my colleague who identified as a trans person) hand and place it on his cheeks. 'Can you feel?' he would ask. Then, he would lower his face and say, 'Feel now, feel.' Then, he would look at him enquiringly.

'What?'

'Today, I have shaved again.'

'Yea.'

'Do you feel the roughness?'

Sometimes he would ask, 'How are these pants?' Then he would turn around and, peeping over his shoulder, he would say, 'This is the fashion these days, you know, drain pipes.' Turning around on one leg and facing us, he once pulled out a pair of goggles from his pocket. 'Look at these,' he said, handing them over to me for a closer look. Sometimes he would lean far back in the café chair and proudly shove his feet right under our eyes to show us his shoes, 'Just bought these...'

'Expensive, huh?'

'No, these are from the seconds shop...'

But it was the women who gave him a high. 'Look there,' he would say, and then quickly add, 'No, no, wait, not right now, don't turn around.' Then, after a few minutes, he'd say, 'Now you can look, look at that girl over there, not so hard, don't stare, just casually look at the third table from us, she is in yellow.' He would whisper whenever he spotted a smart middle-class girl, 'Pretty, isn't she?'

Sometimes, Indira would come under his radar, 'Look at you, just look at how you dress...'

'What?'

'Can't you take more care? Work on your looks a little? You have the frame of a man. If only you would take care of it! I tell you; women will come to you.' Often, our conversations ran along these lines. We generally met once a week. But once mobile phones made for easier contact, we spoke more frequently, though not in person.

Virat had the effect of evoking contradictory emotions of both affection and irritability at the same time. One day, he turned up at Vikalp's office during his lunch break, like he sometimes did, just for a casual chat and to share details about his new girlfriend. 'Give me something to read, something good,' he repeated with emphasis.

'What is "good"?'

'Well...something about us, I want a story about us,' he said, pointing his finger at us and at himself. 'About us, about people like us, some story? Is there one? My friend would understand if she reads something about us.'

'Now you know why I have been asking you to share your story.'

He smiled. 'I know what you're trying to say. I will come tomorrow in the afternoon and sit with you. Will it be long?'

He came the next day. Dressed in his usual jeans and shirt, his face was tanned from all the cycling he had done in the summer. His large eyes twinkling, he settled down in the chair and wiped his hands on his jeans. 'It gets very hot. I cycle nearly forty kilometres in a day. See,' he said. Pushing up his sleeves, he showed us his arms proudly. 'Can you see the muscles? If I rode that scooty, I would not have got these.' He pointed at his muscles. He added, 'Not having money for the petrol is fine. So, I am here till two-thirty, I can talk until then. I can stretch it till three, but after that, I have to get back to work to follow up on the customers. Should I begin?

'I was born right here in Baroda, though my family is from Firozpur in Punjab. I had a happy childhood. My father was an autorickshaw driver, *Beeji* (grandmother) was a nurse in the Air Force, and my grandfather worked in the Railways. We were reasonably well off. We were two sisters. When my mother left, she took my youngest sister with her. She was very young and small, so my mother took her away with her. I sometimes wonder how she is. Although my family does sometimes tell me that she is not fine, and I keep thinking why. But no one really talks about my mother. Her parents took her away because after my father died, my grandmother and others wanted her to marry my *chacha* (father's younger brother). My father died of cancer when I was five or six. One year before my father's death, my *dada* (paternal grandfather) passed away. Slowly, the family situation changed. *Beeji* adopted me after my mother went away. I was very young. I grew up in my grandparents' house, which is across the road from my parents'. People who work in the Air Force can have their children enrol in the Air Force school, and that is how I was admitted. It was a good school, English medium. I completed my tenth class from there. In 1994, my *chacha* got married and then slowly, everything started to go…the situation became worse…. The atmosphere in the house began to change. *Beeji*'s pension was just enough to take care of food, but we could no longer afford that school. My *chacha* separated from us and began to live elsewhere. Then, only the three of us lived there—my grand-mother, my sister, and I.

'I wanted to finish my education and secure a job. I got into a lot of arguments with *Beeji*. She wanted me to get married, but I did not want to do that before finishing school. Even now, we argue about it…but I told myself and *Beeji* that I would marry only after I completed my schooling. *Beeji* would not hear of it. "I want to see you get married before I die. I am growing old," she grumbled. And it is not like the pressure has gone away now. Once, she arranged a meeting with a man. I met that man with a male friend of mine, and I told him that this friend was my "boyfriend" whom I intended to marry. But it is hard to refuse all the time. A couple of times, when we were looking at the family album, *Beeji* began to cry when she saw pictures of papa and our youngest sister. She misses her son, and I think she feels that she would be completing her son's duty and fulfilling his wishes by getting us married. We fight about this every day—my marriage, I mean. Even my sister—she argues a lot with *Beeji* too. She wor-ries about us, I guess. But she goes on and on, saying the same thing repeatedly. I have learnt to turn a deaf ear, and I tell my sister to do the same, but she does not stop retorting. Nor does *Beeji*. No one listens, so there are outbursts every now and then in our house.

'Now, I am sure that I will never marry. Thinking back, I'm sure my idea of marrying after school was just a temporary way to deal with the pressure *Beeji* brought upon me. After coming here and meeting others like me, I know better than to get into a marriage with a man. From the beginning, ever since I became aware and can remember, I was drawn to women, never to men. Then once in Firozpur, I kissed a girl… It was a kind of confir-mation for me. I knew for sure that I wanted a woman as my partner. When a man touches me, there is no sensation. I have many male friends, and we all look at women. They treat me like

I am one of them, they call me *bhai,* and I use a razor hoping that I will grow a beard. People say if you use a razor, a beard grows. But nothing happens; I do not get any hair.' He touched his chin ruefully.

'I did not like it at all when my menstrual cycle began. I think it is such a waste on me—this *bachaydani* (womb) and all its processes. Someone else could benefit in my stead. I did not feel like myself when I had long hair, I mean, it felt so strange. I wanted to look like a man. After passing class ten in 2001, I felt I'd had enough of school and books and I wanted money of my own to do the things I wanted, like cutting my hair. I first cut my hair in 2001, and now it's been three years. I'm 21 now. My first job was in a thread factory, where I had to stand for eight hours at a stretch, for 30 rupees a day. I lasted a month there before quitting. Then, I did a number of short stints in marketing, selling daily-use items such as creams, powder, and utensil cleaning powder. It wasn't an easy job. I'd go door-to-door in villages with a male colleague of mine, trying to make sales. Once, he gave me a drink mixed with something… It was the first time I had taken anything like it. Fortunately, I threw it all up. His intentions were not good. I had difficulty getting home.

'People look at you in all sorts of demeaning ways. I wanted a better job. For that, I had to learn Tally, but I did not have enough money to pay the fees, and I knew *Beeji* would not give me the money. Since I hadn't followed her wishes and instructions, I knew asking her would be like stirring up a hornet's nest. Instead, I asked that male colleague to lend me money, and I was shocked when he demanded a sexual favour in return. For me, this was a confirmation of what he had intended to gain from offering me that drink. He suggested I do sex work to earn the money.

'I quit that job soon after. But to find another job, I had to borrow newspapers from my neighbours once more to search for suitable vacancies. *Beeji* was still not easy to handle. "You either go to school or marry. Don't dare to step out to work." This is what

went on day after day, and I would ignore it. At times I tried to get
around her; if she got up to get water, I would run and get it. "Here,
hold the glass. Listen, *Beeji*, listen, times have changed—it is not
the same. Am I saying no to marriage, just wait!" She would pull
me close and say, "You are the older one and my favourite." So, we
both blackmailed one another. "You are the best," I would tell her.
She really is the best. I will tell you why. When my father was alive
and things were better off, we bought two plots. On one we built
the house we live on, and the other is still vacant. I wanted to make
a garden, but *Beeji* would not allow it. But a few days later, I dug
up the soil and planted some saplings. *Beeji* grumbled, "I will dig
them all up." And one day, what do you think happened? I heard
her asking our neighbour if she would water those plants. We have
this kind of relationship—even between heated arguments and
counter-arguments, we manage to look out for one another.

'I knew I needed to work to be independent and free of social
pressures and *Beeji*. A friend of mine helped me get this job as
a telephone operator for 2,000 rupees, and alongside I took up
telemarketing with Vijay Motors Ltd in Karanpur. My work involved calling up clients for service reminders. During this time,
I also applied for admission to a six-month Bachelor Preparatory
Programme.

'It was then that *Beeji* threw me out with all my clothes. As
if I meant nothing to her. She was convinced that, having fallen
into bad company, I had taken to sex work. She thoroughly disapproved of my mobility and occasional late return home. After she threw me out, I had nowhere to go after the office and
my classes. Can you imagine, nowhere to go? No shelter, no…
nothing. I stayed with the night watchman. He was a kind old
man and stayed in the campus where I was taking classes. For
two days, I stayed with him, wearing the same clothes and with a
near-empty stomach, until I reconciled with *Beeji*.

'It was the end of July 2004 when I first met her. I was actually interested in another woman whom I would look out for

during class. When this woman did not come for classes, I was unable to pay attention. I would keep looking at the door, waiting for her to appear. One day, I was late for class and could find no place to sit, when I saw this other girl make a place for me. I sat with her, but my heart and head were elsewhere. As my luck or ill luck would have it, this other girl was not interested. I mean, she was friendly and all that, but nothing more. Shila, on the other hand, was really forthcoming. A fine girl, I told myself. It was she who asked me for my address first. Gradually, I got to know her and would occasionally call for a friendly chat. Nothing more.

'It was the accident that changed everything between us. It was March then. I was crossing the road on foot and a Gypsy cab hit me. The front tyre of the cab came to rest on my right foot, just before it braked. I had a hairline fracture. I had to stay in bed for four days. I called Shila and told her about my accident, and she came over to see me. Prior to this, there had been nothing between us.' Sighing softly, he said, 'Well! She came over to my home and everything changed. When I say home, I mean the one room that I had rented near my workplace. I had moved out of *Beeji*'s house once again because of all the fights and tensions we were having.

'Another friend of mine, Rachna, who was just a friend, had also come to see me. When Shila came, we all sat talking. I had a heavy head, so I asked Shila to press it for me. She sat next to me and began to softly press my head. It was a wonderful sensation, her warm fingers pressing down on my temples, the slight brush of her finger occasionally picking a strand of my hair, and then moving on from it. I could smell her and feel her breath. A tingling sensation gripped me. I felt like I had no bones left in me. Once Rachna left, Shila and I were alone. She was running her fingers through my hair, I touched her gently and, reaching across, hugged her, just lightly. She held my hair in a tight clasp. I could feel her excitement. I asked her to kiss me. She kissed me on my forehead, got up quickly, and then said "I have to leave".

'I had no time to recover from the shock. It was not intended that way, I told you earlier. I had felt drawn to another woman, not her…and suddenly, it happened. For a long time that evening, I kept thinking about her. At night, I dreamt of her.

'The next day, I got up and clambered off to work; I was limping, but I managed. I called her from there and asked if she regretted what had happened. "No, if it were so I would have told you." I felt so relieved. I wondered about her becoming my partner, and it seemed too good to be true. "Wait, watch and see what happens." Another friend suggested, "Give yourself time."'

But Virat was in love, and in no mood to pay heed. A few days later, when Virat returned, he was excited and eager to share the 'story of my life!'

'She called me to her house. Yes, to her house! I did not anticipate such a turn of events. We sat and talked to each other, and then she took me to her room on the third floor and began to talk…then she came out and stood on the balcony, and, with her hair loose, she began to comb that thick, dark hair of hers. She is good-looking, slightly stout, soft, and full of passion, with large eyes, yes, she has such large eyes. That day, when she let her hair down, down to her hips with her face turned towards me, I felt that she was doing all of this to get my attention. She looked at me smiling, and I called her inside to where I was sitting on the floor. "All this is wrong," she whispered. But she came up so close….' Virat stopped midway, and then after a while, he continued, 'Even as I am talking, I feel like she is near me, I could touch her, I feel her so close right now and my stomach has a nervous, tingling sensation. I miss her…

'Then I asked her what was so wrong about it? I stretched out my hand, palms turned out. She put her hand in mine. I pulled her close and we snuggled up close, just sitting together in silence. She ran her hand through my hair. I began to kiss her. I could feel her excitement. I asked her if I could kiss her on her lips and she simply nodded. This was my first real kiss, if you know what I mean. I had kissed her before, but not like this. She held me with passion.

'This was the beginning and, I can say now, the end. Our relationship did not last long. In August it all ended. I saw her the last time in a cybercafé. "Let us go someplace together, somewhere further away."

"Fort area?"

'She agreed almost immediately. We were barely a few kilometres away when it began to pour. It was a heavy downpour and we stood under a tree. I wanted to kiss her. But we were by the side of the road, in full view of people. She pulled out a raincoat from her scooter and we covered our heads. We kissed then, under the raincoat, with the raindrops sometimes falling inside. It was a heady feeling. I noticed how she clung to me. We went a little beyond the city, but the traffic and the rain were both so heavy that we could not reach the Fort area. On our way back, we stopped at the Rose Garden and sat on a forlorn bench inside. By now, the rain had eased off. Cars went by on the road, throwing shadowy sparkles of light in her face. Droplets of rain stood out bright on her round face. That image has stayed with me,' he said, sighing. 'I can see her so vividly.

'I put my arm on her shoulder and pulled her close. She turned to me and we hugged and kissed. Then I began to kiss her neck. I do not know why, but I had not kissed her on the neck before that. When I kissed her on the lips, I could feel her surrender herself to me, as if she were about to pass out. I kissed her for a long time. I went insane and felt like I could not stop kissing her. Then suddenly, she broke free and got up from the bench. She asked me to get up too, and we walked together to the little stair leading out.

'The next day I called her to say I wanted to take her away. "Why don't you?" she replied. We talked frequently, but after that outing in the rain, she became restrained. She would allow me to kiss her, but it was never the same again. I sensed it but kept hoping she would come around.'

He had a sudden brain wave. 'You can convince her. Meet her,' he insisted. 'Tell her about people like us, ask her what's wrong, why she doesn't talk to me.' Although we did not think that this was the best way to go about it, we gave into his persistence. Having just begun working with same-sex relationships, it was still an unfamiliar ground for us. Virat said that we should try to catch her outside her computer class. He stood behind us, impatiently pacing up and down. When he saw her, he pointed her out in the distance, saying, 'There, she is there, that one!' We walked towards her, but cutting us short, she looked at her watch and muttered 'class', walking away without another word or glance.

Virat was crestfallen. 'I do not understand. Everything was ok and now she withdraws without talking to me. Why? What happened?' Not willing to give up yet, Virat said, 'Can we try to meet after her classes?'

'This is neither a good time nor a good place,' we reasoned with him to leave the girl alone for some time. 'Maybe she was afraid of us, or her family. We don't know. Give her and yourself some time,' we repeated. Shaken by the girl's reaction, Virat nodded without much thought or resistance. For a few weeks, Virat did not come to the office like he usually did. We called him, and he sounded despondent. He promised he would come within a day or two.

Instead, we got another call from him later that very day. He was calling from a police station, asking us to intervene, to 'help sort this matter'.

'What sort of matter?'

'The same one.' Then, he whispered into the mouth piece 'Ladkiwala.'

At the police station we saw Virat standing before the Assistant Police Commissioner. The man in uniform left us with no doubt as to what would happen if Virat did not cease to harass the girl, 'I'll have you behind bars...' We saw Virat straighten up and shift his weight onto both his feet; drawing closer to the ACP's table, his stature looked like he was all set to confront the big man in khaki. He gave us the impression of an ardent fellow facing the world of uniforms and lock-ups without the taint of cynicism, with hope-filled eyes that imagined the world could be changed if one tells the honest truth. Before we could stop him, he had uttered the blasphemous words. 'Sir, but loving someone is not a crime, sir. I...'

'But, Virat,' we hurriedly interrupted him, trying to stave off more harm, 'harassing someone, especially a woman, is a crime. Sir is right.' Suddenly finding an endorsement of his view coming from a side opposed to his, the Commissioner turned to us and gestured us to sit in front of him. Now that the battle lines were slightly blurred, the ACP raised no objection when one of us pulled Virat away from his menacing stare. We took out our organisation's cards and assured him that Virat would no longer bother the girl. 'We have known him for several years now,' we explained.

Once safely out of the police station, we told Virat that love like ours is outlawed, and it is indeed a crime. Virat could not believe it, 'I thought it is not used...'

'You are right. The law is commonly not enforced, but it is a law that exists, so it is still a possibility. But tell us, what have you been up to that a police complaint had to be made against you?'

He burst out, 'She just would not take my calls. So, I wrote to her, letter after letter. I went to her locality outside her house with my friend, but they beat us up. They came to my company and made a complaint to my top bosses. Everyone got to know. Her mother, father, and her brother know everything. They saw the letters. She told her mother everything. After that, her father complained about me to the police. All I did was leave flowers for her every day. I cycled to her place and dropped off the bouquets. I am sure she knew who brought those flowers, day after day. I was there early in the morning every day, when the newspaper guys deliver the newspapers. Actually, I think it was they who must have described and reported me. That is how the neighbours caught us, my friend and me. They surrounded us and began to make threats. Finally, my friend showed his Air Force card, and we were let off.'

We reasoned with him, 'Even if it is flowers, Virat, it is against her will. Since she did not ask for them, she will experience it as harassment. Besides, she is making it clear that she wants to end the relationship.'

'End, indeed, end the relationship, how come?' Virat flung his arms in frustration. 'She wants to end it without saying anything? I don't understand?'

We tried to calm him down. Then we tried explaining it to him, 'She is not saying it in so many words, but don't you think she is communicating something to you? You were the one who noticed that she seems withdrawn and changed, didn't you?'

'No. I mean yes. But you see, this is not it, I am looking at all that has happened between us... How one can change so fast? She is the woman in my life. I will not give up. She promised and now... I am telling you—she is under pressure from her parents.'

'How do you know this for sure?'

'I made my sister call her. She talks with her, yes, yes, very nicely. Why would she talk to her if she was not interested in me? I am telling you, she is a sensible person, very understanding. But that brother of hers, he used to threaten me, saying that he would have me beaten up. He would come looking for me in our locality, but of course, he could not find me, or my house. He tries to control her, so naturally, she does not like it.'

Virat would not believe that the girl wanted to break up. Instead, he read her withdrawal as a sign of parental pressure. The next time he dropped into the office, he looked distraught. We asked him how he was faring in his attempts to reach his friend. Was he able to talk to her?

'No. She does not talk to me. She talks to my sister. Her parents tried to stop her, but she has become very daring. She talks back to them. What I do not understand is why she stopped seeing me. If it is on account of our intimate relationship, and she wants to withdraw, that would be fine by me, I have no problems with that. But she should continue to be my friend. After all, we began as friends first. I am not insisting on or interested only in a physical relationship. All I want from her is her love and friendship. What can be wrong with seeking a friendship? I wish she would understand what I am saying. That is why I wanted to talk to her. But she still refuses to see me. My sister is asking me to forget her.'

Not long after, Virat was informed by his sister that she would be getting married, and learnt that her family had made tight security arrangements for the event. 'I am seen as a *Dada* now! As if I would do any harm.' After a while, Shila also stopped taking his sister's telephone calls. She got married, and this gave Virat a sense of 'finality', diminishing his hopes of ever finding out the reason behind her withdrawal. 'I have to tell you this—in this whole affair, I have lost my job. I felt so down I was unable to keep up with work.'

Virat, who was usually so talkative and friendly, grew sullen and silent. When his visits to the organisation dwindled even further, we were worried. We went to see him in his house on the periphery of the city. At the end of a long, narrow lane, lined with small houses that stood shoulder to shoulder, was Virat's house. Single storied, with a roof of tin, it was towered over by another house on one side. On the other side, there was a smaller house, outside of which a woman sat washing her clothes; she was bathed in white sunlight that slanted away across the courtyard to Virat's house, where it slipped under the curtain. We stepped inside the house, and a tiny figure, barely discernible in grey salwar and kameez, looked at us enquiringly. We asked where Virat was, saying that we were his friends.

His *Beeji* turned away from us and called out to him, but there was no response. She hurried inside, instructing us to sit on an iron cot in a flawlessly clean room, the shelves lined with utensils in the order of their height and size; not a speck of dust lay on the family photo frames, TV set, or fan. Money plants framed the two large windows. Behind us, we heard Virat drag himself out of the room. He stretched out a hand, a look of happy surprise on his face.

'He has been like this for days—look at his shirt and pants, so crumpled.' Turning to Virat, she asked, 'Is this the way you dress to receive your friends?' Without paying attention to his *Beeji*, he took us inside to a room that served as both kitchen and sitting room. Pictures of actors and actresses from glossy magazines beamed at us from the wall. The kitchen led on to a small space. Virat turned to us. 'Come here,' pointing to the mango tree that stood in the open ground, he continued, 'Look at it. It has been with me ever since I was a child, like my friend. I talk to it, especially these days. Look down, look at the way it fills this space with these dancing shadows. But you know, in the night, the shadows are scary. I snuggle with *Beeji* and wake her if I have to go to the loo.'

We returned to the kitchen and saw Virat's *Beeji* with teacups. 'Yes, he does wake me up, I have to accompany him. This one needs to grow up.' As we resettled, Virat continued, 'When you came inside, you could not have imagined this open space, could you? This is what I like, the unexpectedness of the space and the tree out there. It is my favourite place in the house. *Beeji* grumbles because it messes up the place when the leaves fall, but when the flowers blossom and the fragrance fills our house, not a murmur passes her lips.' While we sipped tea, we persuaded Virat to come and help in the organisation. Having got him to agree, we left, satisfied that he was safe under his *Beeji's* watchfulness.

For a few months, Virat remained involved with the HIV/ AIDS programme. But not for long. 'I prefer to work in my own field of automobiles.' The need to bring home a heavier pay packet compelled him to search for another job. Although he was beginning to re-anchor himself in a routine, you could still tell he was yet to recover completely from the heartbreak, still wondering why his girl had left him. 'I joined this automobile company. Even though my pay is not good, I said yes to them…I told myself what you tell me, "Go, get on, pick yourself up." I threw myself whole-heartedly into work and was noticed because of it. There was this other auto company whose owner's wife would come to our show-room, and she offered to take me on with a better wage. I considered it at first, but I thought about how my employer had taken me in when I needed the job, so I felt a kind of loyalty to them to stay on. I did leave, but after a few months, and then joined this TVS company. It was while I worked here that I bought myself a Star Deluxe, my first vehicle paid for with my own money.

'I was a supervisor there, but when an opportunity came to take training in Basic Services, my boss sent a new guy. I was his senior and the older of the two of us. I was so upset, remember? Then it was you who suggested talking with my employer. I did. Well, he had an explanation too. I did not have the Basic Services diploma that my colleague did. I saw the importance of the diploma and began to prepare myself for admission. But the diploma people did not accept my application. They didn't even offer a reason for why they had denied me. When you two came with me to demand an explanation, they said, "Girls do not normally go in for such jobs; we are not accepting her application for the same reason." It was a great feeling when we went there, and you told those people that you were an organisation working with women, demanding a written letter that cited these reasons for them not accepting my admission. The next day, I got a call and I got the letter that admitted me for the training. This is how I finished my diploma.'

Months went by, and Virat was still trying to overcome his 'rejection', as he called it. He continued to think of reasons that would explain his friend's sudden withdrawal. 'Do you think…' he wondered aloud, 'my previous girlfriend left me because I am a woman. Do you think the other one also withdrew for the same reasons?' He looked for an answer from us.

'Maybe, but one cannot say for sure. Perhaps you know best why she has withdrawn.'

'Women get married, and we lose our partners. That is how it works.'

Over time, his wish to become the man he was grew intense, with more urgency and clarity. Having found a space and community members like him, he wanted to know more about gender change, asking and seeking answers to questions that bothered him. He talked about it all the time. We were fortunate that our friend, Satya, who had been through a gender affirming surgery, came to a nearby city, and the four of us went there to meet him. But when we met with Satya, Virat hardly asked a question. As we conversed over cups of tea, Virat stayed quiet. For someone who never stopped asking about the subject, his silence puzzled me, until I caught him looking intently at Satya. 'Is that beard real?' he asked.

Satya was open and willingly shared his life, understanding perfectly where the questions were coming from. Smiling, he leaned forward. 'Touch and see for yourself.' Virat and Ankit touched it, and I saw them, all the three trans men, exchange smiles. I felt so privileged to be present at that moment of brotherhood.

Ankit broke the spell. 'Your parents…' he hesitated for a while. 'I mean, your parents, didn't they try to stop you?'

'Well…did they?' Impatient for an answer, this time it was Virat who did the asking.

'I spent time talking to them, telling them how I felt. Before that, I did a lot of research and reading, seeking out relevant information. I also went through a lot of online material made available to me by my cousins who were training to be doctors.'

'What was the cost?' Ankit wanted to know.

'It would probably cost you three to four lakhs. I had top surgery to get a flat chest and began to take hormones, as advised by my doctor. These have helped in the growth of my beard and moustache. I spent around 20,000. I paid for it all; I would not take a penny from my parents. My mother and sister both supported me.' He went on to explain the whole procedure at length and opened a window to the possibility for one to live the life of their choice.

Feeling more comfortable with one another, Virat asked, 'Do you mind showing us your bare chest?'

'No, not at all. But I would like these two (meaning me and my colleague Indira) yes please, both of you, to go out of the room.'

It was several years later that Satya cleared my understanding of why he had asked us to leave the room. 'I asked you and Indira to go out for different reasons. You, since this was a need of those in the room who identified as trans men, and Indira, since there was no expressed desire, like from the two trans men, to see the results of such a surgery.'

A little later, we re-entered. Feeling more at home now, our conversation veered around our bodies. When assessed through the stereotypical masculine and feminine frame, our bodies did not fit in. Yet, we kept coming back to these ideal bodies, weighing ourselves on those scales. It was a realisation that Satya brought home: 'How many of us would have that ideal masculine or feminine body that we see on television, in the films, or in the models that walk down the ramp? There cannot be one line of definition for anybody. We see tall females and short males all the time, don't we?

'While the change has been positive for me,' he shared, 'when I travel, urinals are a problem.'

Ankit said, 'Yeah, urinals are a problem for me too. Because of my appearance and the way I dress, when I enter the ladies' washroom, I am eyed with suspicion. I fear that someone will shout and there will be a *hangama*…and that attention is the last thing I want. But that apart, I wanted to ask you, what would you say you are?'

'I call myself a trans man.'

We lingered for a while, talking more about our lives, echoes of similar struggles, and identities that best defined each one of us. 'It was such an enjoyable session,' Virat and Ankit both remarked before parting. We thanked our friend for sharing his journey of transformation as we bid our goodbyes. With that, our sojourn was over, and we started on another journey. 'More than lesbian women, we are trans men, just as he said he was,' Virat spoke after a long silence.

'Yes. Though we love women, we do not identify as women.'

'I do,' I said, the odd one out.

'Well! The three of us here are not…we are not women, and if we identify at all, it will be nearer to men. So, we are trans men.' After our return from meeting with Satya, Virat was charged with an enthusiasm that did not falter with time. 'Call me Virat.' And from then on, we did.

Then there was another long absence in his regular visits. Since the first absence had ended in a trip to the police station, we were worried for what lay in store this time. He called a few days later and announced that he had to talk. When he came, we huddled into a quiet corner. 'This time it is no girl problem. It is about sex change. Seriously, I want to go for sex change,' he emphasised. 'How can I get it done? Can you help?'

Over the following weeks, we talked endlessly through the mesh of likely hurdles, what the operation would entail and its consequences: his family, specifically his *Beeji*, sister, employer, the state, doctors, hospital, his own health, and the costs that such an operation would involve. These were not easy conversations. Neither was the act of putting these ideas into action. Anger and frustration plagued us. As a team, we were walking on pathways we had not even set foot on before. I remember our visits to the government hospital, from this department to that department, then from one private hospital to another, then back to the government hospital, for this test and that test. It never seemed to end, all this running around.

'I have examined her. She is a girl,' stated the endocrinologist during one such visit. 'She menstruates, and in every other way, her body is completely that of a normal female. All she needs is counselling. How can we go against nature when there is no problem?'

'Madam, all she wants is to change her appearance to a male. It is not about her body,' we tried to explain. 'What we mean is, it is about her feeling about herself, about her body.'

'Did you see that girl who entered the room?' We nodded in affirmation. 'She is not a complete female. Her body is producing male hormones, her voice is becoming heavier, and the lower part of her anatomy is changing too.' We did not even dare to exchange glances, least of all with Virat. This doctor's reference was critical if we wanted to get the referral for Virat's surgery in a government hospital. I noticed Indira's shuffle towards the doctor, attempting to speak again, but the doctor continued, almost unstoppably, 'This child's parents want her as a female. So, in her case, an intervention makes sense but...' as she paused, Indira managed to muster the syllables, 'Madam...'

There was so much to say but this doctor was not listening. Suddenly, I had an awful sense of panic for people walking through these doors, for us sitting here, and for those who would be next. The doctor was not listening at all. And worse, I thought to myself, what if this child later chooses to identify differently? But the doctor was continuing in a voice that knew it all, 'In your case, marriage may help.'

'Madam,' this time Indira's voice was loud and sharper, 'All she wants is a male appearance. I have a friend who felt the same way, and he had a vasectomy done and an operation of the ovaries that kept the uterus intact. Every month, he takes a hormones maintenance dose, and now he is happy to have an appearance he identifies with.'

The doctor turned to Virat, 'God has made you like He did all of us, a man and a woman, and how can we go against God?'

When Virat replied, it was without the slightest trace of rebuttal, anger, or rancour. He said very simply and softly, 'But it is God who put this feeling inside me.'

That day, we returned to the office and sat in a huddle with Virat, wondering if he would be able to bear the weight of such a cross-examination. This was only the first step; how many more were we to take? We looked at him.

'Do you think you want to continue?'

'We do not know for sure what the people in the government will say.'

'They will ask for some elderly member of your family to be there.' This time it was Virat's turn to fly into a rage; he banged on the table, and glass tumblers toppled over and pens and pencils rolled on the floor.

'Tell me, are you people with me or against me?' He grabbed his bag and walked away without turning back, leaving us wordless and shocked. He called us the next day. We didn't speak about what had happened the day before. He had a dream and a sense of self that resisted denial. We went with that.

After two more visits, the endocrinologist agreed to refer us to the government hospital and asked us to meet with one particular doctor. He was the psychiatrist, grey and smiling, and with a personality that restored the confidence of ordinary citizens milling in the government hospital. In a state medical institution, it is rare to find someone so understanding and open. Virat withstood the agony of postponement from week to week, of standing in the long queues as one of the hopefuls to take out his 'case paper'. With those papers in hand, he spoke with his employers and shared with them the changes that would follow. Their ambivalence was hard to label as positive or negative. The wait and visits that proceeded were a test of our patience.

Finally, the date of Virat's surgery was fixed. 'My second birth,' he called it. We approached it with some anxiety. Pre-operation documents had to be signed by 'family', and Virat had decided to delay the disclosure to *Beeji*. 'My secret is safe with my sister, until we fight. Then she will spill the beans. No fighting with her until then.' He said solemnly, 'But *Beeji* will not sign on my operation papers.' We decided that Indira would sign as an organisation, but it had to be approved officially. The state could turn whichever way it felt, and we were unable to predict what whim they would take that day. But it worked. It was 2007 when Virat had his surgery.

'I feel complete now.' He was lying in a hospital bed, only wincing occasionally and closing his eyes to indicate he was in pain. 'This moment has come, after a lifetime of dreaming about it.' He looked 'at home' as he made plans, 'Now I will go to the gym, and once I start taking hormones, my muscles will build. And shaving, that too is going to be for real. But I am still unsure how I will face *Beeji*. She has no idea. She thinks I am out with you for a workshop.' Pulling himself up on the bed and buttoning his shirt up to his neck, he said, 'Look at me closely, what do you say, are the bandages under my shirt covered properly? Is anything… I mean, is there anything unusual you notice that might draw her attention? If she knows that this was what you did, we have had it. She will never want to look at you, nor allow you or even me inside the house.'

So Virat returned home after staying only two days with us, still with his bandages and a dull pain. '*Beeji* did not notice anything, but I know she was a bit puzzled at my odd behaviour. When she noticed me hiding in corners to change my clothes, she stared at me as if she were about to ask me something. But I hurried away and stayed out of her sight. Though of course, I could not avoid arguments with my sister over the housework—we are always fighting. So, she lifted my shirt twice and called out, 'Look what has she gone and done. Look at her!' Thankfully, *Beeji* is a little hard of hearing, so I escaped that day. Even now, we have not spoken to one another about it. Maybe she knows or maybe she doesn't, it does not matter anymore, to me or to her. We have reached reconciliation after many years.'

Weeks later, the doctor's experienced hands cut the knots until the bandages unwound off his chest. The moment was awesome. It was a man's chest. He ran his hands gently over the space where his breasts had once been. 'Those were like weights that pressed me into suffocation—gone,' he said, smiling at us, an infant awakening to the newly born universe before him.

'When I rang up my boss, she called me by the female name and I said to her, "I am Virat."' Though Virat felt safe and welcomed in the familiar, life in the workplace would continue to open up wounds he thought would suture with time. 'I noticed the male customers steal glances, at me and amongst themselves, wordlessly naming the secret between them. There was a bond of brotherhood that I knew I could never break into. But I continued on. Then one day, I noticed my colleague, this guy at the repairing site, unbuttoning his shirt, deliberate and slow, and lifting up his arms to show his biceps. Opening his pants, he stood in his underwear, pulling its elastic intermittently, staring at me. His gaze settled for a while at the centre of my pants before he slid on to the floor below the car.'

A few months later, Virat went through his second operation, followed by an agonizing wait for the moustache and beard he so hoped would grow, meanwhile suffering the insidious insults and whispers that followed him around the workplace. At home, the silence did not allow him space to unburden himself. 'But for nothing in the world would I go back. It is said that to see heaven, you have to die first. Whether my life is shortened or it ends, or whatever else happens, this was my life's goal and I have arrived here. Not all days are bad but there are days...' We could see the toll that even the not-so-bad days were taking on him. On those days, when he had to return to his office, he would sigh, 'Now I don't feel like going back.' We saw his feet drag, and the wave of his hand was drained of all energy. Going by shared experiences of others who had gone through sex reassignment surgery (SRS), we suggested a change of place. 'But my *Beeji*, and my sister's marriage, and my job...' his tone betrayed his affection for them. When pushed to think through his rationale for staying on in the same city, he acknowledged, 'I was born and raised here.'

After much persuasion, he changed his job. But like all professions, the world of automobile showrooms and workshops was a circle of known people. News of Virat's gender change reached before he did. But he still stuck to his city, the city of banyan trees with roots splitting into more roots, each one as visible as Virat's sinewy ties of attachment. He lacked the cunning to cover up his vulnerabilities, and so suffered in more than one way. Even when he wooed the women he fell in love with, it was beyond him not to act so overly eager. For every yet-to-be-lover, his wishful imagination often resulted in a wallet far lighter than he could afford. But his single status stayed unchanged.

It was at this point in life that Virat expressed a wish for some change and greater exposure to the queer community. A few months later, when Vikalp was invited to conduct a workshop, he was happy to join in. At the venue that first evening, Virat stood transfixed. The tension in his body seeped through to me, and I relived those moments of my own, when I too had once whispered, 'So many of us.' The first day, he sat with us all, paper and pen in hand, listening attentively. The next day, I noticed Virat's distraction and his close companionship with a trans woman. That night, the bed next to mine was empty until the early hours of the morning.

Much later, he shared his experience of that night. 'I allowed myself to succumb. She showed such interest in me. It was my first experience with a woman like her. I was attracted to her. No doubt the touch and the smell of her body is different… I mean, from women, but she is a woman, if you know what I mean. I needed her warm touch. We were all sleeping in dormitories though, so all we could do was snuggle, kiss, and hold one another—no more. I was looking for a partner then. Her closeness helped me pass those days in the office as our relationship developed over distance. After a while, though, it petered out.'

Three to four years later, Virat's younger sister was married, which reignited *Beeji's* desire for Virat to do the same. He decided to relocate, for reasons of the 'heart alone'. He had met a girl through a common friend living in another city, who had told him about her unhappiness with her current trans partner. So Virat began speaking with her. 'We exchanged pictures and talked on the phone for many days at a stretch. I convinced her to come and live with me. But there was a problem—she did not have the money to buy her ticket. I arranged for her ticket and she came. She came, you know. I went to receive her at the station. My heart was beating so loud, I felt like it could be heard over the roar of the engine as it pulled in. I saw her get off. She is not broadly built; she's light and small, with big eyes. That was my girlfriend, Mitra. I picked up her bag and as we drove off on my bike, shivers ran down my body. Sitting behind me, she could feel me trembling. She slid her hands through her bag and held on to me, tight and close. Taking her home was the hard part. But I had prepared *Beeji* earlier. She was a friend in her eyes. When the night came, *Beeji* allotted the separate room in which I slept to my friend and asked me to shift in with her to sleep. "She is our guest," she said, refuting any logic that I gave against our guest being alone in an unfamiliar place. It was difficult to get past my stubborn old woman, proffering the same logic as I did, "But she is our guest."

'Instead of turning in, she and I, we sat awhile talking, nursing our nocturnal separation and planning a way out of it. We had to turn in. A little later, as planned, my friend called out to me. I waited for her to call me again. I tiptoed out. On returning to *Beeji's* room, I said, "She is scared to be alone," and I picked up my pillow and sheet. It was a night to remember. Right there in the open doorway, between whispers and our furtive exploration, she pulled me suffocatingly close and kissed me, lip to lip and mouth to mouth. A current ran through me. It was like...' spreading his fingers, he said, 'What can I say it was like...like, I mean like, nothing I can describe. How happy and proud I was that night of my flat chest as she ran her fingers over me, and when she rested her head against it. We never shut the door so long as we lived with *Beeji*.

'I used to go for work and she stayed back at home. Soon, differences erupted between *Beeji* and my friend. I tried to maintain some balance, but what do you do if one wants to eat rice and the other wants chapattis? Between their choices of tea and coffee, rising and retiring time, everything became an issue. *Beeji's* complaint was that she was on the phone all the time, with little or no help from her. I realised this arrangement was not going to work. I moved out and set up a house on the periphery of the city.' It was a cosy flat that Virat moved to, with two windows overlooking trees, a windswept vacant ground, a big balcony at the end of the two rooms, and a kitchen. 'This house owner was a friend's friend, and he let me have it for a lease of 11 months.'

'It is a rare find' we had told him when we went visiting the couple. 'Keep it.'

But it was not to be. Virat soon found that the frequent calls that *Beeji* had accused his friend of making were mostly to her ex. One day, Virat noticed that she had left her Facebook messages open on the computer. Not able to resist reading them, he found out that she was still in love with her ex. 'I woke her up and made her sit in front of the computer. She said he had kept calling her because she had left without a word. She had left just like that to come here. She wanted ten to fifteen days to bring closure to her previous relationship.' Reluctantly, Virat agreed and booked her tickets both ways. But days went by, and then a month, but his friend did not come.

His friend kept postponing her return. 'Financially, my family situation is not good, so I will have to take up a job,' she said. Virat kept hoping. 'She talks vaguely and does not really say she will not come. I don't know if she will.' It was hard for him to accept that she wasn't coming. He continued to call her, and she continued not to respond.

A few months later, Virat broke the news. 'Finally, I am moving out of Baroda to a new city, to be with her. She said, "If you come here, we can be together." So, I am going. I have managed a job interview with the company I am currently working with. But since my documents do not reflect my gender change, I am worried. I thought having a known reference will help and the rest I can manage, my identity documents and all.'

When he arrived in this new city, his friend told him that she had moved out of the rented place because of differences with the owner of the house, so she was now living with her previous partner. 'So, I ended up staying with the friend who had originally introduced us. My friend would meet me in the evening after work and we would go out. I did not like the idea that she was staying with her ex, and we often landed in awful arguments about it. I told her, "Whatever you do with him, do not bring him before me." But she did one day. I saw him when she came to pick me up in a three-wheeler. He was sitting there right beside her. What's a guy to do? Oh yes, we got into a fight. Hitting and screaming at one another in that small space of the three-wheeler. The driver tried to intervene, and so did my friend—or rather, I should call her "our friend". They both tried to pull us apart. I was so angry that I even hit her, and then began walking away. I bought myself drinks and returned to where I was staying. My friend followed me. We made up. And a few more days passed in peace.

'I had recently been exposed to sex work, so one evening, I asked my friend with whom I was living if she was into sex work too. From my perspective, it was a simple query without any insinuations, but she thought otherwise. This threw her into such a state of fury that I was taken aback. Before I could get my wits about me, she was shouting at me, "Get out, get out this minute, and how dare you!" She asked me to pack my bags and leave. I tried to explain and told her I would leave first thing in the morning, but she was adamant and began throwing my things out—whatever stuff she could lay her hands on. It was unbelievable. I was still trying to pick up my scattered belongings when she called the landlord to ask me to vacate. Of course, the landlord thought I was a man, and what could I tell him, he ordered me out.

'I was new to Bangalore, and I had no idea where I would go. I stood outside for some time, wondering what to do next. Some of my stuff was still in the house. Hoping she would relent, I knocked on the door to collect my remaining things. But the door did not open. Finally, I went up to the top floor to the landlord and asked him to mediate so that I could at least retrieve my sheets and other belongings. It was late into the night, dark and still. I thought of going to my trans woman friend who had welcomed me into her place before. I was amazed to see that she had three floors. She is a mother to so many trans women living there, often rejected by their families. They find a home there. But the humiliation and shock prevented me from calling.

'I spread out my sheet outside a medical store and lay down, sleepless and scared. I could hear the dogs howl, coming up close. Somewhere in the distance, I recognised the brawl of a drunk. As I searched my contact list for names in the dim night light, some boys thought I was writing a suicide note. I told them I needed a place for the night, and they suggested I go to a nearby building that had PG accommodation. I was worried because it was the end of the month, I did not have enough cash to pay them. I slowly walked down the road, thinking that I would not tell them about the cash shortage, but instead say that I would pay in the morning. My biggest concern, however, was having to share accommodation with boys. I turned and walked back slowly. It was still night, but by then I had gathered my senses and called my trans woman friend. She said that I could stay with her instead of a hostel, what a relief. As dawn broke, I made my way to her three-floor building.

'This is how I began to live with her, amongst her family and now my family too. It was good but different, how can I explain, the sheer openness of sex, desire, money, competition, and comradeship. There was so much going on there, and I learned so much, their contradictions and mine. As days passed, they became months and then a year. She was the boss there and because of my association with her, I was treated differently. Sometimes I just could not tolerate the many people who came into her life. We planned on getting married—perhaps it was a way to deal with our anxieties. We got engaged but it had to remain a secret as, in there, no marriages are allowed. It was becoming hard to cope with my surroundings. Late in the evening, when money had to be collected from the trans women, it was quite a scene. It was never a smooth transaction; there were tempers, tears, stories of street violence, of blows and beatings, of harassment and abuse, mostly from policemen. To add to my discomfort, our relationship now began to grow weary as we fought regularly. I was drinking every day. One positive did come out of my stay there though—my friendship with a trans woman named Lily.

'Finally, I had gathered enough courage to seek out a hostel, but it had to be a boy's hostel. Whilst there, I would have to wake early and finish the morning rituals before anyone else was up. Or I would linger around till the washrooms were empty, and I could use them without intrusions. If I reached my office late, I would stay on longer in the evening. But there were always occasions when I could not manipulate situations to suit my reality. I was always haunted by the paranoia "What if I am found out?" I was constantly gripped with fear and tension. More than ten of us had to share three washrooms. Once, someone pulled the door so hard that the bolt inside gave way. I did not want to be that person inside the washroom. I knew that many of them thought I was a *chhakka*.[28] I left that hostel after a few months, but during my time there, I learnt how to read signals and navigate masculine spaces.'

With time and close observation, Virat was intoxicated with the taste of freedom that this period gave him. No curfew time, the freedom to meet and bring over friends that he chose, the hairstyles he changed, the clothes, rings, and chains that he wore, and the sheer anonymity of a big city with its spoils and dazzle. He grew familiar to the new city, its ways, markets, places, and language. We used to see him every Diwali when he visited home. He was now a member of a trekking club, taking trips all over the southern part of the country. 'The rivers, the mountains, cooking on the beach side, the nights and days spent out...' Heaving a sigh of sheer satiation, he said, 'You know, in less than two years, I have travelled to more places than I ever did in over three decades of my life. Funny, that I feel so settled now. A job in a different city with a different culture, and with the travelling that I do. There is a sense of finding a home away from home.'

In the months that he was away, we kept in touch telephonically. One day, he called. 'I am back and I have been here for a month now. This time, it is for good.' This was indeed surprising. The last time he came, he seemed so well-settled.

'How come? What happened?'

'I will come over and tell you.'

So Virat came over and shared: 'In that new city, just as I was becoming well-acquainted with it, a jolt shook me. I was transferred to a new office and found a colleague with whom I fell in love. She felt the same. Every evening after work, we would go out. That was wonderful. It made the city so much more comforting. Until I realised, she already had a boyfriend. I stopped

---

28 *Chhakka* is a derogatory term used for queer people, primarily in North India.

seeing her, but in the office, we had to continue to be cordial. We still ate lunch together. Two months later, I found out that she killed herself.

'She did not appear to be someone who could take such a step. Her presence had become a habit with me. I would look for her to then realise she was no more. Her desk was empty, leaving me strangely lonely. We were no longer lovers, and yet… Anyway, I am back. *Beeji* insists I should stay, and I might. She is also getting older and irritable. She may not have given birth to me, but she is my mother and I, her son. At times it seems that she understands my sexual preference and gender identity, and other times I think she must not. We have never spoken about it. My beard, moustache, and new deeper voice are there for her to see and hear, and though she still calls me by my earlier name, I know that she accepts me—she even tells my neighbours to find a girl for me! The neighbours too use my dead name, but still, I can tell there is some kind of acceptance. The funny thing is that all the youngsters call me Virat. There is this small boy in our locality, I have a special corner in my heart for him, and he calls me Virat Bhai. I love it when he calls out to me and shows me his drawings. His mother is enraged when she finds him drawing and colouring pictures instead of completing his schoolwork, I have seen her tear pages out of his exercise book. He is a different sort—he also loves animals and slips out to feed the neighbour-hood stray dogs and cats. I hear his mother call after him, and then the little fella scampers back, the dogs following him. He is dragged inside as the dogs bark in protest, his mother's shouts getting muffled behind the shut door. I can tell you it is quite a scene, this. He also has a great fondness for trees and plants. He is different from the other kids, like I too was different. I mean, not different in the sense that he is like me, but just a different kind of guy from the others. So, you see why I am especially fond of him. I suppose I am of many facets to people here: a man of two cities, of many cultures, from west to south, a Punjabi-Gujarati if you will, with one heart and many heartaches, single and looking. Single and still looking, yes, looking still; if you think the years of loss are behind me, then no, not yet.

'Now the law has changed, it is possible that I can legally validate the identity which has always been a reality for me. I could get it on my documents, with the *sarkari thappa* and all that, but at the end of the day, it is the people here who make my life, mixing my old and new names.

'I do not like it—this mixing—but you know, I like them still. I am known here, my truants as a child, my late nights; I am known as that queer kid who turned male. This is a city, where I found people like me, here in this locality is where I call home. In any other place, I have to watch my own back, but here, there is always someone else watching out for me too. I cannot say that of any other place.'

A Collective Coming Out

When we first met Virat, he identified as lesbian; there was no other word available to describe his love for women. Before meeting Satya, he had never heard of the word 'trans'. Though I never claim to be a spokesperson for trans men, nor say that I have lived the same experience, I can draw parallels with this revelation as I too lived the first part of my life without a name to describe myself. When I did find it, the comfort was immeasurable.

Over fourteen years, we have watched Virat's transformation in more ways than just the physical: moving from his grandmother's house to his own rented apartment, from a small city in the west to a metropolitan in the south, from identifying as a lesbian to identifying as a trans man. And as an organisation, we too have transformed, from Parma—an anonymous post box that we used to have—to an active group with names, faces, and each one of us with histories as deep as the roots beneath the earth. As we uncovered more of those 'like us', a group emerged under the name of Sabrang. We went from anonymity to now having faces to match the names. The coming together of the group helped in breaking down the isolation and myths about gender and sexuality. We realised that the oppositional binaries carrying prescriptive gender roles were not the only valid choice for men and women; some amongst our group and in the wider communities where we worked did not prescribe to these binaries. We learned to notice the diversity that surrounds us all.

Numbers began to rise, and Vikalp as an organisation became involved in counselling, organising meetings, joining Pride parades, discussing the Section 377 of the IPC, imparting information on SRS, approaching government hospitals for desired gender change, intervening and taking action to support eloping couples, strategising ways to secure itself and the community against police action and attacks, providing shelter, preventing family violence, and undertaking sensitisation sessions both for the community and the larger society.

As one of the earliest members/supporters of Parma, Virat was one of those who advocated for greater openness, stopping only when others reminded him of the risks they would run on account of him. 'You have to use my name for my story,' he insisted, relenting when he was reminded by other members in the group that 'our association with you may reveal who we are, and many of us here may not want that.'

'How are things going to change then?' he argued.

Our organisation went through a similar process as the queer individual: after self-discovery, it came to a point where it was time to 'come out'.

If our 'coming out' could be pinned to a certain event, perhaps it could be the Gujarat Social Forum (GSF) held in Ahmedabad in 2006. After LGBTIQ+ featuring as a central point of discussion during Mumbai's World Social Forum in 2004, there was a kind of ripple effect throughout the country and a tangible increase in visibility—a phenomenon that was undeniable when our GSF workshop on gender and sexuality drew in 700–800 attendees. People were spilling out of the tent, and the speakers could be heard beyond the thin canvas walls. Members of Vikalp's trans community attended as out and proud.

However, as the movement began to gain momentum, the 'ripple' mentioned was yet to be felt in small towns and rural villages. The plight of queer couples and individuals remained a challenging terrain to navigate, leaving many with few options other than to elope.

11

'Who Will Believe She Ran Away with a Woman, and That She is Still...'

This story goes back to 2006, when we were barely two years into our work on queer issues. It was the first day of the year 2006 when Monu and Reema eloped from a small town Ratangarh, a block situated at a distance of 100 km from Baroda, within the district of Panchmahal. We learnt of them only three days later, when the story appeared in a local newspaper.

Reema, the paper said, was 21 years old and was the eldest child of Metabhai. She had a younger brother. Monu was a 19-year-old, the daughter of Gurmeet Singh and Jasbir Singh. She had a brother and a sister. Monu's father worked as a security guard in a company in a town not too far off from Ratangarh. He lived in the premises of the factory. Monu lived with her mother in Reema's rented house. Over time, the neighbourly friendship between the two developed into love.

Besides their elopement, the report also talked of Reema's parents levelling charges of abduction and theft of valuables estimated at Rs 55,000 and Rs 15,000 against Monu. Having escaped with the valuables, both were untraceable.

The news generated a lot of discussion within our new group that was emerging from being a post box to a small presence of queer people in Vikalp. While some of us expressed the desire to go on a fact-finding visit, Dev, one of the earliest identified trans persons in our group whose relatives ran a hair cutting salon in the same town, said that 'the elopement scandal was doing the rounds from the day the couple had disappeared. The news in the paper was a trifle late. The reason why I knew about Monu specifically, even before she hit the headlines, was because she had come for a haircut at the salon my relatives ran. My relatives had called me at the time, saying, "Today we had a client who was dressed like you, and her hair was styled like yours." This piece of conversation elicited smiles of recognition from some of us, but Dev was quiet, with a frown. He was uneasy when his relatives had called him the first time to tell him about his similarity with their client. But he let it go: 'After all, nowadays even girls have short hair and wear jeans and all that; thinking the whole matter would die a natural death, I did not allow myself to get agitated.' But on the day we met, the paper carried Monu's photograph along with the news that she had eloped with a girl, and Dev was worried. He had come over to talk about it. His relatives had called him first thing in the morning to tell him that the client who looked like him had eloped with a girl. 'Why are they calling me and telling me all this?' He turned to the group, saying, 'I cannot help thinking that they will find out about me and my friend, by the way he dresses and because of the story about running away with a woman.' Dev's involvement with a woman compounded his worry. The story held a fear for him that he would now be categorised with the 'look-alike people in dress and behaviour'. His friendship with a woman would be seen in conjunction with Monu's, and it would then be exposed as being more than what met the eye.

Fear has a quality of contagion; I detected a fear similar to what Dev had expressed amongst the other trans men as well. Dev's forthright articulation helped the group to talk about it and arrive at some rationalisations. Like the waves that return to the shores, fear kept returning every now and then throughout the time we were involved in following Monu and Reema.

The news report mentioned the town and the name of the factory in which Monu's father worked as a security guard; this encouraged the trans men, who argued for a fact-finding visit. 'Let us try to meet the father to get more information.'

Another one said, 'It is a quiet town, no one will notice us.'

They decided to approach Monu's father because our shared experience showed that generally, the families of trans masculine persons reluctantly accepted the gender identity of their child. We imagined that if we could get him to talk, we could make some headway into supporting the couple in staying safe. Having gone there, they found that he had left the place two days earlier. No further information was available. 'It is confirmed that he did work there. He lived in a one-room hut, which had absolutely no material possessions in it. Just a string ran across on one side, with a few clothes straddled on it. The dilapidated low door was hardly able to support itself. The condition said something about the family's financial state. Maybe that is why he had to leave his own state and live in such conditions away from his family.'

The next day, the papers carried the news that the girls were still untraced, giving us hope that they were successful in their getaway. But the papers also said the search had intensified. Every day, the papers carried some information or news about the couple, as if refusing to let them go out of sight—they built an aura of suspense around their disappearance, giving a different meaning to our everyday invisible queer lives. Their survival and safety became our collective hope. We held our breaths. Unable to wait any longer, the following day, two of us decided to go to the town from where the two had disappeared.

We initially met with Reema's parents. We spoke to them, several other relatives, and the larger community, who immediately gathered around us and told us somewhat triumphantly that Monu's parents were held outside the Ratangarh police station. 'But they (police) are not doing anything. Simply holding Monu's parents will not help until they take action.'

Reema's family was convinced that Monu was biologically male. Substantiating their belief, one of them demonstrated the shaving action and said, 'He shaved.'

'We know he is male.'

Someone else intervened, 'We know because he used to go in the mornings to defecate with the other boys.'

'Whom did he go with?'

The ring of people surrounding us parted and a small boy shuffled right up to us, pointing at himself, 'With me. He used to go with me every morning.'

Others explained, 'He is Reema's brother.'

In lieu of his alleged 'crime', the Marwari community had built enough pressure to prevail upon the police to act. Consequently, they had detained Monu's parents on the premises of the police station. Fear of further harassment from the collectivised power of the Marwari community prevented Monu's parents from protesting the illegal detention.

Reema's family alleged that Monu's parents had abetted the elopement. According to them, when they found Reema missing, they realised that even Monu's mother was not in the house. Since she was their tenant, it did not take them long to discover her absence.

Alerted, they collected a few relatives and immediately rushed to the place where Monu's father worked. '…And there, we found them both ready to leave. We asked why and where they were going if they were not involved.'

'We know,' they repeated emphatically, 'we know the girls are in Punjab—that is where they were going. You can talk to them and find out.'

'We would like to do so,' we said, and as we proceeded towards the police station, we were followed by the whole contingent of the enraged community. We wanted to speak with the detained parents alone. Taking a chance when we reached the police station, we made it clear, 'Everyone will have to wait farther away while we talk with them alone, to hear their side of the story.' Initially, the suggestion was rejected outright. However, we insisted.

'To be fair to all,' we said, 'it is important to listen to the other side.' Reema's father conceded and the crowd stopped where they were. When Monu's parents saw us approaching, they got up and came out of the shed. Peering through the fading light of that winter evening, Gurmeet Singh recognised that one of us shared similarities with his daughter. 'You are just like my daughter, just that Monu wears pants and a shirt and you are wearing a long kurta...you could be Monu...'

Over the distance of allegations and counter-allegations, silences and suspicions, and the illegality of our relationships, here was someone sharing something that reached us more in symbols than in open words. This was the recognition that Dev had feared, but here, the recognition worked to establish a bond and helped in the realisation of a reality that lived deep inside us; just for a while before we drew our breath again, we stood in that moment of profound intuition and the magic of connection. There is a side to vulnerability that perceives more than the eye sees; sometimes, it even reaches the powerful and the dominant and encourages them to read the text right and lay out a safe plan. Perhaps it was something in that shared moment that also told us that the young women were indeed in Punjab. Before we went back to the larger crowd, we told the couple that being detained at the police station by virtue of simple association with the 'suspected' was illegal and that they could file a case. He knew of the law. Before joining the factory as a security guard, he had retired from the police and that is where he had learnt of the law. 'It is a practice that is followed,' he told us. 'But these are powerful people—they can do anything.

'They are blaming us and my daughter. She does not identify as a woman. This is not her fault, you see that, don't you? If I could afford an operation, I would get her operated. We have heard that it is possible.'

We could hear the crowd behind us getting impatient, so we warned the parents, 'For now, do not say anything to the people here about what Monu feels. Let us go and talk to them.'

We brought the two warring sides face to face. 'I do not know where my daughter is.'

'He knows.'

Another one loudly claimed, 'He is protecting his son.'

'She is a girl.' The father countered the allegations of Monu being talked of as a boy who had kidnapped their daughter. The mother spoke up, her face turned towards us, 'Monu was always like this. Ever since she was a child, she did not concede to wearing girls' clothes. She always dressed as a boy and wore her hair short. She was withdrawn and often kept to herself, aloof and quiet. She really had no friends. She did not even complete school because…'

'But she can speak English,' her father quickly interrupted and concluded proudly.

But Monu's mother whispered in our ears, in an aside, 'During the day, she would stay by herself up in the loft, and only when it got dark would she come down and go out. She is very quiet and prefers to be on her own.' Coming up close, she added, 'I did not even know when her periods came.' Monu's mother did all the talking about her daughter, as if answering all the debates, doubt, and rumours that were being spread about her. She wanted us to understand that her daughter was not the kind of person who would abduct anyone.

The community gathered menacingly close. 'You ask him, he will listen to you; ask, we are telling you, ask, ask him to make a call to Punjab. We are telling you that is where our daughter has been taken. They do not belong here—they are from Punjab and they have taken our daughter there.'

The community did not give in and continued to aggressively pressurise Gurmeet Singh to call his relatives in Punjab. He said he did not have a phone, and as the arguments raged on, threatening to turn violent, we intervened and nudged Gurmeet Singh to listen to them and make a call to ease the situation.

He looked uneasily towards the police station, as if seeking permission. Once again, insistent voices prodded him to make the call. We all went to a payphone close to the police station. He dialled a number and spoke in Punjabi. The phone was handed to us, and the voice at the other end said that the pair was not there.

Reema's community stood sullen and disbelieving. They shared, 'Reema had called us from a number in Rajasthan, and when we went there, we found that it was a booth number at the railway station. We think that, having made the call, they may have boarded a train to Punjab.'

We returned that day and discussed the whole episode within the group of five people. Most of us felt that we should intervene to free Monu's parents from the illegal detention. We framed a letter to the Collector to intervene in the detention of Gurmeet Singh and his wife. On revisiting them, we learned that Gurmeet Singh had appointed a lawyer. We contacted his lawyer to follow up on his situation. Within a day, they were both released. However, every strategy that we conceived to reach out to the couple fell through because of lack of information about their exact location. The only way to reach them was to build enough trust with Monu's parents.

We attempted to meet them but they were not traceable. We went once again to the factory that Gurmeet Singh worked at, but neither of them was there and no one there knew of their whereabouts.

We met again with Reema's parents to attempt reconciliation between the families. But one of the relatives, who did not favour any reconciliation, dominated the dialogue and refused to even meet midway at a compromise. 'Our daughter's honour is at stake...'

We tried to reason and approach him in a more acceptable framework of hetero-patriarchal norms, 'But the one she has gone with is a woman...'

'Your saying so does not turn this man into a woman...'

'We are not saying it. The press, the television, and others in the locality are all saying she is a woman.'

'That is what we are hearing today, but tomorrow, who will believe us if we say that she ran away with a woman, and that she is okay; tell me, who will believe it? For whoever hears of such things, is this any better? A daughter has to be married; if rumours spread, then who will marry her? You tell me. Anyway, man or woman, we want our daughter back. We do not want any compromises.'

We returned with a heavy heart that day.

Another fortnight went by and there was no news of the couple. We crossed our fingers, hoping that they would manage to stay undetected. A sense of unease lay upon us, and we were not quite sure how to find a way out.

'We can do nothing at this time,' a member from the community cleared the air for us. 'We have done all we can do, now we wait, watch, and then act.'

'In case they are caught, we can bring them here.'

'But how can one know?' another one asked.

'We wait.' We went around in circles, unable to unravel the knots. As the days passed, we realised that we could only intervene when the two were found.

We learnt from the media that the Marwari community gave a letter to the Collector demanding action in locating Reema, requesting a CBI intervention, and complaining of police apathy. The Collector promised action. Photographs were given out to CID Crime and Railways. This implied that the couple's pictures would reach different parts of the country, helping in their identification and finally leading them back to the town they had fled from. The month of January ended, and we realised that the net had been cast wide enough to trap the pair.

The newspapers consistently followed the development on this story. Unknown to us at that time, we learnt much later that Monu and Reema's getaway became every queer couple's inspiration, with people nurturing a secret hope that the two were not found, ever. In the meantime, the Ratangarh police, on their job, had spoken with the DIG Ludhiana, and the hunt had intensified. Each day, the information that came through the media confirmed that it was not long before the lull gave way to a storm. In March, the Ratanpur police went to Punjab on a suspicion that Monu and Reema were seen in a village in Ludhiana. Our worst fears were confirmed. We knew that the couple would be tracked down and brought back here from the place they had fled to and, in all probability, separated.

Before the first week of March ended, the couple was located—the paper reported that they had surrendered and were brought back to Gujarat. The news spread like wildfire. When the train came to a halt at the station on the morning of 7 March, just a day ahead of Women's Day, there was the jostling of an unimaginably aggressive crowd. It swept one off the feet; perhaps some people were present merely because they wanted 'to get one, just one glimpse of this couple'.

Some amongst them were there because Reema and Monu's love aroused a memory of denial or ignited a dream of love, or maybe it was a bruised dissent harboured under cover, a non-compliance that did not quite speak out openly, and now sought comfort in seeing the defiant couple and secretly rejoiced in their daring. They had the gumption to do what many of us only fantasise about. Some wanted to check Monu's gender identity for themselves. After travelling a whole day and night in the train, the couple was instantly whisked off from the station and into the jeep which we know often drives the people in it to the

police station and the lock-up. The media had unleashed an unprecedented curiosity in the public mind through their regular
briefs on Monu and Reema. It was a story that, having begun,
needed an end. But the story did not end there.

Anticipating that the couple would be produced in the
court the next day, ironically on International Women's Day,
two of us rushed to the town and made our way straight to the
police station, still unsure of what our next step would be and
where it would land us. Once there, we waited for an opportune
time to see the couple, hoping they would be brought there to
be produced in the court. While we hung around, we heard that
Monu had fled earlier with another girl from a minority community.

But at that time, the matter had ended quietly. We also heard
that Monu's sister and her husband had come to the police station. We searched them out and learnt that the parents had deliberately kept away to avoid censor, blame, and further custody.
Monu was accepted in the family as 'difficult' because of her 'difference from normal girls'. Nonetheless, they said she was a 'part
of us, we cannot simply desert her'. It was from them that we
learnt there was a possibility of one of them being cited as below
18. We wondered if there was some connivance in the assertion
of the police that one of them was a minor. By showing one as
underage, the intent to separate them would have a validity that
could not be questioned. But if there was evidence on the contrary, separation of the two would amount to violation of the law,
because the papers had reported both the girls to be above 18
years of age. As adults, they had a right to make decisions about
their lives. 'Perhaps this is an opportunity we can use?' we told
ourselves.

The swelling crowd outside the police station kept the police personnel on their toes. They were not letting anyone inside,
and visitors were being strictly scrutinised. Posing as journalists
from different newspapers, we asked to see the two girls. Sur-

prisingly, we were let in. Finally, we were able to meet the couple in custody. But the hovering presence of a woman constable who kept a hawk's eye on us and them did not allow much of an open conversation between us. Nonetheless, we told the woman constable we wanted a private word with the two of them—she refused. Instead, she moved up closer to stay within earshot and chose to watch over us. Our only hope was that she would look away and we could slip our cards to them. Having anticipated such an impasse and the constancy with which the visibility of a different gender identity had ironically created and broken down barriers at the same time, we had planned to go as a team of two. One of us was distinctly androgynous and I was the woman. We hoped that they would find a reflection of themselves in us and recognise us as allies. We quickly slipped an upside-down visiting card of our organisation beneath our palms and, bending close, we said, 'Do not reveal your relationship, except as female friendship. And hide the card. Contact us if you need to.' They had been photographed hand in hand, looking at one another as only lovers can do and feeding each other bites of food. Even the write-ups that followed left no doubt about their relationship; their own voice, however, would matter in the court. We left with a hope that they had heard us, and if questioned in the court, they would stick to the version that we had given them.

Once back to the main room of the police station, we let it be known that we knew the law and inquired from the police about the delay in producing the women in court and the likely day and time they would be produced. We learnt that there was a strong likelihood of them being produced in the court that very day. Having got the information, we located the court where the couple was likely to be produced and left.

Our next step became clearer after this visit to the police station. As discussed in our group meetings, our aim was to ensure the couple's safety and prevent their separation unless they wished otherwise. Taking guidance from our activist lawyer, we wrote out a letter to the Magistrate in the District Criminal Court about the malafide intent in showing the women to be below 18 years in order to prevent them the right to mobility and freedom to choose where and with whom they wished to live. We also attached the copy of the news item from the newspaper that talked of the couple being adults. We decided to wait for the hearing to hand over the letter to the judge. We sat right in the front row, in the centre chairs that faced the honourable Judge's table and chair. The courtroom was almost empty when we entered. But as we waited, people thronged in. We wondered if all of them were from Reema's community. Soon, the court filled to its full capacity, and people stood along its walls. What we did not know was that even outside the court, the streets were overflowing with people. The usually deserted premises of the court and the area in its vicinity had not witnessed such a mass of people: they were sitting on treetops and terraces. The rest were packed in whatever places that appeared to them. Reema and Monu's story was on everyone's tongues, thanks to the papers that did not let a single day go by without carrying their names and stories.

Inside, we awaited the arrival of the judge. Suddenly, there was a hustle of footsteps. We saw the policewoman in the corridor outside the door from where we sat. Reema and Monu were being brought in. We rushed out and quickly waved at them to let them know we were with them before they were pulled away in the back chambers. A little later, the Honourable Judge walked in, and as he sat down, we got up and handed him the letter. He read through it but he seemed angry, and said, 'I will look into the matter myself.' We retreated into our seats and sat through the proceedings.

The judgement was path-breaking. It read, 'Reema and Monu are above 18 years of age. Both have the right to live their lives independently and as per the rules of the Indian Constitution, there cannot be any restrictions on them.'

After the judgement, we drove out immediately. Stone pelting had started, and the police had to resort to lathi charge. We saw, for the first time the massive crowds that had gathered around the court. That day, all roads led to Ratanpur. The small town was in the grip of a sensational story that had ended on an unexpected note.

'It is time for us to leave. We should not be recognisable,' Indira said.

I was puzzled. 'But why us? Should we not meet them?'

'No need. They will knock on our door tonight, that is why.'

'Now they are free, why would they come?'

'Where else can they go? Look at the situation here, they are not free. We are not free.'

We returned to our city. The same day, in the dead of the night, the phone rang. It was the police calling us. They wanted to drop off the Ratangarh pair at the Vikalp/Parma office. We ran to the office. At midnight, there was a knock at the office door. We watched through a crack in the door—Reema and Monu had come in the police jeep full of uniformed men and women.

The police had tried to prevail upon them to go to a government shelter home, but the couple had refused stubbornly. Even though the judgement had given them the right to live wherever they chose, the family had tried to pull Reema out from the jeep. She had screamed loud enough to put the onus of protection on the police. They had pulled her back in, and then she sat between two policewomen. The crowd began to pelt stones and some people stood in the way, blocking the jeep. It could only move at a snail's pace, while hands that groped inside looking for Reema had to be pushed back to stop them from taking a hold on her and pulling her off the jeep. Battling the tug of war, the police had brought them back to the police station and tried to convince them to go to a women's shelter home. 'But I refused point-blank,' Monu shared, 'How could I go there?'

'I knew no other place that would have been safe for us. We could not stay anywhere near my family. So finally, we showed them the card you gave us, and they called you and brought us here.'

The police took it from us in writing that they were dropping them here.

That night, our list of visitors went up, and continued to go up as people from our community and allies came to share our joy. The couple stayed with us for another two days until the telephone began ringing and we began to fear for their safety.

The next morning, we celebrated their safe arrival and willingness to live as partners. We held a small ceremony to welcome them and acknowledge them as 'partners' before community witnesses. As we talked over their decision to elope, Reema shared that 'the idea was initiated by me.' Her experience of family was one of oppression, discrimination, severe restraints, and neglect. With Monu it was different. He did not appear to be dominating and demanding. 'I was afraid I would be married to someone who was controlling and compelled to live with him for a lifetime.'

Monu was a quiet person, exactly like his mother had told us. He identified as a man but he simply shrugged when addressed in feminine gender. However, when clothes were bought for them, he refused to wear the jeans because 'it is a woman's pair.' It took him another two days to tell us that his preferred pronoun was 'he'. 'I often have dreams that I have grown a beard and all the other features that make a person a man. I want to undergo sex change. The first thing I will do when I have the money is to become what I feel I am.'

It was after several interactions, without looking at us even once, that Monu shared, 'A male doctor had physically examined me to verify my sex. Both of us were put through intense interrogations to verify our age.' As news continued to spread about them and speculations of their whereabouts were rife, their safety became our paramount concern. Especially when we began to get crank calls and some that said we were destroying family lives and misleading young women. The couple, having been photographed extensively, was recognised by people around the organisation.

We looked for safe spaces for them. Sangama, a group based in Bangalore, supported our efforts and showed willingness to have them there. We hoped it would give them some space and time to be with each other without the burden of being caught and taken away. After careful consideration and strategic planning, we booked their tickets on a train which would leave in the morning at a time when few people are about. We then dropped them to the railway station, well-guarded and protected. They stayed in Bangalore in the shelter for two months. During this period, Monu re-established contact with his family. Both of them missed being in familiar surroundings. Differences in food, language, and surroundings created adjustment problems. Having waited till the end of May to let things settle, they returned to Gujarat and stayed another three days in the organisation before Monu's father came to take them. A formal letter was signed by Monu's father that, in taking Monu and Reema, he would be responsible for the safety of them both. The family had moved further away from Ratanpur. After staying with Monu's family in a village in Bharuch for about twenty days, there was conflict in their family. We were contacted to help in setting up the couple in their own space.

One of the community members had an apartment where we hosted the couple. Before moving in, the community supported them by contributing basic starter materials like food, furniture, utensils, sheets, and mattresses. In these months, several efforts were made to search for jobs and to include them in organisational work as well. Relationship seemed to improve between Monu and his family, which led them to shift with them once again. They took up the job of selling vegetables. Buying in bulk from the wholesale markets, they went around the localities selling vegetables. But the income was not enough and jobs were not easy to come by—both had dropped out from school early on. In the meantime, tensions within the family began to surface again. We also intervened in the tensions that the family went through. But with each passing month, the relationship began to show signs of falling apart. There was love and passion, yet the lack of adequate role models, economic struggles, and absence of full family support began to slowly take its toll.

Then one day, we received a call from Monu. He wanted one of us to come immediately to his place. He explained, 'I have also called Reema's father, asking him to come and take her. We cannot live together any longer.'

When we reached the house and stepped inside, a pall of silence hung over the huddled figures of Monu's brother and mother as they sat on the floor. Clearly, a storm had left the two figures we saw frightened and tense. The seven men from Reema's family who had gathered outside also spoke of things gone awry. We went out and asked them all to go inside the house to avoid drawing more people into the situation and creating a stir. They entered the house where Monu and Reema had been living together with Monu's parents. It was a house with two rooms, one small and another large simply by comparison. We asked to speak with Reema first.

Reema explained, 'I was afraid when I saw my father. I do not even know when Monu called them.' In a voice and eyes that held bitterness and anger, she asked him, 'Why did you?'

'I had to call them. Day after day, it keeps getting worse. You know it.' Then turning towards us, he said, 'Yes, I called her father because they fight a lot—my family and her. Then the both of us fight, and it never ends. It is better if we separate.'

In the meantime, Reema's brother, sister, and her mother had arrived.

'You did not even bother to tell me.'

'How could I have told you? Was it possible in the middle of this fight?…And we had decided that we would take a decision if this kind of fight happens again.' We heard the irritable note in his voice.

Reema stormed out of the room. Her body stiff with anger, she began to collect her things.

To drive home the reality of their decision, we then began to write a statement that everyone had to sign, where Reema's father ensured her safety, stating that he was taking her, and that we could call Reema to check on her. The statement also explained that the couple was choosing to live separately of their own will as their relationship had deteriorated. Reema's family signed the statements.

Reema returned and signed alongside her father's signature.

But when Monu was asked to sign, he became hysterical. He threw things and then ran into the bathroom and poured kerosene on himself. His brother wrestled with him to keep him from finding matches, saying that, like his parents, he too would be sent to jail if anything happened to Monu or Reema. Monu was sobbing and mumbled, 'I have done so much for Reema, stolen, lied, quarrelled with my parents, done things I would have never done. I want to kill myself. She is going and I do want her to... but it is impossible to keep her.'

Reema wrapped herself around Monu in front of everyone and said that Monu just had to ask her to stay, and she would. Monu did not ask. His silence was neutral; it did not speak to her.

She retreated. Bending down to pick her small bag up in her hands, she walked slowly away out of the door, surrounded by her family.

Several months later: Reema's departure left Monu alone and angry with his family. For someone who was generally quiet, now, he often sought us out to talk about Reema. He would call, or at other times, we would meet him. 'I want to get Reema back.' We knew her parents had taken her to a village whose name or location the family did not divulge. We told him that, in all probability, she had been married off. He talked about what he liked and disliked about Reema. He said he liked to pamper her, to indulge her, and to discuss his sexuality freely. But he never really trusted her, because she flirted with other men and despite that said that she loved him. 'What was I to make of it?' he asked angrily. Sometimes, if asked, Monu would say that if Reema returned to him in old age after marriage and children, he would want to be with her. At other times, he would say he wanted no one in his life. 'Not even Reema.' The whole incident had left him grappling with a lot of unresolved issues; the break-up had been too abrupt, even though he seemed to have initiated it.

It has left us deeply uneasy that we were able to see Reema only once since she went that day. Over time, Monu settled down and has since been in touch with us. As we reflected over the graph of events, it saddened us. But like Monu, we too came to rest on some realisations: the partnership may not have worked out, but our intervention had made us wiser and bolder. The legal route that we took of upholding the right to choice and mobility did create a space for the couple; even though it was short-lived, it made a difference. We learnt to arbitrate for the families, and importantly, we were able to stand together in making a voice heard across our community, and saying that we support those who are marginalised because of their sexuality and gender.

While we learnt all this and more, there are moments of deep sadness, a collective memory that continues to hold Reema in our conversations—someone so young, passionate, and outspoken of her love, where is she? Tied in a marriage to a domineering man she did not want? Did she find someone of her choice? Is she happy…? Oddly, the lingering questions that are so hard to simply shrug off are the ones that keep us together.

12

Of Elopements and Maitri Karaar

As mentioned, we did not know at the time that the press reportage of Monu and Reema's story served as inspiration for several queer couples to be as bold as them and to elope—a decision that requires great courage and sacrifice. Vikalp has intervened in more than 15 elopements, and we know of 25 couples who have all eloped (some of them twice or even thrice). And out of those who do elope, some have survived the onslaught of family, state, and the larger society. Others have had to separate due to family interference or the strains of adopting new identities; facing different cultures in unfamiliar cities with no moral or economic familial support creates a struggle at multiple levels. The decision to elope is one that impacts their livelihoods and the opportunities they get for the rest of their lives. Navigating harsh realities with nobody on your side often takes a toll on relationships. Sometimes, retreating to the family home remains the only option. Here, if acceptance comes at all, it is attached to conditions that are far from comforting.

As citizens, shouldn't we all have the same opportunities to dream up a fairy-tale love for ourselves and live it in our daily lives with legal validations? For some couples, turning to the practice of Maitri Karaar has been a loophole in which to achieve this union.

As mentioned briefly in the introduction, one cannot talk about a queer Gujarat without a mention of Maitri Karaar. Maitri Karaar's origins derive from an even earlier custom which gave an official legitimacy to a temporary relationship between a man and a woman before they were married. To begin with, Maitri Karaar contracts were used primarily so that men could give particularly valued helpers or maidservants a kind of legal recognition. The contracts were given legal legitimacy in that they were stamped and signed by both parties, the SDM, and the sub-registrar of marriages.[29] As it grew in popularity, mainly with ministers and senior bureaucrats, the nature of Maitri Karaar arrangements became tarnished as it was utilised mostly by the wealthy and powerful as a convenient way of keeping a personal mistress without disobeying the Hindu Marriage Act.[30]

However, Maitri Karaar was also utilised by women. These special contracts, completely unique to the state of Gujarat, were seen as useful by many women as they allowed for them to enter relationships with married men and secure themselves financial support, should any children come out of their relationship,[31] albeit that custody would be granted to the father.[32] As well as supporting 'other' women who could be seen as 'sexual deviants' for their failure to subscribe to monogamous marriage norms, Maitri Karaar was also used by other 'deviant' women: those in same-sex relationships.[33] For instance, in May 1987, the *Indian Express* ran a story on the Maitri Karaar of two women, which the paper reported was the second of its kind. Both of them were around

[29] "'Maitri Karar": Now Illegal Gujarati Custom of Keeping Mistresses.' September 14, 2019. https://drishtikone.com/blog/2013/01/03/maitri-karar-gujarati-social-custom-of-keeping-mistresses-by-circumventing-hindu-marriage-act/
[30] Ibid.
[31] Baxi, Pratiksha. 'Feminist Contributions to Sociology of Law: A Review.' *Economic and Political Weekly* 43, no. 43 (2008): 79–85. http://www.jstor.org/stable/40278106.
[32] Singh, Chander Uday. 'No Cumbersome Divorce Proceedings, People of Ahmedabad Opt for Maitri Karar Contract.' November 3, 2014. https://www.indiatoday.in/magazine/living/story/19811215-no-cumbersome-divorce-proceedings-people-of-ahmedabad-opt-for-maitri-Karar-contract-773519-2013-10-24.
[33] Baxi, Pratiksha. 'Feminist Contributions to Sociology of Law: A Review.' *Economic and Political Weekly* 43, no. 43 (2008): 79–85. http://www.jstor.org/stable/40278106.

the age of thirty, one a resident of Vadia and the other of Varsada, and they had met at teacher's training school in 1978. 'During all these years, the two women had been living together,' according to the *Express*, 'since they did not wish to get married and wanted to continue living together, they decided to enter into this friendship contract.' The women stated this in writing and did so in front of a notary public.[34] A convenient loophole for certain women, it seems almost ironic that it was feminist lawyers who initiated a backlash against Maitri Karaar, the reason being they did not provide women with any real benefits or rights.[35]

But one could make the argument that even if the contract offered no benefits from a financial perspective, it could have at least allowed for same-sex couples to exercise their choices when separated or harassed by their families. The writ of Habeas Corpus is used to secure the release of a person who has been detained unlawfully, including detainment carried out by a private body. Habeas Corpus has successfully been used several times by families to retrieve adult daughters against their will from lovers they have eloped with.[36] In Gujarat, this very thing happened in 2008 to a couple of primary teachers, Raisa and Vina. Raisa's brother filed a Habeas Corpus petition saying the women were 'abducted by unknown people and illegally detained'.[37] False claims such as these do not seem to anger the court, nor have families been accused of wasting the court's time; instead, they work very much in the families' favour. A newspaper article reported that Raisa simply 'said she would go back to her brother' and just 'walked away with her family members back home.' Her

[34] *Indian Express*, May 6, 1986

[35] "'Maitri Karar": Now Illegal Gujarati Custom of Keeping Mistresses.' September 14, 2019. https://drishtikone.com/blog/2013/01/03/maitri-karar-gujarati-social-custom-of-keeping-mistresses-by-circumventing-hindu-marriage-act/.

[36] Thangarajah, Priyadarshini, and Ponni Arasu. 'Queer Women and the Law in India.' In *Law Like Love: Queer Perspectives on Law*, edited by Alok Gupta and Arvind Narrain. Yoda Press, 2011, p. 330.

[37] 'Runaway Lesbians Return Only to Split.' *Times of India*, June 26, 2008.

partner 'stood a mute witness with tears in her eyes'. No attempt
is made at revealing the real tragedy and heartbreak we know it
would have been for the two girls. The headline of the story read
'runaway lesbians return only to split',[38] the connotations of 'split'
insinuating that the break-up was mutual and their decision. The
legal powers that 'blood relatives' have via Habeas Corpus allow
families to exert power over these women even into adulthood.
And it is not a two-way street: in Kerala, two women tried to use
the writ to be reunited when one of them was captured and tortured by her family, but it was immediately dismissed; a woman
cannot file for another unless they are related 'by blood'.[39]

It is not too far-fetched to say that a Maitri Karaar contract
could have helped the women's case. Although said to 'not offer
any real benefits',[40] would a Maitri Karaar perhaps annul a parent's filing of Habeas Corpus against a same-sex partner? Or allow a same-sex partner to file Habeas Corpus for their significant
other? Again, as this is a hypothetical scenario, so we cannot say
yes for sure, but neither can we dismiss it as an outright no. In
the 1970s, Maitri Karaar allowed for an unmarried Hindu and
Muslim couple to be reunited by the courts via a Habeas Corpus
petition, much against their families' wishes. Narrain and Gupta draw parallels with these kinds of relationships and same-sex
relationships: they challenge the collectivist societal structure, as
the individual's own self-fulfilment is given greater importance
than what the individual is expected to deliver to the family.[41] If
a same-sex couple in possession of Maitri Karaar were also to file

---

[38] Ibid.
[39] Thangarajah, Priyadarshini, and Ponni Arasu. 'Queer Women and The Law
in India.' In *Law Like Love: Queer Perspectives on Law*, edited by Alok Gupta and
Arvind Narrain. Yoda Press, 2011, p. 330.
[40] '"Maitri Karar": Now Illegal Gujarati Custom of Keeping Mistresses.' September 14, 2019. https://drishtikone.com/blog/2013/01/03/maitri-Karar-gujarati-so-
cial-custom-of-keeping-mistresses-by-circumventing-hindu-marriage-act/.
[41] Narrain, Arvind. 'Queering Democracy: The Politics of Erotic Love.' In *Law
Like Love: Queer Perspectives on Law*, edited by Alok Gupta and Arvind Narrain.
Yoda Press, 2011, p. 3.

for Habeas Corpus, should the court also allow for it as it did for the Hindu and Muslim couple?

Writing on Maitri Karaar, Baxi said that it 'remains an open question whether the rules [on Maitri Karaar] do not prohibit the registration of partnerships between women, presumably since the contemplators of public policy and morality deny the existence of lesbian sexuality altogether'.[42] But what if the legitimacy of Maitri Karaar was calculated on the same factors of a wedding, which is: 'if it looks like a wedding, and seen and understood to be a wedding, it is a wedding'. To decide, judges will examine photographs and testimonies of priests, witnesses and guests.[43] This is not saying Maitri Karaar is like a marriage; however, accounts of these unions between women have been reported to include the exchanging of garlands in a temple,[44] and if the contract was to be proved on the same principle that weddings are, then a ceremony like this could have it accepted as official in the eyes of the court. Baxi is right, in that it remains an 'open question' as to whether or not same-sex unions would have been recognised by courts in the 1970s or 1980s; however, it is said the Maitri Karaar between the two teachers did not excite much media comment, so there can't have been much public outrage or backlash against the idea.[45] Today, if the decision was to be based solely on 'public policy and morality', it should surely be accepted, given the recent law reform regarding homosexuals and transgenders.

---

[42] Baxi, Pratiksha. 'Feminist Contributions to Sociology of Law: A Review.' *Economic and Political Weekly* 43, no. 43 (2008): 79–85. http://www.jstor.org/stable/40278106.

[43] Vanita, Ruth. 'Democratizing Marriage.' In *Law Like Love: Queer Perspectives on Law*, edited by Alok Gupta and Arvind Narrain. Yoda Press, 2011, p. 343.

[44] John, Thomas. 'Liberating Marriage.' In *Law Like Love: Queer Perspectives on Law*, edited by Alok Gupta and Arvind Narrain. Yoda Press, 2011, p. 364.

[45] Baxi, Pratiksha. 'Feminist Contributions to Sociology of Law: A Review.' *Economic and Political Weekly* 43, no. 43 (2008): 79–85. http://www.jstor.org/stable/40278106.

According to online and scholarly articles, Maitri Karaar was banned in 1983;[46] we know, however, that Maitri Karaar is still very much used in practice. Within our community, there are more than five couples that I know personally who have obtained Maitri Karaar via the courts and with a lawyer present. A friend of mine also told me that whilst he was in the court getting his, another unknown trans individual walked in for the same purpose, 'and we struck a friendship there and then'. So, it is not a unique occurrence to only our circle and continues to be used by couples in Gujarat to this day.

When we first began our explorations around same-sex relationships in 2003, we heard vague whispers of two women in Mehsana district. They had entered into Maitri Karaar. Naturally, we were intrigued and looked out for more concrete information.

'They had been together around the 80s,' some said. Others claimed, 'It was the 90s.'

'Their names?' we asked.

'One of them is Patel, the other Christy.' Their full names and their exact location had faded away from most people's memories.

Another one wondered, 'Are they alive?'

No one seemed to have any exact information.

---

[46] Ibid.

13

The Life and Times
of Mansa Patel and Dalphina Fernandez

'*Ek fiat gadi levi che, Dalphini bahu icha che anay mari
Dalphina ne emma besadi ney mane Goa ley javu che.*'

'*I want to buy a fiat, Dalphina is very keen, and I want to
make my Dalphi sit in it and take her to Goa.*'

We went on making discreet inquiries, all the more because if this
was an older couple, we wondered how they had managed to live
together. Those times were harder, so was it their Maitri Karaar
that gave them some space? We asked ourselves, wouldn't their
Maitri Karaar be noted somewhere? We hoped that such a contract would have their address as well. Desperate for any leads to
meet and know them, we looked for anything and everything that
would tell us more about these pioneering women, especially since
this contract of friendship unique to Gujarat was generally entered
upon by men and women. This one was between two women, perhaps the only one of its kind. How many women could have done
it then? What was written there? we wondered to ourselves. Turning to the lawyers, we asked, 'Can it not be tracked down?'

'But that document would be with the persons concerned,'
lawyers told us when we approached them in Ahmedabad, 'It is
between two people. We cannot know what's written there.'

Clueless about the exact place and the full names of the two women, we were at a loss. Like a familiar line of a song that keeps playing on loop in our minds, Mansa and Dalphina's story, with an imprint upon us, kept haunting us in its incompleteness and anonymity. We asked about it, looked for it, and went about talking of it amongst ourselves and to others, because the lives of these two women had a resonance with our own and with the people we worked with and who contacted us. We continued to look for hints and leads that could tell us something. Was there someone out there who knew them? Now more than before, doubts, questions and speculations pressed us on: Were these women in love with one another, and where were they now?

In 2006, just before the year ended, the tide turned. However, it was under the most unfortunate circumstances and through long-winded processes that we chanced upon some information. In September 2006, Gujarati newspapers carried the news of an alleged suicide committed by two Patel women in the Gothva village of Visnagar Taluka in Mehsana district. A trail of a violent end to same-sex love stood out; with no remedial entitlements and no punishment to the guilty, it reinforced the message of the adherence of one rule for all, and it was encrusted with silence. Between overcoming the shock of the two women killing themselves against the denial of their love for one another, awaiting a lull in the scandal, and strategically planning a quiet visit to the site, between following up and attempting to locate our own sources for more information, by the time we reached Visnagar, it was November.

The journalist who had covered the recent suicide of the two women told us that some years ago, another such incident involving two women had happened in this very district: their names, he said, were Mansa and Dalphina Fernandez. Their full names tallied with the half names we had in our records. He told us that they were no more. However, the journalist himself had no further information. What happened and when? And why?

The question that kept coming back to us was this: could it be because they loved one another? Though faded and fragmentary, the small glimpses we got into their lives left a profound sense of unease and sadness in us, pulling us into a past where the footprints of people like us, though barely discernible, pushed us to go on seeking answers about them. For putting on record the erased and invisible lives and to stake a claim in the history of 'We the people of India'.

'I know there was a report in a local paper that detailed the whole story,' the journalist shared. Our spontaneous reaction was to ask if he had the name and contact number of the reporter. Though he did not have it right there and then, he promised us to give them to us.

Later we followed up with the journalist for weeks, and several telephone calls later, we got the local reporter's number. His name, we learnt, was Kaushik Pachani. Having the telephone number was as good as gold for us. Hoping that the number worked, we tried it timidly. And lo, it did, it worked. The bell rang clear and sharp. Not knowing how open the man on the other side would be, we had prepared a story. Knowing that Mehsana district and the Patel community had the dubious distinction of having the lowest sex ratio in the state, we presented ourselves as researchers from an NGO who were looking into the reasons of suicides and deaths of the females in that district. Given this context, we wanted to know more about Mansa and Dalphina's deaths. He expressed willingness to talk to us about both of them.

After fixing a time and date for our meeting with him, we reached Visnagar on 23 January 2007, in a little over three hours after covering a distance of 200 km from Baroda and locating the address given to us. The reporter's wife stood in the lane outside their house to direct us. Welcoming us warmly, she invited us into the neat one-room kitchen flat, and as we entered, Kaushik Pachani introduced himself.

Since all our enquires about Mansa and Dalphina had earlier been met with a blank or with half-truths, we wanted to know how the journalist had heard about him and through him, of Mansa. 'He named you as a much better source of information. Did you know Mansa?'

'It was my first wife, Seeta, who really knew her. She was a member of the Mahila Suraksha Samiti (MSS) so I got to know her through my wife, who helped Mansa. But she is no more. In fact, both of them are no more, do you know?' He looked at us enquiringly. We nodded, and he continued, 'Two years ago, I had published the story in my weekly newspaper. It is my guess that this is how the decade-old story was revived. I have the copy of that paper somewhere in the house.

'I published it as an unsolved case of unnatural deaths in Visnagar. This was a case of a lesbian relationship. Mansa lived with her friend Dalphina. They entered upon Maitri Karaar; although I do not remember the exact date and year, this was the incident after which the trouble began for them and finally led to their death. Even earlier, she was the talk of the town as someone who lived with a woman, wore short hair, and drove around on a Bajaj scooter.'

Several questions passed through our minds as we listened to him, and when we opened our mouths, we both did so at the same time.

'You called their deaths unnatural. How so...?' I found no appropriate words to ask anything more.

'I have written the entire story with all these details in the article in my paper. I will get it for you.' He got up and rummaged through his files and papers, stooping low and then straightening up to look through the bottom and top shelves and other places around. But he could not find it. He turned to us and shrugged, 'It has been some time since I wrote their story. You can leave your address with me, and I will search for it and post it to you.'

Just when our hunch had been proved right and we were beginning to get some information about their relationship, we were cut short. It was hard to simply write our address and leave abruptly. Still worse was the thought of waiting and the indefiniteness of getting the paper from him.

While one of us wrote our address for him to post the paper to us, the other asked him, 'And Dalphina—did you know her?'

'No, I did not know her. She worked in the Visnagar Civil Hospital as a nurse. All I know is that she came from Anand, or rather, when she was last seen she was boarding a bus towards Anand. Since then, she has not been seen.'

'Not seen!' We repeated, 'What do you mean, not seen?'

'She disappeared.'

'Disappeared? Meaning…? Where, what happened?'

'When did this happen?' We could not stop ourselves.

An irrepressible desire for closure and a hope for justice goaded us, 'Who was responsible? Was anyone caught?'

He did not answer our questions that had sprung up as shocked reactions. 'You will have the story from me,' he promised. 'I will look for it. It is a long story, very long and complicated.'

It was a signal for us to stop probing for more. But we persisted, 'When did she disappear? Where could she go?'

'I do not recollect exactly, but around the time they entered upon Maitri Karaar, she disappeared or was kidnapped. No one really knows. My paper covers it all.'

We sat for a while, unable to move and waiting for more. But it was hard to get more of the story from him. It was time for us to leave. We got up and thanked him. He was our first significant informant who had changed hearsay and our hunch to a fact of reality. We owed him a lot and expressed it in our profuse thanks to him. We had feared asking him directly about the nature of the relationship between Mansa and Dalphina, but the first thing that he did was to refer to them as lesbians, a word that rarely found utterance without labels. He was using it conversationally, conveniently, in an almost 'normal tone'. As we bid goodbye, we reconciled ourselves to a wait rather than ruffle him with more questions. He was the only source of more information, and we thought he had best be left to his choices.

While we waited and made follow-up calls to Kaushik Pachani, we were looking at end of February. In March, we decided to go to Anand because Pachani had talked of Dalphina boarding a bus towards Anand. We knew our decision was somewhat foolhardy, since a name alone was too tenuous a thread to go by. But we went with that, hoping to add the 'Maitri Karaar' event as an identifier and as a possibility of an opening to gain more information.

Fortunately, a new member of our staff was from the Christian community based in Anand. Seeking the new staff member's support, we landed in Anand. There, we met with Brother Francis in St Xavier's school. He had been in Anand for more than 15 years now. When we asked him if he knew anything about the disappearance of Dalphina and the whereabouts of her family, he was not able to recall anyone remotely connected to such an incident of Maitri Karaar. Our visit to Anand brought us back to where we were after meeting the journalist. Now, he seemed to be our only source of information.

By the end of March, we finally heard from Kaushik Pachani. He had sent the weekly paper *Our News* by post. It was a front-page story written in Gujarati in the year 2005, headlined as lesbian relationship and further worded in more provocative details such as Mansa's unnatural death and the mysterious disappearance of Dalphina, a nurse in the civil hospital. It also had a picture that clearly showed scant reverence for the dead—even though the article presented itself as well-intentioned towards women and the readers, the picture of a half-naked woman seemed to be there to score selling points. Whatever may have been the genesis of the news story, it brought us a step closer to an unknown past, that of two women who loved one another in a day and time when it was profoundly prohibitive to do so.

Since the article focused on Mansa's unnatural death, it was centred on a flawed investigative process, barely letting us into the rest of their lives as partners. Of the two, Dalphina remained in the shadows. We carefully picked our way through the report and wove together dispersed details, the discrepancies, the silences, and some questions whose answers were possible to find through the internet; then, we built our first legible narrative that allowed us a glimpse into Mansa's life and the complex intersection of her sexual choice, wealth, inter-religion relationship, caste, and family honour. She was way ahead of the times that she lived in, way ahead of the town of Visnagar in the 1950s, the years in which Mansa grew up, matured, and fell in love. The story that emerged through the report, and our own summarisation of it, is as follows:

Mansa was the youngest of four sisters, with a brother younger than her. The second eldest sister, Sheila, was active in politics. She was married to man named Mehar Chand Bhai. He was elected as an MLA from Janta Dal between the years 1985 and 1990.

Though married herself, Mansa chose to leave her marriage after two years. Born in a family of Patels, Mansa belonged socially and politically to a powerful dominant caste and class of Gujarat. Indeed, Mansa's father was well known in Visnagar of Mehsana district. Later, we learnt that he was a philanthropist and freedom fighter, heading the taluka panchayat. In 1975, he was elected as an MLA for a term of five years as an independent candidate. He also founded a cooperative bank. He had 250 acres of land in Banaskantha district. On his death in 1986, Mansa inherited 45 acres of land.

This inheritance became an eyesore for Sheilaben and her husband. Pachani narrates an incident when Mansa's brother-in-law, Mehar Chand Bhai, whose political stars were on the rise then, used his influence and tried to transfer out Dalphina from the Visnagar Civil Hospital. Mansa stood up against the order, demanding justice. At this time, the chief minister of Gujarat was from the Congress party (1985–89). Overcoming this complex nexus, Mansa went to the Ahmedabad High Court to make an intervention in Dalphina's transfer. She was successful in finally stalling it. It was after this incident that Dalphina and Mansa began to live together in Mansa's bungalow in Sarovar Society in Visnagar.

Sheilaben, like her father, was also a politician. She was a member of the legislative assembly and had been elected twice to the assembly in the early 1960s. When Jitendrabhai Desai was the chief minister, Sheilaben was known to be very powerful.

Around 1965, in one of the *talukas* of Mehsana district, a person had broken the law known as the *Mehman-Pratibandhak Dhara*. He had invited over 35,000 people for a feast. The police brutally assaulted the people who had gathered there. When an investigative committee was formed to look into the police atrocities, Sheilaben was successful in stopping the inquisition by just making a few phone calls while sitting in the Mehsana police headquarters. Judging from the information available, she was probably in power at the time. When Sheilaben shifted away from politics, her husband Mehar Chand Bhai stepped into the limelight. It was once said of Mehar Chand Bhai that he was the husband of the queen, but not the king. However, Mehar Chand Bhai proved the adage wrong; he won the elections as an independent candidate and grew to be a powerful politician. As public figures who belonged to a well-known family from a dominant and caste, Mansa's inter-religion friendship with Dalphina could not have gone down well with the family. Later, their Maitri Karaar clearly added fuel to the simmering fire of antagonism.

However, missing singularly in Pachani's narrative is the year when Mansa and Dalphina made their contract of friendship. He puts down 1988 as the year when Dalphina disappeared.

Pachani cites two complaints filed by Mansa after Dalphina's disappearance: The first one was filed on 13 July 1992. It was made to the Vice President of Gujarat State Mahila Suraksha Samiti (GSMSS). Mansa gave a copy of this application to the Home Minister and to the police station in Mehsana district, but it was disregarded both by the home ministry and the police department.

Four aspects stood out clearly in this complaint: 1) Mansa mentioned the highly influential nature of her family which prevented her complaints from being registered to the police station. Here, we see her rationale for approaching the GSMSS. 2) She mentions the resentment of both their families to the Maitri Karaar and even names them as conspirators in Dalphina's disappearance following their Maitri Karaar. 3) She accuses her family of attempting to usurp her property and fears for her safety, suspecting them of even killing her; critically important is that her application seeks protection. She was well aware of the danger she faced, and indeed, she did meet a gory end.

Lastly, this complaint also helped us calculate the exact year of Dalphina's disappearance. Mansa specifically mentions two years and three months as the time that had passed between Dalphina's disappearance and the complaint. Going by this date, Dalphina disappeared in 1990. The reporter, however, mentions it as 1988.

The second complaint was filed on 17 March 1999 to the Visnagar police station, seven years after the first complaint and nine years after Dalphina's disappearance. One wonders at this long gap. Perhaps she filed more complaints and these were not heeded? Mansa's brother-in-law was an elected MLA for two consecutive five-year terms: from 1985 to 1990 and from 1991 to 1995. During these years, he may have used his influence to prevent investigations into Dalphina's disappearance, or perhaps he had a hand in it. Perhaps by 1997, Mehar Chand Bhai did not have the kind of power he enjoyed earlier, and so Mansa's second complaint survived.

Geeta Pachani, a member of GSMSS and the first wife of the reporter, accompanied Mansa when she went to file the second complaint in 1999. Here, once again, she talks of being threatened and harassed in her house. She even writes that she recognises and knows their names. Instead of disclosing these names, the reporter then uses dots and goes on to say that, in the complaint, she asked for appropriate action to be taken for her protection. On the day of the complaint, she gave this reporter a written letter. In the letter, she names John Christian as the person who comes to her house, steals things, and even threatens her. The name suggests a link to Dalphina. We learnt later that he was indeed related to her—he was her brother. On reading the report, we called Pachani regarding the letter that Mansa had given him and the discrepancy in the dates of Dalphina's disappearance, but we felt discouraged by his response. We tried to locate other sources to verify facts, such as popular Gujarati magazines like *Abhiyaan*, *Chitralekha*, and newspapers' offices for the availability of back issues. The former often asked us repeatedly to get back to them. When we did, we got no answers. Some newspapers did not have records that went that far. Until that time, we had still not resolved the issue of discrepancy of the dates. This meant that until April 2007, we still did not have the date or the year of Mansa and Dalphina's Maitri Karaar, nor a second source which would corroborate the year of Dalphina's disappearance.

Nonetheless, the dates of both the complaints were critical in providing some frame of time in which these events unfolded, and of the kind of people who were involved. Set against those times and the people, Pachani's report uncovered for us a narrative of incredible courage in the face of the odds that Mansa battled. Outside of these complaints, the report brought to the forefront the relentless pursuit of Mansa's family to thwart her deepening and gradually emerging 'out' relationship with Dalphina. It was evident at first by what happened when Dalphina moved from the nurses' hostel to Mansa's bungalow and later entered into a contract of friendship before a press conference called by her—it created a sensation in the wider circles, including the domestic in-fighting over property ownership with her family and her family members abusing their state power to try to transfer out Dalphina from her job, after their Maitri Karaar. All these events occurred during the period when Mansa's family was in power. Did the politically powerful family have a motive in enabling Dalphina's disappearance, and in Mansa's murder? Pitched against the powerful clout, we get a hint of Mansa's long and lonely search for Dalphina when she approaches GSMSS and names both their families as conspirators in Dalphina's disappearance. At this juncture, we could only speculate if Mansa had to wait until 1999 to get her complaint registered.

Once again without mentioning the exact date and year of Mansa's death, Pachani goes on to write that soon after she filed the second complaint, Mansa was found dead in her bungalow, naked, with her neck, head, hand, and thighs burnt. On the right side of the body, there were three pairs of slippers, and beneath the body, there was blood. If the post-mortem had been done following the right procedures, the cause of death would have been known. Pachani points out how the rule of law was flouted in this case: cases of violence against women have to be registered with the police. The police has to give a report to the civil surgeon upon which the post-mortem can be done. This procedure was flouted. Additionally, Visnagar had three women members of the state-run Mahila Suraksha Samiti—even then, none of the members were asked to be present at the time of the post-mortem. According to the news report, the post-mortem was done at the site itself, even though the hospital is hardly three minutes away. The news report says that the doctor of the civil hospital did the post-mortem at the site of the murder; the question the reporter asks is, why was the post-mortem not done in the hospital? It is known that Mehar Chand Bhai was the trustee of the school in which the doctor's father was a teacher. Interestingly, Pachani goes on to mention that a newspaper correspondent went to the Visnagar Civil Hospital and contacted the doctor there; when questioned by him about the post-mortem procedures and its report, the doctor's response was one of anger. The reporter then wonders why the doctor showed such anger when asked about Mansaben's post-mortem reports. Indeed, Pachani's report raised deeply troubling questions that had no concrete answers, and the possibility of finding these answers receded further as time went by, the concerned people passed away, and memories dimmed and faded.

While the news report gave us an idea of how deeply enmeshed sexuality and gender, power and honour, wealth, politics, and criminality are in everyday life, it also showed us the possible connivance of state actors with well-connected families, and of these families using their clout to pressurise those dependent on them to toe the line, like the doctor whose father was a teacher in an education trust run by Mehar Chand Bhai. The inclusion of Dalphina's family as possible suspects in Mansa's murder, especially after Dalphina remained untraced, seemed harder to understand. What would they stand to gain, particularly against a powerful and socially well-placed family? Besides, Mansa's property was under dispute. The legal road to justice is long and costly, which only the rich can afford. We wondered if Dalphina's family was as powerful or rich. We knew too little about Dalphina, and even less about her family, to be able to come to any neat conclusions. On the other hand, what we knew about Dalphina without doubt was that she was a nurse in the government-run civil hospital in Mehsana.

In our effort to find out more about Dalphina and her disappearance, we decided to file an RTI on 8 May 2007. We hoped to know more about her family, the year/date of the couple's Maitri Karaar, and most importantly, how long after it Dalphina disappeared. We also wanted to get some corroborative evidence of Dalphina's exact year of disappearance to put to rest the difference that came up through Pachani's news-report and the application that Mansa gave to GSMSS. We hoped that however indirect or off the mark, the information that the RTI would yield may help us understand the rationale for Dalphina's disappearance, which we suspected was due to a relationship that was beginning to get 'more visible' with its demand of 'entitlements'. Through the whole process, we hoped to get some idea of, or leads into, Dalphina's life, however patchy or shadowy they may be.

Amongst our several queries was one that asked for dates of her joining the hospital, how long she worked, when she stopped coming to work, and evidence of her being relieved from her duties. According to the response, Dalphina joined on 8 March 1988 and stopped coming to work in April 1990. By this response, Dalphina's year of disappearance could be put at 1990. This tallied exactly with the gap of two years and three months that Mansa mentioned in her 1992 application to GSMSS. This is also part of the same period when Mehar Chand Bhai was politically powerful.

The pegging down of Dalphina's disappearance to 1990 led us to conclude that their friendship contract was made prior to 1990, almost three decades ago. Compared to those years, the times we live in have undoubtedly changed. Though the queer community was still struggling under the label of criminality then, even the mention of same-sex love was prohibitive socially—it stigmatised people who were seen having such relationships and created a scandal for the families associated with them. A formal contract, which was mostly prevalent between a man and a woman, being made between two women of those times must have created an unprecedented upheaval in the larger society and their families. Looking back, one realises that even the privileged status of this couple was no protection; it helped only in briefly restraining an open confrontation, leaving a simmering hostility that hit out in the most brutal way imaginable when an opportunity came.

The response to the RTI reached us on 30 May 2007. It mentioned that an FIR No. G.U. R no. 17/90 had been lodged at Visnagar police station on 5 April 1990 regarding Dalphina's disappearance. After four years, the hospital authorities issued a public notice to Dalphina on 19 February 1994 asking her to present herself at work. But in the absence of a response, she was relieved of her duties from 1 April 1990. These details confirmed Dalphina's year of disappearance. But the RTI did more. It opened a window in the wall and gave us a glimpse into Dalphina's elusive life.

A copy of the letter which relieved her of her duty was sent to us following our demand for it. That copy had the residential address of Dalphina's family. At last, we had located a source who could possibly give us more information on the mysterious disappearance and perhaps share details that would help us draw a fuller picture of Dalphina, who was dimly and yet so alluringly present in the story of this partnership.

We went to her village and walked into a house that was occupied by her eldest brother. Ajay Fernandez was the name by which he introduced himself. We learnt from him that Dalphina was the eldest daughter of the large family, consisting of her parents, four brothers, and six sisters. Growing up in a financially precarious position, Dalphina took upon herself the responsibility of meeting the needs of her family in more than one way. She was supporting the education of her siblings, ensuring that the bills were paid in time, and there was food on the table. She used to send money home every month. Her brother vaguely acknowledged his sister's contribution. She was working in Visnagar hospital, and it was there that she met Mansa. In his tone, one could read traces of regret and unhappiness at 'what' the oldest and the 'most mature' of the siblings had done, going down the road which everyone could see would be ruinous. He suspected the involvement of Mansa and her family in Dalphina's disappearance. 'We did everything we could to find her... She did not come here that day. Mansa and her family claimed that she had come here, but she did not come here. We learnt much later that she could not be located... She was with her, Mansa was always with her, both of them were together always. She and Mansa would come here together on her two-wheeler, yes, all the way from Mehsana. And then they would return the same day, with no stopover for the night, riding more than 200 km back and forth. We would tell them not to take such risks, but they did what they had to; Mansa hardly ever listened.' He said that Dalphina maintained a diary of all the expenses incurred. Though he had those, he did not share them with us, but he did let us know that she was an equal participant in sharing the household expenses. It was from him we learnt that Mansa died in 2002. Later, this information helped us find the story done in *Sandesh* that Pachani had mentioned in his report.

This was 2002, the same year when the minority community was massacred in Gujarat. As so many were being killed for being different, Mansa too met with death. Perhaps she was also killed for her difference, a minority in her daring difference, someone whose voice had to be silenced to make all things level and uniform? But like so many others, Mansa's death drew no mourners or court appeals as she struggled to uncover the disappearance of her partner.

Dalphina's brother told us that one of the journalists who had met and done a story on them immediately after their Maitri Karaar had asked him to send all the papers to her and that she would write about the whole incident and draw media attention. But soon after that, she returned all the papers by post without writing a word on the tragedy. When we inquired if the journalist had given any reasons for not going ahead with the story, he said he had no idea.

Though difficult to prove conclusively, we wondered if the story had been deliberately suppressed because it hurt people who were well-connected, wealthy, and powerful? Learning about the papers that were returned to him, we asked him if he was willing to share them with us. He gave us some news stories that were published prior to Mansa's death and allowed us to only photocopy them, which we did and returned, relieved that we at least had some papers that would tell us more about the two courageous women.

The other news story that we looked for was the one published in another newspaper that had been mentioned in Pachani's report. The meeting with Dalphina's brother gave us an idea of the date and year; now, we needed to look for it in the back issues of the newspaper. However, its earlier issues were neither available in their Vadodara office nor online. The other newspapers did not have the back-dated issues either. We were lucky that one of the papers that carried the news of Mansa's death did have issues dating right back to Independence Day, but those were in their main office in Ahmedabad. We went there, and the librarian, proud of his work, was more than happy to help; he also allowed us to photograph the report.

Looking at the newspaper/magazine clippings which Dalphina's brother gave us, we searched for the journalists who had written about the couple. We tried to contact them. Except for one of them who wrote in a popular magazine, the other reporter, Prith Kumar, remains impossible to locate. Besides, the story from the newspaper did not have a by-line, which would have helped us meet the reporter and follow the story. It merely said 'by a representative'. The journalist whom we were able to trace had done the most endearing story about the partnership of these two courageous women, and she was based in Mumbai. We travelled there to meet her. We were eager to let her know that her article was amongst the very few documents that had recorded queer history; even though we knew the end, the story told right from inside the home of the couple resonated with truths about our own lives. It wove in details like having separate bedrooms, and then the journalist painstakingly being shown the two rooms as evidence of their relationship being 'only a friendship'. Even the romantic verses that she recited for Dalphina and the letters of longing that she wrote while wooing Dalphina, were all in the name of being 'friends only'. When we met the journalist, the one thing that she was able to recall of that interview was Mansa's penchant for reciting romantic poetry. She did not remember more and asked us to send her the article so that it could jog her memory for details that the written version of the interview did not have. On our return, we e-mailed her the article twice, and a third time too, and then waited. We did not hear from her.

The story that we piece together, with our summarisation, is taken from interviews, an article that was written by the Mumbai-based journalist before Dalphina's disappearance and published in a popular Gujarati magazine, and from Prith Kumar's feature that was written after her disappearance in another magazine which is no longer in circulation. We also looked at the news report published in the Mehsana edition of the Gujarati newspaper of June 2002.

Prith Kumar, in his article of August 1990, wrote that two years earlier, in February in the city of Visnagar, Mehsana district, two middle-aged women, Mansa and Dalphina, vowed to live together as friends through a Maitri Karaar entered upon a ten-rupee stamp paper. Going by this article and what the Mumbai-based journalist writes, the friendship bond was signed on 24 February 1988. (Dalphina disappeared in March 1990.)

Through these interview-based articles, we get a vivid picture of Mansa; though it is to a lesser extent, Dalphina or 'Dalphi', as Mansa called her affectionately, also emerges out of the shadows. Mansa is referred to as being forty-five years of age in both 1988 and 1990, and Dalphina as 42 years old, telling us that

Mansa and Dalphina were born in the mid-1940s, on the cusp of pre-independent India, when hopes ran high on building a new India. In their story, we hear the names of Dynora TV, Godrej cupboard, Bajaj scooter, radio, and Fiat car, reminiscent of an earlier 'Make in India' era. Mansa was a graduate in pharmacy. She participated actively in her father's social service activities and used the returns from her investments for daily expenses. Dalphina, often called Nurse Dalphina, had obviously completed her degree or done a diploma in nursing. She worked in government hospitals prior to her transfer to the Visnagar hospital. Dalphina was the eldest daughter of Christy Peter, who belonged to the Anand district. She had five sisters and four brothers.

Though placed in different economic and social positions, both the women were not only financially independent but they also lived on their own, unlike most women in India even today. Mansa moved away from her family residence in 1969 around the age of 24. Her father had given each of his daughters a house. Mansa inherited the much-talked-of five-roomed bungalow in a prestigious society. Mostly, she lived there alone, before Dalphina began living with her in 1980.

As a nurse, Dalphina too had moved out of her parental home. She went to the places where her job took her. She lived off her salary and even supported her family. In their day-to-day lives, each of these two women took decisions of their own reckoning and faced the consequences of these choices: Dalphina's decision to stay single to better support her family, as well as Mansa being a woman who chose to separate from her husband in the 1950s. The two women staying single when it was scandalous to live outside marriage in those times tells us another story of their struggle and courage. Later, upon meeting one another, and despite facing stiff opposition, the two nonetheless forged a partnership that challenged the norms of religion, class, and caste; an entire heterosexual model was upturned with their decision to live together.

Mansa was well known both because of her family and due to her own strong sense of self. Right from childhood, she was brought up as a boy—we do not know for certain what exactly being raised like a boy means. Does it mean that she engaged in work that was considered male or it did it simply include being allowed to dress in male clothes, or was it she who chose those? Hard as it may be to refrain from identity labels, the fact is that we know too little of her interiority/subjectivity to box her into a category. Those who described Mansa and those who knew her said she was always wearing male outfits, either a safari suit or pants and a shirt, with a hat and goggles. She wore her hair short. Driving through the city on her Bajaj scooter, she came across as fearless and carefree, riding past curious bystanders. Her father sold her scooter because she would be out driving the whole day. Prith, the Mumbai-based journalist, who spent more than 18–20 hours with the couple in their house, tells us that Dalphina was wearing a green *kurta* while she sat watching TV and describes her as having thick, shoulder-length hair, occasionally streaked with grey. She had a light complexion and appeared to be a delicate woman who fitted the Gujarati model of a *namni nar* (delicate woman).

In the two pictures of the couple that have been used by different magazines, Dalphina appears to be lean and is seen in a saree, unlike Mansa, who has been described as rough and tough and appears to be heavily built. Dalphina had health issues related to her kidney. The doctors had advised her to keep a fat-free diet with no spices and salt. Dalphina seems to be meticulous and with an eye for detail, for she maintained daily diaries noting the expenses and events—a habit that requires discipline and an ability to reflect and be with one's own self. These were qualities that she brought to work and even to the bungalow, which Mansa says became a home only after 'Dalphi' began to live there. She filled the large space inside the compound wall of their bungalow with flowers in the front, and in the backyard, she grew vegetables. Dalphina did the weeding, sowing, and taking care of the gardens in general, but it was Mansa's responsibility to water them.

Professionally, Dalphina was skilled and known for the quality of her work. Before joining the Visnagar hospital, she had worked in the Ahmedabad Civil Hospital. They met one another when Mansa got admitted in the hospital for an operation for treatment of piles. Post-operation, Mansa was wheeled into the ward that Dalphina was in charge of. As a dutiful nurse, Dalphina would regularly check in on her patients. When Mansa saw Dalphina's caring and gentle demeanour, she felt drawn to her. Conversing with the journalist, Mansa recollected, 'Dalphina used to come for duty in my ward. That was the time I first met her. When I was awake because of the pain, Dalphina would come and touch me on my forehead and console me.' After the operation, Mansa had to stay in the hospital for 15 days. During that time, the relationship which began as a friendship became so intense for Mansa that she felt she could no longer live without Dalphina. 'But that time,' Mansa confided to the journalist, 'my attraction for her was one-way traffic. Dalphina did not have the same feelings for me.'

Just a little before Mansa stepped into the hospital and during the intervening months of the couple's friendship blossoming into love, Dalphina, who had stayed single, was finally considering marriage. She was in correspondence with a man in America from her community of Protestants. They regularly used to exchange letters, and Dalphina was coming around to seriously settling down with him when she met Mansa. Dalphina confessed to the journalist that she could not write love letters well, so she would copy the letters that Mansa wrote to her. Mansa was aware of the existence of this man.'

Mansa nodded, 'I used to even go and post those letters of Dalphina. But in my heart, I was convinced that ultimately, Dalphi would be mine.'

Recalling the days gone by, Dalphina added, 'I considered Mansa just a friend. But after she was discharged, she would write me long love letters. These really surprised me. I had never in my wildest dreams imagined that a woman could be so madly in love with another woman.'

The journalist writes that, for almost six months, Dalphina kept oscillating between the American guy and Mansa. However, in December 1980, the ultimate deadline to take a decision had come. The American man was coming to Ahmedabad to meet Dalphina to further their marriage plans. In the meantime, Mansa, who had been discharged from the hospital, wrote poems and long letters, often two a day, asking Dalphina to come and meet her. Mansa would wait for hours in a park outside the nursing hostel where Dalphina lived and, if she did not turn up, she would give in to tears.

Mansa's waiting, interspersed with the long letters, poems, and later, the wooing, made Dalphina change her mind. She called off her marriage plans and later moved in with Mansa.

When the two began to live together, there was opposition from all quarters. Dalphina's family is specially mentioned as being opposed to this move. Perhaps her earnings went in a large measure to support her family; the fear that they would no longer be available added to the ignominy that the family faced. While the reports all mention extraneous opposition, one can sense several levels of internal conflict spiralling outward, joining the antagonism outside and taking a toll on the couple's everyday lives. Dalphina was speculating marriage and writing letters to the American man; even though Mansa was posting these, it was probably hard on the relationship as the two got increasingly involved. It appears that Mansa too was involved with another woman. Perhaps she was also dealing with a break-up in a friendship that she had struck up with a girl who grew up in the orphanage set up by her father. The two shared a close relationship. Even after the girl got married, and returned, Mansa used to support her financially. Dalphina's hovering presence during and after Mansa's operation angered the girl. When Mansa and Dalphina sat in the park, the girl too would be around, hiding somewhere close by. When Mansa got deeply involved with Dalphina, the girl is said to have protested publicly. Public display of tensions in these relationships probably had negative consequences for Mansa and further angered her family. When this subject came up while conversing with the journalist, the tension between the couple was slightly revealed—Mansa rebukes Dalphina angrily for digging up the past of a person and says that this does not help in making friendships last.

It is clear that without support from close friends and family and with a hostile world outside, these relationships have no anchors to rest on, burdening them with an excess of inward dependence.

This couple navigated some of these conflicts, arrived at some strategies to deal with them, and stayed together for eight years before the blow separated them. Sometimes, when Dalphina would get very angry, Mansa would go off alone outside for an hour or two.

She would return when their moods had stabilised and the food was ready. No matter what the conflict, even when they stopped talking to one another, they had an unwritten rule that they would not let it reflect on their meals. They believed that food helped to cool down anger. Meals were an important part of their expression of love and togetherness. In most Indian homes and relationships, meals are a part of an unspoken subtext of communication that is often used to convey emotions that are difficult and inexpressible.

Generally, Dalphina returned from the hospital for lunch at noon. If Dalphina came home at three sometimes due to work, it was rare for Mansa to have eaten. 'Dalphina is hungry. When this thought crosses my mind, I cannot swallow a morsel,' Mansa confided to the journalist. She had even switched off the fridge so that the doctor's advice for Dalphina to have room-temperature water was followed strictly in their house.

Living with Mansa, Dalphina felt cared and fussed over, and when she shared some of these moments, her face lit up with love.

'In the beginning, when I had just moved in with her, she carried me about the house and took me everywhere with her.' They had been living together for eight years when the journalist came to meet them. But she notes that their love, unlike most husbands and wives, had not grown stale. Both were living their dreams together and envisioning a future together that they attempted to secure financially; as they bought insurance, paid instalments for flats, and acquired one in Ahmedabad—each had put the other's name as the second name in all of these ventures, worried for the other person in case one of them died.

Until Mansa came into her life, most of Dalphina's life had revolved around taking care of her siblings and parents; now, she had a partner who showered care and attention upon her. Mansa would get immense satisfaction from buying the things that Dalphina liked, and as a result, Dalphina's cupboard was bursting with Ahmedabad Handloom silk saris and imported mid-length frocks. Dalphina's birthday fell on 1 May, but Mansa had already bought her an advance gift. According to the reporter, no husband could be as devoted as Mansa was to Dalphina.

Though the writer sees them through the lens of man and wife, and the gender roles that she sees at play facilitates this categorisation, the reciprocity of power and love between them does not quite meet that model. For example, the oral and written narratives say that Mansa always dressed in male clothes. But the pictures accompanying the reporter's article and those in the newspaper show her in a sari and salwar kameez. One wonders at this contradiction between the visual presentation and the oral and written narratives. Would it be appropriate to make a connection between what the reporter observes in the interview and the pictures of Mansa in order to understand this contradiction? Or is it a contradiction at all? The reporter says that, using her 'power like a police man', Dalphina insisted that Mansa, who always wore a shirt and pants, should begin wearing salwar kameez when she goes out. Is it possible that, in deference to Dalphina's wishes, Mansa had stopped wearing male clothes outside home, so the pictures we see of Mansa are in female clothes?

While narrating a related incident, Dalphina says that when they recently needed to take a picture in their house, she had tears in her eyes as she requested Mansa to wear a sari. Can we speculate that wearing female clothes outside or inside the home was against Mansa's sense of self?   While the others around her refer to her as a male person, we do not have a single word from her that would tell us of the gender she identified with. Can we then conclude that wearing female clothes was not simply a change of clothes for her? Or that it was the male clothes alone that defined who she was? And in wearing them, was she asserting a 'self' that the rest of the society denied? Or was she an individual who walked the spectrum of identities that changed with age, contexts, and the demands of a relationship? Most importantly, we see a space in their relationship that allowed for suggestions and choices to prevail between them.

The couple's relationship at an intimate level may not have been as simple as the narrative reads. To grasp the multiple levels at which the couple struggled and still survived as a pair, one has to read the subtext. In the article, the boxed caption says Mansa was from a 'happy Patel family', which we know is not entirely the truth, 'who fell in love with Dalphina', who is then described as a 'poor Christy nurse', which is an unnecessary and demeaning detail. Saying that they have both decided to live together for a lifetime through the legal means of Maitri Karaar, there were descriptions that created visibility for all those components which challenged the heteronormative structure and, in all likelihood, aggravated an already worsening situation.

Since the writer is engaged in highlighting the life of the couple that is different, its cover page has a title on the extreme right that reads, 'Women of Visnagar who live like husband and wife'. The framing embeds two subjects that are taboo: sexuality and same-sex love, the unmentionable secrets of shame; by labelling the two women 'husband and wife', the sexual innuendo is almost immediately evoked, and juxtaposed with the word 'women', it subtly reinforces the myth of 'unnatural' that is attached to same-sex love. Tapping into stereotypical prejudices, the title ties the reader's imagination to a familiar grid, but the text of the interview also leads us into deeper complexities by presenting a contradictory picture. When asked if they had a sexual relationship, Mansa denies it. 'We are not the kind who would think of sex between two women. Even if we sleep near one another, we cannot cross our limits.' Yet, after their death, the reports about the couple all mention and imply a sexual relationship between them. What is surprising is that this denial of a sexual relationship had surprised the reporter. Even though she herself had broached the subject timidly, expecting an acknowledgment of a relationship that was unacceptable to the larger society would indeed be 'crossing limits' of whatever forms of acceptance that the couple had. Perhaps denial of their sexual relationship was the price they paid for acceptance? Or maybe it was the truth? These are intimacies and identities that are difficult to label in the absence of the subjects' own description.

Using the word *bhaibandh* or comradeship, Mansa projects true friendship as the basis of their partnership. Perhaps Dalphina's insistence that Mansa wear female clothes stemmed from the hope that the cultural space accorded to female friendships would be available to them if they both looked like women?

We get a sense of the larger oppressive reality that the couple lived in when the reporter, at the end of the interview, says that her revulsion to such relationships had reduced after meeting them. By implication, the fact that she harboured and continues to have those negative feelings is a measure of the pervasive homophobia that existed, the danger lurking even from those people one imagined to be open. Even when the two went ahead and publicly proclaimed their Maitri Karaar through a press conference, it was a proclamation of friendship and was perhaps done more to counter the resentment of both their families, as well as being evidence of their commitment for one another and for inheritance purposes.

Both Pachani and Prith Kumar wrote that the contract was the talk of the town and that it created a 'hue and cry'. Even the reporter's visit from Mumbai to interview the two women seems to be propelled by the same piece of news. The larger context and practice of Maitri Karaar in Gujarat gave it a sexual colouring, because it was a socio-legal contract that was often made between a married man and an unmarried woman, both of whom agreed to live with one another under enumerated conditions. In this context, no matter what the given name of the contract indicated or what was said by this couple, or the larger public, it was, by implication, a sexual relationship. They may have decided to enter upon the contract because they had to feel that the legitimacy of their relationship was being questioned increasingly and because of the insecurity it created for the couple for the future. Just prior to Mansa and Dalphina's Maitri Karaar, two women in Gujarat made a Maitri Karaar, and this was followed by the news of two women police constables—Leela Namdeo and Urmila Shrivastav—tying the knot in December 1987, in Raipur in Madhya Pradesh; this news spread throughout the country. These incidents may have acted as a catalyst to concretise their own action plan to seek some form of legitimacy to their relationship? Perhaps on taking legal advice, they may have found that Maitri Karaar was the best option for them? Within two months of the two constables' marriage, Mansa and Dalphina made this contract. They may have thought that a public announcement of their partnership would pre-empt any form of risk by entitling them to some rights.

Clearly, the Maitri Karaar that the two friends had entered upon reflected a bond deeper than what their kith and kin were willing to concede. We know of the earlier attempts made by Mansa's brother-in-law to deter Mansa from deeper involvement with Dalphina. So long as there was a denial of a relationship, they were ignored by the families, though not without disapproval. However, the Maitri Karaar, in its public proclamation of life-long commitment, perhaps altered that subdued note of silence and compliance to heterosexual norms. Though the contract itself rested on legal ambiguities, perhaps the documentation of an oath of commitment on a stamped paper unsettled the family's assurance of inheriting Mansa's property? Or maybe the permanence of the relationship between the two women, being harder to deny now, 'dishonoured' the family?

Mansa shared with the journalist, 'My love is so steadfast that I do not need a paper contract, but I have done this for my Dalphina. Tomorrow, if I am no longer here, no one should harass Dalphina, and no one should be able to take her out of the house. We made this contract keeping in mind such an eventuality in future.' In the last paragraph of the Maitri Karaar, it is clearly written that in case of Mansa's death, all decisions related to the house are with Dalphina.

As readers, we know that both women, in making financial investments, were putting the other's name as the second name. Steps such as these may have let word spread about their intentions about who would be the future inheritors of the properties owned by them, unleashing speculations and a fear regarding inheritance.

Importantly, such a friendship, especially after Maitri Karaar, would have been seen as a deterrent to the political ambitions of Mansa's family. This is evident from Pachani's news report. He talks of Sheila and her husband going to Mansa's house soon

after the event of Maitri Karaar and having a heated argument
with her regarding her inheritance, which was worth crores. One
wonders, did Mansa name Dalphina her inheritor? Mehar Chand
Bhai also filed a suit of property dispute in the land revenue department at Ahmedabad, preventing Mansa from getting possession of her land.

When the two signed the contract and held a press conference, it created a sensation, perhaps because it involved Mansa,
who was well known around the town for the person she was and
because of the family she came from. Two years later, Dalphina's
disappearance did not allow the 'scandal' to simply fade away
from the public memory. The person that Mansa was, with her
indomitable drive and focused will to find Dalphina, kept the
matter alive.

She stood her ground even against her powerful brother-in-
law; knowing that he posed a threat to her life, she stubbornly
pursued her search for Dalphina, going on to file complaints after
complaints to the police for her safety, entitlements, and equality. She did not bend to their will. Though powerless, she had
a strength that stemmed from a strong sense of self, from her
outrage at the injustice.

In the interview article, Prith Kumar, specially mentions
that while Mansa's voice held a gentle humility, her words were
sharp like an arrow. In this description and in the rest of the story, Mansa emerges as an outspoken and bold person who did
not mince words and continued to take steps that did not go
down well with her family. Her persistent search for Dalphina
and the interview she gave to this magazine are clear examples
of her bold but lonely rebellion. Her family would certainly have
resisted any publicity that recalled a relationship that brought
'shame' upon them. Here she was, openly saying that, except for
her mother, who understood her grief, the rest were all happy
at Dalphina's disappearance, telling us indirectly that her family
did not stand by her. She did not spare Dalphina's family either.

She mentions that Dalphina's parents, sisters, and brothers were all very angry with her and wished for their separation; one of the sisters is seen as prime suspect in having a hand in abducting or locking up Dalphina. It is from this interview that we learn that on the morning of 31 March 1990, Mansa saw Dalphina off on a bus going to Ahmedabad. Dalphina had earlier expressed a desire to visit her family. So, she had taken some time off from work, and Mansa had agreed to this brief period of separation. Dalphina was to return on 2 April. She never did.

In this interview, we learn of the extent of antagonism the couple faced. Instead of condolences, Mansa experienced complete isolation when Dalphina went missing. She mentions her single-handed search for Dalphina, without help from any avenues.

We learn that within two months of Dalphina's disappearance on 31 May 1990, her relatives went to Visnagar Hospital, broke open the door of her room, and took things worth Rs. 30,000 from there, including a Godrej cupboard, a Dynora colour TV, clothes and other domestic things, and bank-related documents.

Making use of the information obtained from the bank passbooks, they wrote to the bank and asked for all transactions to be put on hold.

We see that this news story also carries names. Each of Dalphina's siblings is mentioned by name, including their professions and their place of work and residence. Names of the policemen investigating the case are also given. She accuses Kheda police of having taken money to do a rough, shoddy job regarding Dalphina's mysterious disappearance. It seems that the naming was deliberate, perhaps to shame the concerned people and build upon them some pressure to act.

The interview also seems to be an appeal or an effort to reach out to Dalphina. The report specially highlights Mansa saying that 'three months have passed since Dalphina's disappearance and my heart says that whatever be the odds, she will come to

me by Diwali.' Anguished by her absence, she woke up at three in
the morning and stayed out the whole day as every corner of the
house held memories of Dalphina. When she went into the garden, she saw Dalphina in every plant; the flowers that bloomed
had withered away without water. Mansa took a vow that until
Dalphina returned, she would not have tea and sugar. She had
even locked up the VCR refusing to touch it. Waiting for Dalphina, she said she would watch the film of her choice on her return. The reporter notes that pictures of Christ and Krishna still
adorned the walls of the house. The minute details that Mansa
gives in the missing report for Dalphina tells us of the profound
involvement and trust between them. Following Dalphina's physical description, we get to know that 'she was wearing small gold
earrings, a 1967 "Tito" watch with plastic strap on her right hand,
one bangle, chocolate-coloured Bata slippers and a "buckle" in
her hair. She had a mole on her left cheek. She had two sarees in
her bag, a Godrej cupboard key, a keychain with a photo of Lord
Krishna, a small almond-coloured wallet, a bundle of two-rupee
notes, and some other money all adding up to Rs. 325/-.'

This interview is significant because here, as early as 1990,
she fears a threat to her life. She talks of enemies around her
plotting to get hold of her property worth lakhs and the cash she
has; she lived under this threat for more than a decade until the
fateful day of 15 June 2002, when she was, most probably, murdered. The newspaper of Mehsana district dated 20 June 2002
carried the news of her death headlined as 'Visnagar's Doctor in
Civil Hospital Wants to Conceal the Mysterious Death of Mansa.'
The news report says that Mansa's post-mortem was done on 17
June, 48 hours after her death. By this calculation, Mansa died or
was murdered on 15 June 2002, and it came to light only after a
stench arose from her house, where she was discovered as dead.
Two days later, the same newspaper writes in its follow-up story
that the doctor's post-mortem report attributed Mansa's death to
a heart attack. Without mentioning more details on the circum-

stances of Mansa's death, the paper points out that the cause of death as mentioned by the doctor was a subject of heated discussion amongst the general public. Going back in time, the report covers the story of the couple—it talks about when they first met, their close friendship which developed into an attraction for one another, and it also mentions that the two had a sexual relationship. The paper mentions that after Dalphina's disappearance, Mansa was heartbroken and lost her mental balance.

For us, the story did not end here. It was quite by chance that someone we knew who had gone to prison for an alleged default of payment told us that Mansa's brother-in-law had also been there while he was in prison. 'He would hide in the toilet to delay the court hearings, so he could escape the wrath of people who demanded their money back.' It was only when we got this first-hand oral information that we looked up the internet for more information. We learnt that Mansa's brother-in-law, Mehar Chand Bhai, as Chairman of a well-known bank had indeed been arrested for embezzlement in the year 2002, a mere four months after Mansa's death.

As a community, it was hard for us to overcome the unfairness that the women had faced in their life, to reconcile ourselves to their murder and disappearance simply for being different, and then to have no justice for any of it. The only relief we had was the revelation that Mehar Chand Bhai had been arrested. Perhaps his tenure in jail had an attached unwritten sentence for the things he did wrong—a sentence that punished him for not being humane enough, perhaps even for misusing his power to try and end Dalphina and Mansa's relationship, both of whom did him no harm. We do not know. And perhaps, we will never know.

We live with the burden of knowing that we will never know the full truth of this story. We are only occasionally relieved at the thought that perhaps justice has a way of quietly slipping in, mysteriously, suddenly, to heal those of us who choose to live as Mansa and Dalphina.

Many More Like Mansa: Gujarat 2002

No stories of Gujarat would be complete if the genocidal events of March 2002 went unmentioned. Especially in the context of queer lives, and in particular, Mansa's life and her death, which followed two months after the massacre of Muslims in the state.

The precipitating incident of a compartment catching fire in the train that carried Hindu pilgrims returning from Ayodhya became the immediate cause for widespread violence against the minority communities of Muslims; the ideological seeds of a pure monolithic Hindu nation, however, had been sown much earlier. The fire in the train ignited an emotionally charged, hate-filled atmosphere, impacting the vulnerable minority in the most brutal way conceivable. The Muslims, seen as 'non-Hindus', became the demonised 'other', and were named as deliberate initiators of the fire that started in the compartment. In retaliation, widespread killings of Muslims took place, beginning from the end of February and going on until March. The violence perpetuated by such ideologies was justified, self-righteously, on the grounds of seeking revenge on 'alleged present and historical wrongs' done by 'Muslim attackers'. In the mayhem that followed, the law-keepers encouraged the police to look the other way while Muslim households were looted and their women raped.

Knitted into that year's underbelly of brutal violence is a piece of queer history that needs telling, to show how, amongst the larger numbers of minorities, crimes against queer women remain absent from statistical details. If mentioned, these appear only as 'stray incidents' of violence, and not as a structural problem. The irony is that even if the crimes faced by the community are similar in nature to what others may have experienced, these are seen as 'less' of a crime, on the grounds of the queer community being 'different' from the larger heteronormative society. In this messy complex web of intersections, Mansa paid the price of being different, like several other Muslim women did that year.

In the days that followed, wave upon wave of violence swept the state... The victims were primarily Muslims (along with an occasional Christian, Parsi) but also included Hindus who had ties with Muslims by business or marriage.[47]

The brutal killings set a precedent of impunity for the powerful and to all those who subscribed to its ideology. Though Mansa was a Hindu woman who belonged to a dominant caste and class, and came from a well-connected family, her life did not follow any of the prescribed or imposed assumptions of purity: she had broken free of the patriarchal structure of marriage, separated from her husband, entered into a Maitri Karaar with a 'Christy' woman in public, and dared to live with her. Mansa's way of life not only hurt the honour of the well-known Hindu family that she belonged to but she also upset the ideal of creating a uniform, cultural, and political identity.

The acts of sexual violence that were committed in February and March against Muslim women had a pattern which was strikingly similar to the way Mansa was killed. In most instances of sexual violence, the women victims were stripped and paraded naked, then gang-raped, and thereafter quartered and burnt beyond recognition.[48]

Approximately half of the victims were women, many of whom were raped and tortured before being killed and burnt. There are reports everywhere of gang rape, of young girls and women, often in the presence of members of their families, followed by their murder by burning alive, or by bludgeoning with a hammer....[49]

---

[47] Nussbaum, Martha. *The Clash Within: Democracy, Religious Violence, and India's Future*. Permanent Black, 2007, p. 20.

[48] Mander, Harsh. 'One thing was distinctly rotten about 2002 Gujarat riots: use of rape as a form of terror.' April 24, 2019. https://theprint.in/pageturner/excerpt/one-thing-was-distinctly-rotten-about-2002-gujarat-riots-use-of-rape-as-a-form-of-terror/225511/.

[49] Mander, Harsh. '*Cry, the Beloved Country: Reflections on the Gujarat massacre*' (South Asia Citizens' Web, 2002), quoted in Human Rights Watch, '*WE HAVE NO ORDERS TO SAVE YOU*' State Participation and Complicity in Communal Violence in Gujarat (Human Rights Watch, 2002).

The presumption that Mansa's death was a suicide or a heart attack was in glaring contradiction to the material evidence found in her house. She was naked and burnt beyond recognition. A pool of blood from a wound in the back of her head suggested assault. Most people did not believe in the suicide theory that was given as the reason for Mansa's death. Long before 2002, Mansa had been bringing up several inconvenient truths; year after year, she had been challenging the existing norms and power hierarchies in society and her family. In the long years of searching for her disappeared partner, she came far too close to breaking the nexus between politically motivated state authorities and her politically well-connected family.

The newspaper report of that month, June of 2002, pointed out that the particular doctor who had conducted the post-mortem on Mansa had bypassed all mandatory rules. Colleagues and people at the hospital who were interviewed by the reporter shared on condition of anonymity that the doctor who had carried out Mansa's post-mortem was known for dereliction of his duties earlier on, in the months of February and March. Mansa's body bore similar marks of defacement and her manner of death had significant similarities to the women from the minority community who had been raped and killed. How do we confirm that the post-mortem revealed more than what was put out to the public?

Telling Mansa's and Dalphina's stories is important to record the resilience of our community, to put our missing accounts on record on the larger historical canvas, and to see how catastrophes engineered by the dominant hurt the vulnerable communities on the periphery, therefore highlighting the necessity of allies.

14

I am Taking This Step Willingly

The only reason we stumbled upon Mansa and Dalphina's tragic story was because we went to investigate two alleged suicides in the same village, in the same block where Mansa met her demise. It is a dark coincidence that if these two women had not taken their lives, Mansa's death would have remained unknown to us.

We first learnt of the couple's suicides on the morning of 23 September 2006, when the Gujarati newspaper *Divya Bhaskar* carried the headline 'Two female friends having same-sex relationship lost their lives: Childhood friendship between Visnagar's married woman and her unmarried friend changed into love. Pain of separation led them to take the final step.' Underneath the story, a coloured picture showed a policeman and others with covered noses and mouths, standing outside a house where the corpses of the two women had been found. At first glance, 'final step' seemed like an obvious euphemism for suicide. The two women belonged to the Gothva village and were members of sub-castes of a larger community known as Patel. By and large, the Patel community is wealthy and is one of the most influential land-owning dominant castes in Gujarat. A large number of Patels emigrate to the USA and other countries. Patels are also known to have a skewed sex-ratio, with the significant lack of brides compelling many Patel men to seek brides from tribal areas.

The news report mentioned that the unmarried woman, named Mamta, was 22 years of age, a teacher, and had recently got engaged just two months ago. The other woman, Suman, was already married, 21 years old and a B.Com graduate who was still living with her parents. Suman was known as a fast-paced bowler, regularly competing in inter-college cricket tournaments, most often opting to wear jeans and a T-shirt rather than traditional feminine clothes. The two girls were known to be friends since childhood, often seen with their hands on one another's shoulders or sharing food from the same plate at public functions.

According to the report, the two left their homes on 18 September, saying they were going out of the village. Suicide was not explicitly mentioned in the newspaper report itself, although odd details, such as the *lota*, dish, and the purse found with the bodies, were given special mention. Another report from the same paper, dated 24 September, noted that there was an unopened bottle of insecticide. But there were no signs of vomiting, which generally follows the consumption of a poisonous substance. The police registered their deaths as an accident.

It was the end of the report that intrigued us: it noted that the women had been missing for four days, but there was no mention of missing persons' reports being filed by their families. We wondered if this was an omission by the reporter or if there had been no case filed at all. If there was no case filed, this was a troubling prospect; had the parents not been worried about their children's absence? Had a form of code, dictated by caste norms, silenced the families? Or was it a fear of dishonour that had caused the inaction? There were many questions and missing details that motivated us into planning a visit to find out more.

We waited a little while for the dust to settle and then went to visit the journalist who originally broke the story. This all happened during the time when we had to present ourselves cautiously; we would never identify ourselves outright as an LBT organisation. We handed over our card and introduced ourselves as an NGO inquiring into natural deaths/suicides of women for 'research purposes only'. It was not wholly untruthful.

There were different and unmatched narratives surrounding the women's deaths. According to the reporter, Suman was adamant that she was not to go back to her in-laws, although her father asserted that she got married and had gone there willingly. Known to be friends with Mamta since childhood, the 'intimate' nature of their relationship was apparently discovered by their parents only recently. After closer inspection, though, it became apparent that although it was called 'friendship', the reality of their relationship was a somewhat open secret. Most people knew they wanted to be together, including the parents. When asked if they had stopped the girls from seeing one another, Suman's father admitted that it 'was not good for either of them, or our *samaj* (community/caste)'.

Going through my notes, I remembered Suman's mother and how her eyes had filled with tears when I asked about her son's wife, and she told me that she was away at her parents' house. It was only then that I remembered—I had been told that Suman was married under the custom of *Sataa-Petu*, a pre-marriage agreement in which two families 'swap' a son and a daughter. A daughter from one family is promised in marriage to the son of the other family, and in exchange, a son from that family marries the daughter of the other. If either party fails on their half of the arrangement, the marriage of the other couple gets affected as well. Therefore, Suman's defiance in refusing to return to her in-laws had also jeopardised her brother's marriage.

Maybe, caught in the trappings of tradition, the two saw no possibility of living a life of their choice. Or perhaps there was some hope, but it was poisoned, like the breath in their bodies.

There must have been tensions going on between Suman and her family regarding the marriage. We learnt from the father that he had outright disapproved of her friendship with Mamta, and that she had already made a previous suicide attempt. Surely, these facts must have made the family worry about her absence.

The news report had not explicitly mentioned a suicide, and neither was it mentioned by the reporter when we went to meet with him. However, when we went to meet the Investigating Officer and the PI, they refused to show us the case papers and insisted that it was a clear-cut case of suicide. 'See, they had *samlaingik sambandh* (homosexual relationship), and one of them was going to get married. So they thought that instead of staying apart, it was better to commit suicide together so that no one could separate them. This was the reason. Even their parents believe so.' We saw that there were two suicide notes filed in the case papers, both of which made special mention of their death being their own responsibility: 'I am taking this step with my own willingness,' stated Mamta's, and 'I am responsible for this deed,' said Suman's. But Suman's father said he knew nothing about a note. Nothing was adding up.

The beat constable took us to the village where the girls had lived with their parents. On the way, he shared, 'Both of them lived like a husband and wife. They were together all the time. Even in the night, till 12 and 1 in the morning... You know... you understand!'

We were shown the room where the two women had died. It was barely 20–25 feet away from Suman's house. The bodies would have started giving off a foul odour after just one day, and yet, the girls lay there for four days. It seems odd that nobody enquired about the smell. The constable told us it was he who had first reached the village after being informed about the discovery of the bodies by a resident, following which he informed the PSI and locked the room. He also told us that the police filed the case as an accidental death, which was odd, since we had just seen the suicide notes. As we walked back, the beat constable shared the anger he held against the family, furious that he had to pay the funeral expenses as neither of the girls' parents were willing to give the money, or even take the bodies for cremation. He was told 'Do as you wish.' The constable stayed at the house the whole night while the sweeper removed the bodies. The parents did not show up.

We still had no answers, just milling questions and infinite conjectures. The Patel community, in general, seemed not to have noticed the tragedy, even when the inconsistencies were so obvious as to have gotten the attention of our over-stretched and under-financed NGO. Even the head constable was disturbed by the lack of emotion shown by the parents. These women had no personhood in the eyes of the media, their family, and their community. They were important only as pieces in an exchange. This 'fact finding' trip left us with no facts, just more puzzles, all with missing pieces.

If we had not gone to investigate Mamta and Suman's suicides, we would not have learnt about Mansa. It was on this visit that we learnt that the two women we were looking for, who had signed a Maitri Karaar, had belonged to this very block. But both were no more. All four women were from the very same town and belonged to the very same community in which the sex ratio was abysmally low. Could the greatly skewed sex ratio be blamed for the family's apathy towards the daughters? Or was it the women's attempts at assertion and openness? Was it claiming their relationships that had led to their deaths? When we tried to lift up a single small strand, it uprooted roots that were entwined like veins running through a body, making the search for a beginning and a primary cause almost redundant. There were all these intangibles, small wisps of telltale signs, that refused to be patted in and fitted neatly into a story line.

It is a sad fact that reading that article on 23 September 2006, presuming that the two died by suicide is the first conclusion one naturally jumps to. To us, it would not be surprising news. The first reported lesbian suicide was in 1979 when a couple jumped in front of a moving train together, a fate they preferred to being forced to marry men.[50] Since then, stories of lesbian suicides surface in different parts of India every now and then. We keep cutouts of all the stories that make it to the press, though there must be many more that go unreported. One study found that from the years 1980 to 2001, there were 18 lesbian suicides reported in the newspapers.[51] Numbers like this would not be available to us if it were not for the efforts of queer groups putting together reports, as oppressed sexuality is never mentioned in the statistical details of the government as a reason for suicide or death. Our own figures, collected both through newspaper reports and from conversations, show 20 queer women dying by suicide between 2002 and 2019.

Such suicides are often the outcome of forced separations, coerced confinement and marriages, and social shaming. As same-sex couples can be threatened with the severance of all familial ties, disinheritance, being locked in or thrown out of homes, their education getting stopped midway, being sent to villages, or having legal cases filed against them, it can seem like the only way to escape control and violence is by ending one's life. In our own study, we found that 34 out of 50 same-sex couples questioned had considered suicide, and 9 out of 50 had already attempted it.

One such story from Gujarat involved two women who jumped into a river, one of whom took her three-year-old daughter into the river with her. Notes left on the wall of the river read: 'We are leaving this world which will not allow us to be one.' They jumped three months before Section 377 was read down. A case for murdering the child had to be registered against the

---

[50] Malik, Varun. 'Section 377 Of IPC Quit India: The Tension between the Human Rights of LGBT and Normative Values.' *International Journal of Research in Social Sciences* 3, no. 2 (May 2, 2013): 144–150.

[51] Bina Fernandez and Gomthy N.B. (2003) (Humjinsi A Resource book on lesbian, Gay Bisexual Right in India Mumbai Combat Law Publication).

women, but questions of abetment of suicide never arise in these instances.

It would not be far-fetched to blame the patriarchal, heteronormative society and its obsession with 'purity' for the death of these girls. The next story, of Mataji, illustrates that these 'norms' of society find different paths for their expression and lead to oppression; they, however, are intersected with various differing cultural traditions and stories that challenge the overarching structures, providing a much-needed space for a different kind of couple.

15

Everyone Needs a Companion in Old Age

This is the story of 'Mataji', the name connotative of their role both as a devotee of Goddess Dasha Maa and as a mediator between the Goddess and their worshippers. Mataji conducts a monthly ritual on full moon days. In the magic of the gentle, golden light of the moon, Mataji changes their gender to a woman or returns to their gender assigned at birth, using only a *chunri* and a *kada* (piece of red or green cloth used to cover the head and a thick bangle). This is the time when Dasha Maa, the Goddess, enters them, and it is through them that the Goddess speaks to the people, bestowing hope for better times within the domesticity of family life and the fulfilment of cherished desires. The Goddess and Mataji are both single.

We first heard of Mataji through a news story published in a newspaper in Gujarat. The report included a photo of a couple. One of them was seen dressed like a man, with short hair, and the other wore a dupatta across her shoulders, signifying her feminine gender. The words in the report's title contradicted the impression of a man and a woman that the picture communicated. Nevertheless, the news succeeded in arresting readers' attention.

The headline—34-year-old Champaben marries 20-year-old Vasanthi!—ended in an exclamation mark, graphically summing up the satire and surprise with which the entire story had been perceived and written. It focused on the storm it raised, even including distorted information that the two women shared a common hatred of men. A member of Sabrang sent a cutting of this newspaper report to us in Baroda. After following up on the story through personal contacts and various journalists, four of us from Sabrang went to meet the couple. When we entered the couple's two-storied residence-cum-temple, we stepped into a warm and welcoming space. Two cots were spread out under a tin shed with a fan whirring on a rod. The couple was not there yet, but we were welcomed by neighbours and others who assisted in Mataji's work.

We learned from them that the couple, Champa and Vasanthi, had both gone out. We shared with the others present there that we had called them a day before, and that they had expressed willingness to meet with us. We were asked to wait while they set about making calls to the couple informing them of our visit. We were told they would be there shortly.

While waiting, we went up to see the temple. In a modest room, there ran a shelf from one end of the wall to the other. On it were picture frames of gods and goddesses adorned with marigold garlands, and a fragile trail of grey aroma curled up from the specks of light in the incense sticks. Outside, at the entrance, hung a bell. A bunch of unopened coconuts lay on the floor. Inside the temple stood a couple with a child, their heads bowed and palms joined in prayer. Later, in the last glow of the evening, we saw another pair of women come in for prayers. The road across the dirt lane that led up to the temple was lined with shops that sold offerings to devotees: incense sticks, red transparent *chunris* of different sizes, flowers, and coconuts.

Even though the construction of the temple of Dasha Maa was yet to be completed, it was already a part of the daily lives of the people there and the people from the neighbouring villages. Devotees thronged the area. The temple was only a visible part

of the stories told and retold, of miracles and cures, rituals and
chants, beliefs and economics attached to the Goddess, which
have existed since time immemorial.

Interestingly, the genesis of Goddess Dasha Maa's story ap-
propriately fits the context within which it has come alive for the
people living there. It is a story about how power devolves from
a king to a people, compelling his obeisance to the Goddess who
was known to be worshipped by tribal and other oppressed communities. Initially, the king, in his power and arrogance, rejects
the worship of the goddess outright. In turn, she punishes him
by taking away, one by one, everyone that gave him power and
pleasure, including his children. Deprived of everything he valued, he learns his lesson and bows to the Goddess. Symbolically,
the story demonstrates the importance of including the cultural
beliefs of the subject-citizens. At another level, it is also a proto-
typical tale of assimilation of different beliefs, one that empowers
the vulnerable to some extent and helps them address the dominant. Stories such as these form part of folklore and exist along
with rituals and practices. Folk renditions of the pan-Indian ep-
ics and myths not only bring the gods home, making the daily
world mythic, they also contemporise them.[52]

Mataji gave socio-cultural beliefs and economic elements a
place, a name, and an address in a rural tribal area amongst a vulnerable people, in the form of a traditionally recognisable temple
where none existed. And it was open to all castes, genders, and
classes of people. A collective consciousness from the past, as
found in the myth, made the cohering of a community possible.
The temple synthesised many familiar symbols, not only of the
vulnerable but also of those who have been predominantly powerful over generations.

Along the side, in front of Mataji's entrance, was the mud-
thatched *chulla* (oven). The dried twigs, sticks, and logs of wood

[52] Ramanujan, A. K., and Stuart H. Blackburn. *The Collected Essays of A. K. Ramanujan*. Edited by Vinay Dharwadker. Oxford University Press, 1999, p. 547.

neatly stacked beside it and the gleaming upside-down utensils indicated that this was the cooking area. It stood under a tin roof that rested on the low boundary wall on one side and two lean poles on the other. Silence filled the air. Then suddenly, the earth vibrated under our feet, and we saw the train whizz past us in the distance. The dark and light blue coaches shot across, clearly visible through the wide-open spaces between the sparse trees and shrubs. 'This is the railway track to Mumbai and Ahmedabad,' we were told.

A wire fence between Mataji's residence and the huts looked happy to be adorned with colourful, well-wrung-out clothes, spread out on it to dry in the sun. Hay stacks lay around both sides of the boundary. Buffaloes and cows sat sleepily, tied to poles dug into the mud. They seemed blissfully indifferent to their young frolicking around them, their mouths moving and chewing endlessly, and their tails flicking up and down. We lost track of time as we sat watching them until the evening stole upon us, slanting and silent. As we were waiting for the couple to come, the buffaloes romped in languorously. We saw them drink water from a trough placed under the pipe of the hand pump. The people said to us, 'The water gushed out from the earth at a mere 40 feet—no we did not have to dig deep, just 40 feet.' When we expressed surprise at this, they said to us casually, 'Here, most people get their water at this level or just a little deeper. No need to dig anymore.' As the shadows lengthened, more cattle strolled in, and not far behind them came the men, with a stick in one hand and a volley of guttural sounds accompanying their manoeuvres as they guided the animals back into their shelters. It was clearly a *phadi* (area) of Rabaris, the community who reared milch animals.

As we talked on, we sensed that the couple were well-liked here and clearly had a ring of strong supporters around them. The tall and confident man, apparently referred to as Kaka, dressed in the colourful attire of the Rabari community, was addressed so not because of any kinship ties but because of the bonds of affection that held them close as neighbours. He sat with his young sister even as another elderly man walked in. Another woman introduced herself, smiled, and said, 'I help out with the chores, especially when the devotees come.' Caste divisions were blurred in the everyday lives of people here. The two 'women' who married one another belonged to different communities too.

They married on 23 November 2009, in a small village about ten miles away from Surat district. Just a few kilometres away from Dandi and its stretch of the Arabian Sea, the marriage revoked a memory of that spark of rebellion. More than seventy years ago, Mahatma Gandhi had marched through this same pathway for freedom of control over our country's resources. In marrying one another, these two women were claiming freedom of control too.

Around 220 km off the highway to Mumbai from Baroda, at Surat, one has to take a U-turn. On the left side runs a relatively narrow road that almost gets lost in the hustle-bustle of the highway unless one sits up and takes note of it. On the right side of that road, a few miles later, an unobtrusive board proclaims the presence of the couple's village. Trees line both sides of that road. Rising high above to embrace one another and reaching right up to the sun rays, the branches allow the *Uttarayyan* sunlight to come through only occasionally. Now from the left, now from the right, and suddenly from somewhere in the middle, so that the pathway to the village is strewn with furrowed lines, dots, and drops of sunlight between the shadows, swinging and shifting places. 'The wind is not as strong as it was last year, to be able to carry the kites high. This has been a year of change,' says Kaka.

'A year of change.' Indeed, yes, I said to myself. Section 377 had been read down but here, that change did not register in the way we saw it.

When we did get to meet them after hours of waiting, the two of them, Champa and Vasanthi, by their own admission aged

43 and 30 respectively, did not talk of the opposition they faced to their marriage or when they started living together under the same roof. Though they recognised the possibility of simmering disapproval, they felt that their marriage had a social sanction overall. 'Otherwise, why would 200 people come to the wedding?' Mataji was sporting the sword as the bridegroom, rejoicing in their masculinity, and Vasanthi was in all her bridal finery; they exchanged vows and took seven rounds around the sacred fire with the pundit chanting mantras. 'Our marriage was sanctified by a priest. However, only one picture of the wedding remains now, because one of the children managed to lay his hands on the camera and pulled out the entire roll of film before it could be wrenched free from him. There is only one picture of the wedding,' Mataji shared.

During the conversations we had with the others while we waited for the couple to arrive, we expressed our admiration for the couple and the people who supported their decision. Somehow, serenely, they introduced a perspective of the two women's wedding that stayed within the grasp of a normative understanding. 'Mataji has their work of prayers and worship. They cannot do this and also take care of the daily chores. There has to be someone to help them and attend to all the bhakts (devotees) who come here. On Dasam, cooking and serving food to everyone is quite a task. On those days, the kitchen runs round the clock. Who could do the work better than a woman? Besides, everyone needs a companion in old age.'

The last remark slipped in quietly, without any dramatic emphasis. And we who sat there listened and nodded in agreement. One of the neighbours, a woman, said, 'Another woman in this household was an ideal solution. Since Mataji's life is dedicated to the goddess, they will not marry a man. They are not fussy, and they do not expect that to be served. They will get up and take whatever food has been prepared. There are many days when they fast. Those days, they do not a touch a morsel of grain, and sometimes they do not even drink water.' Mataji's spiritual attainment beyond the humdrum of daily necessities was within the given parameters of fasting and penance that spiritually enlightened people undertake. While the public affirmation of their multiple-gendered self is achieved over time, her intimacy with her partner as 'wife' is premised on certain structural binary gender roles.

However, beneath the hegemonic gender notions of work division, a shift of monumental proportions had happened. Here, Mataji finds day-to-day support and affirmation around the shifting gender identities they wear. Though named and called by their female name and known by the female identity of the deity Mataji, the everyday world of people around them does not recognise Mataji as female, even though the name and the god that she represents is female. They are seen by others around them as a higher being. They identify as male with a spiritual calling.

'Ever since childhood, this is how they have been, male,' shared their youngest brother, 'My parents and sisters even burnt all their male clothes that they wore, but they refused to wear female clothes. When my parents pressured them to marry, they adamantly refused. Having travelled places, they are wise. Around the age of 15, they went to Mumbai and lived there for five years. They returned and were admitted into police services on contract basis. It has now been nine years since they left the service to devote themselves entirely to the goddess.'

Later, Mataji filled us in with more details, 'I have learnt judo and karate. I worked in the police—I joined under very special circumstances. Every day, I would run into some trouble or the other, beating the guys, overpowering them, or playing better than most. Every other day, there would be a hue and cry about the fights I got into. Perhaps all this was what drew the attention of the police officer who lived in the same locality. He handpicked me. This is how I came to be in the police, even though I have studied only till the fourth class. Once, when there was a karate competition, my father—who eventually accepted me as a son—told me not to bother to show him my face if I didn't win the competition. I tried my best and when I won, I felt proud of myself. The officer there told me to salute him. He was my senior, and winning does not take away our duty to show respect. But I told him, "Every day, today and all other days, I have saluted you and will continue to do so even in future, but today, I owe the victory that I enjoy to my father. I retain this salute for him." The officer let me off. I returned home and saluted my father.

'I was lucky to have parents like them.' Holding up the large frames for us to see their parents, they proudly showed us their picture. 'They did accept me finally. Originally, we belong to Junagarh, but in the 1950s, my father moved to Ahmedabad from there. I was born there, and so were all my other brothers and sisters. When my father moved from the village to the city, it was a hard life. He worked as a temporary employee in a government job. He died 15 years ago. We were poor. There were seven of us to feed and clothe. My mother worked on construction sites; carrying loads of bricks and mud, she raised us with great hardship. Mostly, she stayed with me. In fact, she died here and has given me an enormous responsibility. She has left everything to me—all the property, money, everything—whatever it be worth, she left it all to me to divide everything between us in a just and a fair way. I propose to call five elderly people from amongst our relatives, friends, and other people, and settle the matter before everyone. For myself, I just want to make Vasanthi's future secure. She should not be in trouble after I am gone. Now, what I dream about is to build an ashram, a place for the old. I want it to be for women only.

'The local leader here from a political party has asked me to join their party. He has sent my papers to Delhi—let us see what happens. But in case I do get in, I will advocate for the poor. I want to be the *Badshah* of the poor, I mean, I really do want to do something for the underprivileged.'

They were thin and tall, wearing a shirt that was carefully tucked into their pants. A thin border of an undershirt, closely fitted around the neck, peeped out of the first few open buttons of the green shirt. Closed footwear, short hair, and an open, affable smiling countenance that revealed a slightly stained row of teeth. The two front upper teeth, whiter than the rest, were perhaps a dentist's work. Perhaps they hid an unmentioned story of a fight or an accident, we did not ask. Time was short and there was so much to share. A meeting like this is so meandering, full of half-uttered sentences, interruptions, and some more questions and more answers that do not strictly match up to each other. The point is that this was not the point. Because, it was imbued with recognition, it did not matter who said what—the excitement of meeting others 'like us' was enough.

It was in this flush of recognition that we went to the beach to get to talk more, separately and peacefully, away from the censure of familiar gaze. Amongst us, we could unburden our secret love and desires. We got into the car. Since it was a tight fit for six people, we opened the front door of the car to allow the couple the larger single seat. Mataji got in and we thought they would move up closer to the driver's seat, but instead, they created a space by shifting right back against the seat; widening their feet, they beckoned to Vasanthi to get in, and she clambered up and settled herself in the space between Mataji's legs, a close twosome, one resting against the chest of the other. When we reached, the couple got out and walked up to the seashore, their fingers interlocked, their bodies almost blurring. 'We come here often and walk up right into the sea. In the late evening, the waves rise and reach right up to the wall. No one is allowed here in the rainy season,' they shared.

Vasanthi, a tribal woman, belongs to a village in the district of Surat. In the beginning, she sat withdrawn. Dressed in a saree, with dangling earrings and three bangles on each wrist, she seemed more distant and difficult to reach. Feeling safe, away from the family and others, we asked Mataji, 'Who proposed first?' But they did not reply; instead, they smiled and looked at Vasanthi, who said proudly and shyly, 'I was the one who proposed marriage.' Vasanthi surprised us all. We all looked at her. Until now, she had not joined in the conversation, but as we talked, her dark face began to glow. 'When I learnt today that some more people were coming to meet us, I said I would not open my mouth. We are fed up of all the attention and remarks about us. After talking to the media, we now doubt if it was a good idea to have talked about our marriage. But now that we have met, I feel this is different.'

In their private world, Vasanthi had another male name for Mataji. Continuing, she said, 'I got to know them when I used to come to the temple and help with the work. It is now more than two years since we have known one another. Then, I began to live here because their mother fell sick, so I looked after her before she passed away, just 15 days ago. It was during this time I got to know Mataji. I liked to work and live with them. I did not see marriage with a man as a viable option for women. There is no guarantee that a woman will be happy in her marriage; on the contrary, almost all the women I know are unhappy, including my two sisters. One of them has returned home to my parents. Though her husband does not drink or smoke, he beats her and suspects her of having relationships with someone else, making her life impossible. When my parents tried to get me married, I resisted until I met Mataji. Marrying them is another matter. They are different. I preferred this idea and life. This is how it happened for me. We both talked about it and then I broached the subject to my father. He came here and all of us talked together. My father agreed after a lot of persuasion. Then he spoke to my mother and brought her around.'

Though different in tone and texture, Mataji too had their story of having resisted marriage to a man. 'When they used to talk of marrying me, I told them I would make that man my brother.' Since they saw themselves as male, when they said that they would make the prospective bridegroom their brother, they were perhaps suggesting that they would tell the man about their preferred gender. 'I had made a vow not to ever marry a man.' They had always projected themselves as having a higher spiritual calling which did not fit the requirements of *grihastha ashram* and therefore, they even overcame the mundane necessity of fitting into a particular gender. It was on these grounds that they were able to argue out of parental proposed marriages. They shared that when they were young, they had been involved with another woman; when the woman got married, an aggrieved Champa of days gone by had asked their friend what the need was for her to marry when they were there for her.

Yet, in the context when we met them, their gender radically altered every month on Dasam, when they re-entered their biologically assigned gender, transforming yet again into a female through the spirit of Mataji. Significantly, the 'male' then wears the *chudla* (thick, heavy bangle) and a *chunri*, the symbols of being female and a chosen representation of the divine goddess. Mataji's everyday world is both of gender fluidity and ambiguity, enveloping them in a spiritual aura. 'Right from the beginning, even as a child, I was spiritually inclined, a devotee of Mataji. Everything in my life has come with her blessings. I follow her orders and she takes care of me.'

Another important change that took place and which facilitated the marriage of the two 'women' was the near completion of the temple of Dasha Maa. It was a temple that concretely stood before the public eye, requiring only a few more additions. In June 2008, Mataji concretised their dream.

'Brick by brick, I slowly raised this temple. Every day for three years, I used to go to the village to take donations. People helped me; they contributed and spread the word. It was my *devima's* (mother goddess) wish that a temple be built here. By her grace, this land of 2,000 square metres, on which the temple stands, has been donated by Samnath bhai. You saw the temple upstairs; it is modest, but it is there. We live downstairs, and when visitors come, they have a place to stay and rest.'

Their spiritual calling elicits respect amongst the people, who are slowly being influenced by Hindu ways of worship and rituals. This trend allows them a cultural leverage which is also enhanced by their higher caste, maybe not given as easily to someone from an oppressed caste. Though belonging to the Hindu religion, they are engaged in the worship of a goddess venerated by tribal and oppressed caste communities, living within a locality largely peopled by them. They are uniquely placed as an insider-outsider to the tribal rural community. Originally as city dwellers, they represent a relatively more powerful group and are an outsider in the rural, tribal area. But like them, their economic status matches the people whose suffering they wish to address and ameliorate.

The temple stands tall near the railway crossing and is perhaps the only one of its kind in the village. Earlier, when we were searching and asking for the right road to reach the couple, we missed both the landmarks, that of the railway crossing and the temple. Stopping on our way to ask where exactly the temple was located, we were told to turn back. There could be no confusion, we were told, because the only known temple in the area was the Dasha Maa temple, the one which we had left behind. Since it was a tribal area, the absence of temples was no surprise. However, this also showed that the temple made by Mataji filled an important socio-religious need, or perhaps it was the outcome of a rising religious trend or an intermingling of the various cultural beliefs of the Hindu, tribal, and oppressed castes. Mataji was born in a family of Darbars, which is amongst the highest in the hierarchy of the Hindu caste structure. Though poor, the fact that they belong to such a caste group and have a demonstrably higher spiritual calling elicits respect amongst the village people. Before the wedding between the two people, their identity as Mataji had already been established. They became a part of its socio-cultural fabric when they actively initiated the building of the temple. They symbolised the shared faith of the Hindu community and represented divinity. Their combination of human and sacred-spiritual qualities, with gender fluidity, also gave them an aura of divinity, thus creating a distance from others. Their singleness by virtue of not marrying a man, just like the goddess, invests them with the value of a higher, more pure form of life. It partakes of a worldview where, by being closer to renunciation, an unmarried person has a better chance of breaking out of the karmic cycle of birth and rebirth. The shifting gender role they adopt weaves an ambiguity around their sexual identity, accentuating their unique and higher calling.

For us, the story, with all its openness, is replete with silences, silences that speak of stories that cannot be retold exactly as they are experienced. It would be of relevance to us to carefully notice where these silences occur in the narrative. Mataji does not refer to their departure for Mumbai. But their brother does so, mentioning even the age at which they left their home. They were 15 years old at that time. This is precisely the age when the body alters. Could this period have been a time of pressure to change their appearance to the female gender that they were assigned at birth? Interestingly, they do not share the episode of how their clothes were burnt. Instead, what we get to hear from them is the parental and social acceptance they enjoy as a 'male' and as a devotee of Mataji. When we met them, they had already overcome what might have been a long struggle in their childhood and adolescence. Maybe even their departure for Mumbai was an act of protest against parental control. Can we read, in between these lines, a narrative of a rebellion?

Having established credibility as a devotee, they have also gained social sanction for their relationship with their female partner. Perhaps going back to that period of struggle, as it really happened, would detract from the overall affirmation they receive. Maybe projecting parental acceptance from the beginning is crucial for getting validation in the current contexts they live in. As part of authority and an institution that is recognised by the society and the state, the family's stamp of approval acts as a qualifier, a test by which the 'moral rightness' of a 'woman' can be measured by others. As a cascading influence, it succeeds in pulling in those who doubt or waver in their support. Those who genuinely support such rebellious acts, but find their approval difficult to defend against the protests of others, can also camouflage their support in a simple acquiescence.

The presence of a 'masculine woman' within a family and society has been often explained in terms of exceptional personhood. Mataji belongs to this category. They rejected marriage with a man because they are spiritually devoted to Dasha Maa. It is a calling that they had to answer and attend to. It is almost as if their role was destined. Mataji portrays their actions as emanating out of a divine will rather than their own free will. Acting under a plan chalked out by the goddess, they affirm prevalent spiritual beliefs rather than self-determined actions, which are often denied to women. Choices that people like Mataji make have to be deftly navigated.

Can we call this an instance of reverse Sanskritisation or cultural appropriation, as Mataji, a person from a dominant caste, takes up the cultural practices of the oppressed? Or is it a process that is so enmeshed and entangled in several overlapping complex processes, that drawing lines of Sanskritisation or appropriation would be missing the enormous complexities of life that cannot be contained or explained, except in fragments?

16

But I Knew That.
I Knew That Others Knew

Ten years have passed since we first heard about Sheetal and Bittu.

Since we are an organisation focusing on queer and particularly transgender issues, their story was brought to us by a newspaper journalist. The two protagonists of the story are a transgender man and a woman who lived together as man and wife. The story found its way into the headlines when Sheetal—the woman in the relationship—was found dead after taking her own life.

The story was complicated further by the presence of the couple's child, Neha. Following Sheetal's death, the prominent question surrounding the story was who should be awarded custody of the child. Should it be the parents and brother of her biological mother, Sheetal? Or Bittu, her father? In the case of a straight and cisgender couple, the answer is obvious: she should live with her father. However, due to the lack of 'biological' relations, Bittu was left without any custodial rights; awarding Sheetal's parents the custody would not only deny parenthood to a queer partnership, but would have also deprived the child of her choice. This issue was the crux of the story in the newspapers; the story you are about to read, however, is focused solely on Bittu and Bittu alone: lived by him, retold to me, and then to you.

Gathering Bittu's story has not been linear or chronological. It has been fed to me in small fragments here and there, the same way in which I wrote and recorded it. Most importantly, the story came into fruition because Bittu wanted it told. 'It's the way I have lived, suffered, and struggled. You have to tell people my story—I will tell you, and you write.' This is Bittu's story, the parts that he willingly shared with us, and the parts which I heard and understood.

The first time we met Bittu, he was a 22-year-old who looked like an adolescent. Five feet tall, his eyes sparkled with an endearing and mischievous twinkle and were framed by thick, curling eyelashes. His tight-fitted red shirt, with two buttons left open, exposed his flat chest and equally flat stomach. He had a curly black crop of hair and a perfect row of gleaming white teeth that were, back then, still unstained by tobacco.

This first physical meeting was almost two months after his story had been splashed across the media. Before this, our only contact with Bittu had been via telephone. It was not until this first face-to-face meeting that Bittu fully opened up to us: 'I have lost everything. With Sheetal gone, I am nothing. I do not understand what happened and why did she do this. The time I spent with her was the best time in my whole life.' He looked away from us. Tears welled up in his eyes and rolled down his face. We sat motionless. There was so much to say, but there were no words in which to say it.

After a long time, I broke the silence, 'Had she made attempts before?'

He simply nodded in affirmation, and then said after a long pause, 'She was right when she said, "You will not find another one who would love you as much as I do." I was alone before I met her, but living with her, I found a family—parental love, sibling-like affection, a partnership, and a beautiful companion. She was beautiful, I tell you, really beautiful. She alone was my family. She was everything for me. The Bittu that you see sitting in front of you is not the same Bittu. Whatever I know, I have learnt from Sheetal—basic etiquette, what and how to wear, eating out, conversing… Before I met her, I was a rustic buffoon! I grew up on the streets, abused and abusive, often drunk. After Sheetal came into my life, I changed. I could not wait to return home every day. She loved me and I loved her. We were a family.

'Now that it is all over, I deeply regret my anger; that night when I lay down with my back to her, without making up with her… if only… how I wish I had turned on my side, then things might have been different. Only days before she died, she took out a loan and bought me a motorcycle, parking it quietly just outside our house. That was on the second of the month. On the seventeenth, just fourteen days after taking out that loan and arriving home to a new bike, she went and did this. Who could have imagined that she would do this? Gone. From right in front of my eyes. I could do nothing, nothing at all, nothing.'

Bittu repeated his words, wringing his hands as he spoke. A grim silence fell between us. That day, we did not continue any further.

A few months passed, and Bittu was introduced to our community group. During one sharing session, Bittu divulged some more: 'My mother, she did not understand anything then and doesn't even now. How important clothes are, yet my mother never allowed me to wear what I liked. When I was a child, she made me wear my brother's outgrown clothes—shirts, shorts, and his vests too. When I grew up, she only allowed me to wear girls' clothes. It was in these clothes that I would be made fun of by my neighbours and peers. I have always identified as a boy, everyone knew me as a boy, and indeed, I am a boy! If someone forces a boy to wear girls' clothes, how would he look? You tell me! Will he not look ludicrous? Stepping out of the house in girls' clothes was an ordeal. I am not a girl, but what could I do to fight against this compulsion to be one? I would wear old worn-out shorts, tying the two torn ends into knots; I much preferred myself in this outfit, even if it meant being beaten.

'I used to be so angry, I felt like breaking everything around me! I could not articulate what was happening to me, and my mother could not understand. She is a double postgraduate, school teacher, and a mentor for so many in the community, but she could not understand me, her own child. All that I knew was that I was a boy—everything else was beyond my comprehension.

'Every day was a battle: the external pressures of conforming and being a girl, being at constant war with my internal longing to be accepted as who and what I *knew* I was. I must tell you one thing though—she made such an effort to teach me how to be a girl. Every time I sat down, she would remind me to keep my feet close together, to keep my eyes down, and not answer back. And I did try to do as she taught me. She cajoled me, scolded me, and when she lost her patience, she would beat me. But nothing worked. You know—if I could, I would have changed.

'Then, there was the nose piercing. I begged, I pleaded, I refused, resisted, wailed, and even ran away to hide under the stairs. But I was caught and dragged to have the needle stuck through my nose.' Breaking the circle, Bittu showed us his nose. 'Look closely,' he said. Bringing his face closer to mine and bending down, he turned the left side of his nose towards me and pointed a finger at it. 'Don't you see it, this spec of a scar on my nose, don't you see it?' Then, turning to face me fully, he said, 'So this is where my nose was pierced. It has been like this, my life, scarred in many different ways. She ruined my life.'

Discrimination against daughters within families is common. Sometimes, it is merely condoned as an economic measure or explained as a means for instilling discipline necessary for their future role as a woman. Depending on the parent, some will allow their daughters to play with boys and wear boys' clothes as children, which is how it was in Bittu's case. Until reaching puberty, it was perfectly fine that Bittu would roam the streets in his brother's clothes and play with whomever he chose, but when he reached adolescence, all kinds of restrictions began to be imposed upon him. 'Suddenly the honour of my family and my community got confusingly attached to me. I had no understanding of this sudden change, both in my mother's attitude towards me and in my own body. My mother kept repeating incessantly: "All will be lost". I just wondered why all would be lost.'

Before Bittu had even managed to comprehend these changes, the noose had already been tightened. 'Wearing boys' clothes was out of the question now, my legs and arms had to be properly covered. Name and honour was the one thing I lived for! My mother would keep repeating it, but I couldn't understand what harm there was in her allowing me to live the way I wanted.'

Of course, there must have been a reason for her insistence. As a single mother, a potential rebellious daughter put her in danger of losing everything that she counted as honourable.

'Perhaps…' pondered Bittu, 'But what has my life come to? I cannot even open a bank account. I do not have a PAN Card.[53] Besides, after everything that has happened, not only have I lost Sheetal but also the only official address and home that I have ever had in my life.' Bittu's snappish open-and-shut response discouraged any more queries. Instead, he moved on, asking 'How can I get my PAN Card?'

I asked him for his mother's address. 'I can give her address, but if and when the PAN Card arrives, she will not give it to me. She detests me. She may even tear it up and throw it away. She is like that, I know her. Is there any other way?' I explained that no one can mess with government documents. If she were to do that, then she would be held accountable.

'How will I know that my card has come?'

---

[53] PAN is short for Permanent Account Number.

'You can call your brother to ask if it has arrived and see how it goes from there. Let's wait and see what your mother does. If she does not cooperate, we can intervene to retrieve the card.'

'How?'

'If it comes to it, we will go and report it to the police station. Together.'

Bittu's brother did confirm that his PAN Card had arrived. When Bittu called his mother, she—as predicted—threatened him with dire consequences if he ever dared to send letters to her address again. We also tried to call and persuade her, suggesting a time and place convenient to her, only to hear the phone being slammed back into the receiver: 'It's none of your business!'

Filing a complaint to the police station then became the only option, though Bittu was reluctant. 'They will ask all kinds of questions...' Eventually, we managed to encourage him to go and we accompanied him. Bearing the callous attitude of the police personnel, we persevered, waiting. Crossing and uncrossing our legs, we sat there, fighting back scrutiny and their hostile curiosity, reminding them every now and then that it was a government document and its denial was a violation of an individual's right. Finally, we secured their cooperation in retrieving the PAN Card.

Bittu's mother arrived at the police station, looking tired. Bittu commented that she must have walked all the way from her house. Dressed in a plain sari, her hair pulled back in a tight knot, taut and stiff, she looked past us. Head held high, she walked towards the policeman, turned on her heel, and stormed out after handing over an envelope.

On the bus ride home, I sank into my window seat and a troubled silence suffocated me. Bittu's face swam before my eyes in the trees, houses, and streets that whirred past. The whole event seemed so ironic—yes, we had managed to retrieve his PAN Card, which was indeed powerful in gaining state recognition, registering him as an addressee and insider of his locality and community. But it seemed so trivial in the face of the opposition he faced, both from his mother and the wider community. Even the state had abetted in his social exile, identifying him as female, denying his true and lived reality of being a male. Although the immediate reasons for his exclusion from the family home remained unclear, my own suspicion was that it was his partnership with Sheetal that had disrupted his family relationships, resulting in him being ousted. Concurrently, the marginalisation of his gender, class, and caste were in a complex interplay, an example of multiplied intersectionality that resisted any categorical summarisation.

As time passed, we learnt more about Bittu and his circumstances. 'You saw my mother that day, right? You saw her,' he reminded us, 'Wasn't she indifferent to me? One thing that I can tell you is that she has nothing for me, she will not give me anything. You tell me I can make a claim against her, but how? She is supposed to be my mother, but she is only ever concerned about my brother. We are only two children, my brother and I. She gives him everything, even now: new clothes for him, hand-me-downs for me; milk and cream for him, dry bread for me; private English medium school for him, government school for me; big fees spent on him, zero cost for me. Sometimes, I wonder how my life could have been if I had studied where my brother did. My mother even bought him a jeep! He was given everything. But he was totally useless. His wife even deserted him and took their child with her.

'One thing I must tell you,' Bittu went on, 'is that whatever I might be—good or bad—I'm independent, capable of taking care of myself. At only 14, I left my mother's house—no, no, it was even earlier! If we count the first time that I ran away to my uncle's house. I thought that maybe my uncle would explain everything to my mother, but he did not. Instead, he reported me straight to her and brought me back home. My mother tied me to a ceiling fan and locked me in the house. To really teach me a lesson, to make doubly sure that I would not escape again, she cut my hair! I mean all of it! "Baldy", that was the name I was given. She gave me sleeping pills too. She knew about such medicines from her work in a government mental hospital. It was a good government job, it used to be my father's, but when he passed away, she was given his job as compensation. I was two when my father passed away.

'So, I was caught the first time I ran away from home, but the second time, I was not. I had realised it was better to do what my mother wanted. I grew wiser. Instead of screaming in protest of her beatings—like after the first time I got caught—I decided to try and win her trust by doing whatever she asked: cooking, sweeping, mopping, and washing utensils. I was already used to doing most of the domestic chores—it was nothing new, only that I was reluctant back then. Now, I willingly did whatever she wanted—or so she thought. I had her convinced that I had changed, and so finally, her vigil over me began to slacken. She wasted no time in looking for a boy for me. Relatives and neighbours all advised me to get married and settle down. I agreed with them—well, pretended to agree—that it was what was best for me and my family. But inside, I thought to myself: Yes, I will go along with seeing this boy to keep things going as smooth as they are. I am leaving home anyway.

'As planned, my mother chose a boy to come and see me. It was an ordeal I went through, simply because I had already made up my mind to leave home. When I met the boy, I told him bluntly, 'I am a boy, brother, same as you. I can do everything that you can. I play marbles, kick the football hard and high, I cycle down to places, go out and roam the streets. I am not a girl.' It seemed that was all that was needed, because the matter soon came to an end. I'm sure he must have wondered about me… the strange kind of person I was. At least, my readiness to meet a boy had convinced my mother that I was truly reformed. She stopped locking me up. She began sending me to fetch milk in the morning. For some time, things continued this way: I did all the household chores, obeyed my mother, and listened to what she had to say cordially. I suppressed my feelings and pretended to be the child that she wanted me to be.

'It was the ninth month of the year 1999. I had planned my exit carefully, calculating the risks and avoiding those that would give me away. I left early morning, before the sun had risen. It was 4 a.m., and it was still dark; the whole neighbourhood was asleep. The darkness would protect me from recognition. I figured that if inquiries followed, then nobody would be able to describe me. All those who knew me were still in bed. I felt a vague confidence that it would take a while for anybody to discover my absence. By the time my mother awoke, I would be long gone, far into the city.

'That morning, I left the house with fourteen rupees in my pocket. Just fourteen rupees, the money I had been given to buy milk for the morning tea. Fourteen rupees is all that I had. Just fourteen rupees,' he stressed. 'Can you believe it? Looking back, I ask myself how I imagined I would be able to survive. I did not consider these things. All I thought about was escaping marriage and the compulsion to live life as a girl. The only clothes I carried were those that were on my back. I was cautious not to carry any extra weight, imagining scenarios in which I had to run to escape somebody that had followed me.

'I had quickly walked far enough as not to be tracked down. Then, I stopped in front of the government hospital. It was here that I began assisting patients and their relatives, running errands for them, filling in time while their families and relatives took breaks. Some gave me money, while others gave me something to eat. If they did not give me anything, I took something from the hospital food that was distributed to the patients. Many bring their own food, meaning that I could help myself from their portion of the hospital meals. Sometimes, that food was enough for me. But sometimes I had to manage with just water to drink and go to sleep like that.

'Finding a place to sleep at night was hard. One night I had to go to the local bus depot...' Then he stopped, mid-sentence, and both of us found ourselves suddenly staring at one another, speechless, for a split second; before I had even realised, he moved on. I had not anticipated that the narrative would go where it had, and neither did he. Caught in the momentum, Bittu had unwittingly touched upon an incident that forbade telling. We both knew that we knew what we knew. I realised, as a listener, how important it is to hear what is unsaid in the stories narrated to us.

Bittu continued, 'I was forever anxious that if someone whom I or my family knew were to see me, I would be taken home to be beaten and locked up. Afraid, I continued to run, this time to Mumbai. I had no ticket, but nobody caught me. I stayed by the station and ate from a lorry. One person gave me food for two days, feeding me *vada pau*. He thought I was a boy. Coming close to me, he asked, "Have you run away from home?" I was terrified that he would go to the police. Two days later, we met again. He asked me to wait at the same place until evening—he would come to fetch me and then give me work. I nodded. All I hoped for was some work and a place to sleep, nothing more. He came back and took me to a complex near Andheri in an auto. He employed me, making bread *pakoras*. I had to sleep on the footpath. I lasted there two days. I did not like it. A bout of homesickness hit me, so to Gujarat I returned. And to wandering in and around the government hospital.

'In front of the hospital was a barber's shop. The shop's owner must have seen me hanging around, so he asked,

"Where have you come from?"

"Khambaat."

"Who is admitted in the hospital?"

"My *Dadi*."

"What's her problem?"

"Kidney."

"*Umph.*"

'He looked at me, and before he could turn and reach his shop, I had disappeared from his vicinity and sight. I tried to avoid him, but after 15–20 days he met me again in the hospital corridor, stopping me and saying, "I have come to see your *dadi*. How is she?" He saw that this made me nervous and asked, "You do not have anyone admitted here? Why are you dressed like a boy?"

'"No, I have no one here," I told him, "My mother and father are gone. *Chacha* has turned me out of the house." I pleaded my helplessness and asked him for employment.

'He responded, "You want to work? Do you know anything?"

'"No. But I can learn," I said enthusiastically.

'I knew I had to work to earn some money, and I was prepared to do whatever was needed. So, this was how I landed my first real job, learning the art of hairdressing. I was not paid for my work. I was a trainee. He gave me food. His house was behind the shop. In the front of the house was a verandah, *autla,* where I slept. He gave me two pairs of boys' clothes. And from here on, I was christened "Bittu".

'In a month, I had matured as a trainee, and I observed closely how the owner cut clients' hair and nails. As the owner's family began to get to know me, their attitude of suspicion towards me eased. They gave me a mattress with a sheet and blanket to sleep in. Two months later, I was "complete", meaning I was now able to cut hair according to the client's wishes, give a massage, cut nails, and even shave. The owner was obviously pleased with me. Now I was allowed to change in his house and use their bathroom. I felt settled. Anyway, I had reached a point that I could attend customers on my own, meaning that my *seth* could not afford my higher salary.

'Any shop has permanent customers, and one such loyal customer ran the public telephone booth (STD booth) in the dental department of the hospital. He knew about another STD booth in which a couple was searching for somebody to work for them. My *seth* was willing to recommend me to this customer of ours, and so the customer recommended me to the couple. I soon found myself working in that booth. Shops were quickly beginning to spring up outside of the city centre and in the suburbs, and moving out here was a relief. I felt safer, less likely to be caught on the outskirts.

'My new employer asked me for details of my address, the name of my parents and siblings. I gave him false names and an address in Khambaat. For a month, everything went smoothly. However, what I did not know was that the couple had made enquiries into the address I had given them. They found out that it was false, all of it—my name, the body I was born in, the street, the city that I lived in. Everything about me was false. Only Bittu was real. But I had no proof of my own self, no ownership of my own identity.'

It was indeed true that according to the binaries imposed by both state and society, Bittu had no means of proving his chosen identity. He had already given up his only home and family, and now that had also cost him his job. But what continued to save Bittu was his ability to strike up friendships. While working at the booth, Bittu had befriended Dilip Bhai, the shopkeeper next door. 'It was his friendship that saved me.'

It is not difficult to picture him becoming friends with Dilip Bhai. We knew Bittu as a great conversationalist, a performer, a satirist, capable of laughing at himself and others. He actively sought out his listeners for their collaborative affirmation, pausing and filling his suspended sentences with their words. Looking directly into your eyes, the manner and tone in which he expressed everyday ordeals, sprinkled with half-uttered abuses, satirical and comical, often mirrored a shared reality. It made Bittu popular company, an endearing individual and friend.

Bittu's masculine appearance and slight frame often cause him to be perceived as a minor and this, often when he rides his motorbike, can put him in awkward situations. He, however,

manages to laugh at himself, thus disrupting any power directed against him, and normally comes out on top of the situation.
Dramatising one such encounter with the traffic police, he strides
out of the group—playing the part of the policeman and taking
centre stage, he begins to stamp his feet and imitates blowing a
whistle, raising his hands as if to stop the driver. Then, changing
places, Bittu shrinks his body and mimes getting off the bike.
Returning to his previous role and performing the part of the
policeman once more, he struts about the place with importance;
waving his stick around, he bellows 'License!' in a commanding
tone. He turns towards us, the onlookers, bends his waist down,
and submissively replies 'Sir'. He continues to mime, this time going through the ritual of drawing out the license from his pocket
and handing it over to the imaginary police personnel. In the
same dramatic manner, he imitates the policeman, who stares at
him and scrutinises the license, looking into the distance, as if
staring at Bittu. His eyebrows knit enquiringly, announcing the
name on the license loudly, 'Manisha Ben?'

'Yes, Sir,' Bittu, playing himself, replies in a respectful, soft
tone. He takes the license from the policeman and pointing to his
chest, he shouts 'I had to cut them!' In his last line as the policeman, he mutters some abuse and finally turns back to his audience, beaming, 'I ran away before the policeman had a chance to
blow his whistle or wave his stick to stop me!' His performance
finishes with narrative, 'I tell myself—Run, Bittu, run!'

In all of Bittu's narratives and performances, his character is
always the hero. The emotions that he expresses within them also
express a substratum of our community's collective experiences.
Laughter healed us and proved to be a release, opening up a level
space that bonded us.

When he lost the job at the booth, the shopkeeper next door
soon invited him to stay at his house, well aware that he was a
girl. 'But within 15 days, I had to leave the house. The shopkeeper's wife became suspicious. My friend made arrangements for

me to stay at his friend's place. He too was poor and lived with his mother in one room and made a living by cooking and selling food off his cart,' Bittu tells us. 'He is still there. Only his mother is no more. I was the only other person who attended his mother's funeral.

'One thing I can tell you is that this unfortunate turn in my life allowed me to learn from this friend of mine. I realised that I too could earn by setting up something of my own, something on the street. I had lived on the streets long enough to know how to survive on them. I knew that before starting anything, I would have to first win over the policeman. So, I ran errands for the traffic police, washed their tiffins, mopped, swept their place, fetched their cigarettes, *bidis*, and packets of tobacco. Pleased with me, they gave me a small space in the *basti* near a hotel. It was along a roadside, just outside some shops, near the *basti*—that was where I started my own business. All I needed was a chair, mirror, and my equipment: like scissors, shaving kit, oil and creams, I was ready to run my shop.

'One thing I tell you,' he said as he shook his head, gazing into the distance beyond my shoulder, 'It wasn't easy. To do this. I tried to work as a domestic help in a *seth's* house. I thought he has a wife and children… but that man, he would not leave me… ultimately, I had to go.' The philosophical edge to his voice altered, instead rising as it adopted an increasingly angrier tone. 'Tell me, you tell me.' He was looking intensely into my eyes and raising his finger towards me. 'Does anybody give anyone anything without calculating for their own benefit? You tell me, does anyone simply give things away without their share of demands in return? I'll tell you; nobody does that! Nobody gives without taking something in return. It is only the demand, and the ways of meeting that demand, that will differ. You have no idea what one has to undergo just to live. You may be like us in some ways, but you do not know what we must face. Your life is different from people like us, very different,' he emphasised.

Less angry now, his tone softened as he attempted to explain, 'I am alone. Where do I live? On the streets. No house. No one to look after me. No elderly person or parent to protect me. I was 14 when I left home. How do you think I managed to live? Did anybody give me a job purely out of concern for my plight? No! Not without a demand. I had no food to eat, no clothes, no home, what could I do? You would not know... But I can tell you this one thing, if there is anybody like me, raised on the street, who tries to say "I am clean and pure", then they are lying! I can tell you. They cannot be clean. I am telling you that I am not clean. Growing up on a roadside means hunger, humiliation, rape.

'There were times when I went to sleep in the bus depot, and the police would not leave me alone. I was easy prey. The railway station was the same—there is no safe place. They know whom to catch, where, and how. I've had to undergo abortions. Don't ask what happens, because you would not know. Even I had no idea. How could I have known what I would have to face? But what could I do? Go to the police? I tell you this: going to the police does nothing for people like us. I am a loose woman dressed up as a boy! Even if I tried to resist them, did that do anything? No. They do not care. Who cares for people like us?

'All my triangles and angles are messed up in my astrological chart. God mistakenly made me a female. I can sit to urinate like a Muslim; it does not matter how short the women's queues are, I will not stand in them. I know how others see me—I knew when I set up my hair-cutting shop. People would whisper, "She is a woman, you know! A woman doing a barber's job!" Whatever they said, that work provided my daily bread. I was making 80–90 rupees a day. Before, if you were to ask me what my dream was, I would reply "just to have enough to eat". That's all. While running my hair-cutting business, what was my dream? To drive a two-wheeler. And it was during these years that I actually learnt to drive one.

'You could not call the street corner on which my business sat a salon—its ceiling was the open sky and its wall a tree—but whatever it was, it served people, and me, a purpose. I gained regular customers, one of whom was Hatim Bhai. Seeing my fingers and hands, he guessed that I was female—that's what he told me. But I knew that. I knew that others knew. The difference this time, though, was that he told me: "go back home".

'I was afraid that my mother still would not accept me. But inside, I had a glimmer of hope—she was my mother after all. I convinced myself: she will accept me, and she will ask me to stay at home, especially if an elderly person like Hatim Bhai can make her understand. I arranged for Hatim Bhai to talk to my mother. He tried to make her understand: "He is your own child. Children make mistakes, but elders overlook them. Keep her with you. She is a girl after all." But she retorted saying, "If you're so concerned, why don't you keep her?"

'Now you see why I was so reluctant to give her address to receive my PAN Card, and even to go to the police station. You see now that she will not give me anything. She is adamant. Beyond reason. Perhaps, if she was amenable to logic and love, I could have stayed there.' He laughed off his helplessness and continued, 'But there's one thing I should tell you—she started coming to see us once I had settled down with Sheetal. Oh yes! She did. After constant rejection, after shutting me off entirely, our deadlock ended because Sheetal took the initiative. She would come over for tea. Now that my house is gone and Sheetal is gone too, she neither invites me nor bothers to see me. That's how she is.

'You know who really helped me?' he asked, and answered the question himself. 'Hatim Bhai. With his assistance, I got my own auto rickshaw. Those who drive auto rickshaws will always park them in specific spots, where we know we can get customers. Once, I happened to park in one such spot where the drivers were talking about a certain woman who frequented that area. *Ye maal achha hai* is how they described her (the material is good). I became curious. I started to hover around that specific auto stand, and it didn't take long for me to manage to catch a glimpse of her. I saw her get into another auto and knew immediately that she was the one that so many had been speaking about. The atmosphere around the auto drivers changed in her presence. Indeed, she was beautiful. This was where I saw Sheetal for the first time.

'I worked out that she travelled to the hospital by auto every day. The next day, I offered to take her there. I dropped her at the door of the hospital but would not take any money from her. She was a nurse. She could speak and understand English very well. I began to take her in my auto regularly. I was there to pick her up, there to drop her off. We began to go out together, getting to know each other, growing closer, and soon, falling in love. Those moments were the best, the ones spent waiting for one another. Isn't it true? Later, it's no longer the same. And I tell you this, when we first started meeting, I thought she thought I was a man. But no, she knew who I was from the beginning, and she loved me, from the beginning! She didn't like men. She was married once, but returned home within 20 days.

'We ran away together. The first time, we were caught within 11 days. We had not planned our getaway thoroughly at all, and we were not helped by the fact that her brother and his wife were in the police. We were bound to get caught, really, but were naïve enough to believe we would be safe, and that her family would finally relent. We were soon brought back, and Sheetal's family kept the matter from going public. The fear of sheer humiliation, loss of honour, and potential loss or interference of their government job is what kept them quiet. When we were caught, both of us were jailed. She was locked up within the four walls of her house, and I in the police station. The police beat me, black and blue, for a "confession". They wanted me to say that I had kidnapped Sheetal with the intent of trafficking her. But no, I stuck to my word, because if I had said something else, like they wanted, I would have been imprisoned. And Sheetal was taking beatings of her own, by her brothers at home. They too wanted her to say she was kidnapped. But Sheetal refused. No case was ever registered, and because I refused to give them what they wanted, I was let off.

'After that, my hunt for Sheetal began. I looked for her everywhere. In and around her house, the hospital. I trailed every possible road and street in search of any traces of her. I never gave up on the search. Every day. Checking out places I had checked the previous day. I just wanted to find her once—just once, I would tell myself. Let me find her once at least, that's all. Finally, one day outside the hospital, I saw a friend of Sheetal's. I waved out to her and pulled over. She had Sheetal's village address—I persuaded her friend to accompany me there.

'In the village, I hung back at the local bus stop and watched as Sheetal's friend turned up the lane leading to her house. I waited on a bench in the shade. But I was unable to simply sit and wait. I paced up and down impatiently, turning my head slightly now and then to look at the lane into which Sheetal's friend had disappeared. There was no sign of her, nor of Sheetal. My gaze returned empty. I decided to not look again. I pulled my cap over to hide my face, just in case someone recognised me. I sat down again with my back to the lane. Sometimes I saw her face swim past my eyes, and I heard her voice echoing inside me.'

Bittu lost track of time as he sat there, with his face pressed between his knees. Then he felt a tap on his shoulder and looked up, startled. It was Sheetal's friend. There was no Sheetal. Before he could even form the words 'where is...' Sheetal emerged. Still standing behind her friend, she gently laced her fingers in Bittu's. The presence of the friend, and the touch of her shoulder against his, became a dam, holding back the couple's tears.

'Sheetal told me that she would be returning to the city soon and asked me to wait until then. Sheetal could not escape from the house, and nor could I enter. So, I used to climb up through a pipe stealthily, then use the stairs to come down. I tell you this, it was very risky. We were in danger of being separated forever should we have been caught or even suspected of being together. This is what led us to make our second escape.

'This time, we were not caught. Abandoning our jobs and familiar places, we moved from one city to another, from one house to the next. I worked as a manual worker. I had no choice but to sell the auto rickshaw, because its number plate was a dead giveaway. We had grown wiser due to our past mistakes. Days passed, and then months too. As time rolled on, a routine set in, giving our lives a semblance of stability. We borrowed money to get a place of our own—we would pay the loan back in small instalments. As the dust settled further, Sheetal got in touch with her mother. Over time, her mother began to come over and visit our house, but we never visited theirs. I already told you, it was Sheetal's doing that my relationship with my own mother was rebuilt.

'She asked me not to interfere, and then went to meet her. She invited them over to our house. My mother never talked to anyone; she thinks no end of herself, you surely saw that for yourself that day. But thanks to Sheetal's efforts, she began visiting us. Gradually, my brother too became friendly with us. Our lives continued to settle further. Sheetal spoke with my mother to try and get me my top surgery at the government hospital. I tell you this, Sheetal definitely had a knack for getting people on her side, and she managed to persuade my mother. Finally, she agreed to sign my operation papers. As an employee of the hospital, my mother and her family could avail of medical help free of all charges. We only had to pay for the medicines. Our expenditure was negligible, and what I received in return was… what can I say…' he gestured expansively, 'total freedom. A sense of self. Hard to describe in words.

'There is one thing; I'll tell you this, deep down, nobody ever really approved of our relationship. They simply closed their eyes, buried their true opinions. On Sheetal's side it was only her mother that cared, because she really loved her daughter, unlike my own mother. When we needed a lump sum of money to re- pair the house, she was the one who readily gave it to us. When Sheetal was around, her mother would come in the day. She nev- er spent the night with us, always leaving before evening fell.'

He had only just spoken of the support from Sheetal's moth- er, but in the next breath, Bittu was voicing his complaints about her. 'My mother-in-law could have done so much more, but she did not. When I think about it, she could have persuaded her sons and her husband to reconnect with their daughter. But in- stead, she chose to not admit her feelings to her family. I feel they would have accepted her, but she did not talk to them.'

Although Bittu felt that his mother-in-law could have done more to fix Sheetal's family relations, I feel that—it is most like- ly—as a woman, perhaps she had little or no decision-making power. I also wonder what she must have told her husband when she left the house for hours at a time. Visiting their son in the city? Or did she use shopping as an excuse? And what if her hus- band decided to cross-check? Sheetal's mother took that risk. On returning home, she may have faced his silence, or perhaps a del- uge of questions.

On one occasion, she was delayed in returning home. Shee- tal's father told her that he had phoned their son to ask how long ago she had left their house; without saying much, he may have implied a lot. Did these layered conversations conceal a disgrun- tled husband, or was he conveying a grudge against his wife for not supporting his ostracisation of their daughter? Did he want to communicate that he knew what was going on? Whatever the exact details of the situation, there is no doubt that Sheetal's mother would have had to bear the burden of all that was said and unsaid. Yet, she remained committed to her daughter, con- cealing her continued support for her exiled daughter from her husband and son. Every now and then, she even managed to give Sheetal and Bittu money from her savings. She carried spices, rice, wheat, and *dhals* for them. Yet Bittu seemed to have lost sight of that support. Perhaps, after years spent on the street and in shanty dwellings, he was too distracted by the novel comfort of coming home and working on the house. Perhaps he was too busy to notice the efforts made by Sheetal's mother.

'She was her father's favourite child,' Bittu went on. 'Right from childhood, she was stubborn, smart, and she had good looks—that added to her qualities. Back then it was Sheetal's mother who grumbled, "Do not pamper her so much." Or she would angrily advise: "Get her married, let her do some house work. All good women do it, let her learn." But the indulgent father paid no heed—he encouraged his daughter to clear the tenth class and take up nursing. But after her departure with me, the same father would not even mention her name, let alone talk about her. I thought he would at least come when he heard of his daughter's demise, but nobody did. Neither he, nor her mother, nor her brother, came to see Sheetal for the last time. Not even to inquire after their own grandchild. On the contrary, they tried to assert their rights over the grandchild, Neha, immediately following Sheetal's death, but not one of them came for her last rites. I completed all the rites along with a friend. Even her mother, she stayed away too.'

It was hard for Bittu to understand that Sheetal's mother must not have had much decision-making power. The family did not want anything to do with Sheetal, making it hard for her mother to support her publicly, no matter how much she may have desired to do so. Despite her position as a woman who was pulled in so many conflicting directions, her support for Bittu and her honesty became evident to us early on. And when we proposed a meeting with Sheetal's mother, she was there. For us, this meeting was a golden opportunity to finally find a way out of the bewildering maze of dilemmas we faced.

When the initial news of Sheetal's suicide stormed the headlines and a custody war between Bittu and Sheetal's parents became a raging issue, our organisation chose to publicly support Bittu as the rightful custodian of his and Sheetal's child. This support was not just for Bittu's individual case, but an opportunity to assert the rights of queer people concerning parenthood in general: a chance to put forward a non-biological, non-conservative, and yet very humane and justice-based perspective of life and these significant issues. We proceeded with our stance on the assumptions that the child had spent her life living with Bittu and would therefore be happier to continue to live with a familiar parent-figure.

Granted, we lacked adequate information regarding Bittu as an individual, and knew even less about Sheetal's family. We were not well-advised nor in any position to be able to assert whose hands the child would be better off in. In the absence of a will left by Sheetal, speculations alone were not sufficient rationale for taking sides. That was why it was necessary to meet with Sheetal's mother. Sheetal's death, and her reason for choosing it, was most likely multi-faceted and complex beyond comprehension. Still, facts that her mother might have known surrounding the circumstances could have at least offered some clue as to where and who the child would be better off with.

Couples, the same as and similar to Sheetal and Bittu, face numerous and multilayered struggles pretty much every single day of their existence. There had been constant rumours about them floating around the community in which they lived, but when the story reached the headlines, these whispers were finally known to be true: this couple that lived as 'husband and wife' were in fact two women! Socially, Bittu was most definitely the underdog.

And this was true legally as well—if Bittu were to be confronted by the rule of law, then based on the ideology that the family lineage can continue only within a marital union of man and woman, there was no way he could claim any sort of custody over Sheetal's child. As mentioned before, Bittu's case was an opportunity to publicly challenge such ideologies, so when talking to the media, we held Bittu to be the rightful claimant of the child. Taking corrective steps was an option both in terms of law and social acceptance, and although the path would be tedious, it did exist.

Sheetal's mother did not have a single complaint against Bittu and bravely shared with us the sad truth of Sheetal's earlier suicide attempts. We learnt that Sheetal's brother had also met the same fate. Perhaps Sheetal was more prone to depression than others? And her suicide was the final, irreparable lethal symptom. Furthermore, we were witness to the parental relationship and close bond that Bittu shared with his child. Here, we laid to rest the matter of where the child would be better off.

'The child is my memory of Sheetal,' explained Bittu. 'Those people have connections to the police service, they have power, whereas I, I am a poor man. A father unable to claim his rightful fatherhood. And why? Just because society cannot accept me. They are refusing a child's right to parental warmth and love because of their own prejudiced views! How do I assert my rights? And what about Neha's? What if they take her away? What can you do, Bittu? My thoughts were paralysed with the constant fear of losing Neha.'

Bittu was schooled on the streets, with neither roof nor master. He had survived solely due to his own wisdom, that he had developed through lived experiences. He learned that the measure of success lay in the hands of those who could wield a rod. What power did Bittu have against such people? The only advantage Bittu had was that he had nothing to lose. He recalled that when he had eloped with Sheetal, a police report had not been filed either of the times. And why? Reputation. Which, for Sheetal's family, was the worst thing that one could possibly lose. This was Bittu's only weapon: 'I went to the media myself and told them everything. Sheetal's family was terrified of any potential "loss of honour," and the adverse publicity that it would bring.

I'm sure they must have thought about their jobs as well. After the threat of such publicity, they retreated. That was how I was able to keep my daughter.'

Though Bittu was able to keep his daughter, the price he paid for speaking out tore his life apart.

Investigators, reporters, TV cameramen, and news gatherers all came knocking on his door. One after the other. They came in a never-ending stream that made it near impossible for Bittu to live in his own house. Rumours ran amok, leaving him defence-less against the onslaught of stories.

'Bittu lives here?'

'Yes, down the road. The girl who goes by as a boy.'

'What does he do?'

'He drives a *chagda ricksha*—'

'No! He does not do anything,' a bystander interrupted. 'He just plays carrom with boys.'

'So is he a boy?'

'I will tell you exactly who he is,' chimed in one neighbour. Lowering his voice, and bringing his mouth close to the ears of the truth-seeker, he said, 'He only looks like a boy, but she is re-ally a girl!' Another chipped in, 'Yes! I have seen *her* with my own eyes in the hospital, in the women's ward! And she told me not to tell anyone about it.'

'What?!'

'Yep, she had just undergone an operation... to be turned into a boy!'

'No, no, he is a *chhakka*. Not a boy, not a girl.'

After swimming through a sea of gossip, the reporters finally managed to catch Bittu and demanded the truth: 'Are you a girl? Your neighbour has told us everything.' 'Who told you? Who...' Bittu kept asking. Defenceless against the onslaught, he answered their questions with more questions.

Now out of its cage, Bittu's 'secret', previously unknown to the community, grew wings and flew through the neighbourhood, dropping whispers of rumours in its wake, including accusations of prostitution and other distorted non-truths. 'Something very wrong was going on in their house,' the neighbours said.

Bittu's recollection of his life with Sheetal was thus. 'I picked up Sheetal in the evening. Together, we rode home. It was routine for us to commute together daily. When Neha was old enough, she would sit in the front and all three of us rode together. We bought vegetables together, and at times we ate outside. Sometimes, we watched a movie in the theatre.' Their routines sound like those of a loving and wholesome family, but others were unable to see them as such.

'Before leaving the house, Sheetal began every morning by reading the Bible. I lit an *agarbatti* (incense stick) to the goddess. Both of us prayed to God and began our day. We celebrated all festivals together, whether it was Holi, Diwali, or Christmas. Our home was decorated with stars at one time, and with *diyas* at another. Neha was christened in a church. We took trips both to the church and to temples. Those were good days. We were happy then.'

The deeper Bittu delved into his past, the more the sharper edges of his story began to soften, allowing for warmth and colours to weave their way into his memories and let them become more beautifully embellished with details and the many hues of his imagination. You see, there is no truth or untruth to stories; it is the experiences, emotions, and the yearnings that take on extraneous forms. As I sat listening, a picture, as if painted by a skilful artist, of a happy family appeared before my eyes, making me even more aggrieved for the loss he had suffered.

Bittu continued, 'Yes, those were good days for us. We were happy. As participants in this game of playing man and wife. We poked fun at ourselves and at the society around us. I don't wear underwear, but each morning I would take the male boxers that I kept and spread them out on a line to dry, for everyone to see! It was almost like an inside joke for us. We laughed, so there was always a lightness and humour to being "outcasts" of society, as if we knew that the problem lay with them, and not with us.'

The fear of being 'outed' as two women living as husband and wife lurked beneath the veneer of everyday calm, and sometimes it leapt up like a flame, leaving a deep, dark smudge between them. There is fear in the certainty of punishment, but the fear in the uncertainty of being caught was corrosive. Laughing at a looming threat may bring some relief, but it does not eliminate it. 'Even while talking about it,' Bittu explained, 'we lowered our voices, afraid that reality may surreptitiously creep up on us.'

Bittu's life seemed to be a carousel—every time he settled down and managed to anchor himself to a routine, he was swiftly uprooted. His temporary 'homes' had included the streets of bustling cities, a veranda of the city's suburbs, a rundown hut on a roadside, to name but a few. For the basic needs that are usually fulfilled by having a home—air, light, bathing, washing, and relieving oneself—Bittu had to look outside of his dwelling place. Bittu lived in poverty, and in such conditions, I wondered if he had ever been lured into the underground world. Where he stood, it surrounded him, spread out uninhibited like an ocean, its waters blue and beckoning, as if bereft of the saltiness for the youth who saw in it a promise of a better life. Would it not be human to step into it? Did Bittu save himself from it? Just as the thought flickered in my mind, I felt uneasy to go where it took me. If Bittu was able to avoid such things, would he have been able to survive? His weathered strength of survival left me without answers or a clue of what the truth might be.

The haste with which the couple sought to achieve the ideals they had set for themselves compromised their dream of idyllic love. Sheetal had been through two abortions, but would not give up on having a child. Whilst carrying the third, she contracted tuberculosis. But she went through the full pregnancy, keeping her end of a promise she made: a child to complete their happy family. Bittu tried his best to earn more: 'I even pilfered some diesel from cars in the night and managed to get some cash.'

But slowly, tears began to appear in the relationship. 'You know, there is nothing like the first time when you love, and your love is returned in equal measure. But as days go by, it's never the same. I loved her, and she loved me, but it was not the same.' Suspicion, like a single strand of hair, seemed to have become caught between them. Barely visible, impossible to hold, and even harder to explain. 'I could feel it. Sometimes, it burst forth in irritability and outbursts of irrational anger. Earlier in the relationship, if there was any kind of dispute, we would make it up to one another. But during the last year or so...' Bittu did not complete his sentence.

Generally, for a heteronormative relationship and family, there is often a supporting ring of relatives present for times such as these. Traditions, festivals, and customs also act as a binding force. But for families like Sheetal and Bittu's, there is no such safety ring. They had to deal with these problems on their own. 'I know she felt I was changing. She told me so. But I could not ask her what was going on. I strongly suspected that she was involved with someone. I was angry and resentful.'

Listening to Bittu, I realised that even though the relationship was sinking into silences and drudgery, I heard the couple yearning to come together, to go back to those earlier times when everything was alright. As Bittu narrated certain incidents, I could see his brows furrow with pain and regret. 'She left me. One day, she left. She did not tell me. Not a word. She did not tell me...she left our house and went away. In a fit of rage, I told her to go, and she did. Neha was six months old. She had just started crawling. The child was still reliant on breast milk, but she left! After all this work and her longing to bring her into this world, she just left.

'I looked for her—morning, noon, and night. Walked every street of the city. Looked in all the places with even the slightest possibility of her having gone there. There was no trace of her. She went to her boss's house. Why? Diwali was just a few days later. I kept calling her. She would have seen my number flash on the screen, but she did not take my call. On the day of Diwali, I sat in our house with Neha. There were no lamps and no light. This was our child's first Diwali, and it was spent in darkness, without her mother.

'She finally returned that evening. I heard a shuffle at the door, I looked up and it was dark, since it was evening. I recognised the shadowy figure immediately. She came in with a box of sweets. Neha spread her arms and launched herself towards her. I threw the box of sweets, demanding to know where she had been, and "with whom" she had been. She did not respond. I could not talk to her. I was so agitated and helpless; jealousy and anger welled up inside me. I remember it too well—that long silence, swollen between us.'

As much as I did not want to linger upon the reasons that may have prompted Sheetal to end her life, I could not help but wonder. Had these everyday tensions and hostility turned all their communications sour? 'I can tell you this—there was no fight, no ugly incident that may have led her to take this step.' Bittu was thinking aloud, 'But when I look back, I start to wonder if perhaps I had stopped listening to Sheetal? We were both busy then. I was impatient too. I wanted to get everything done fast. I felt like I had waited long enough. I used to get angry, so angry. It was a mistake.' Had the weight of life's daily grind simply eroded the promises and commitment they had made to one another? Had joy slipped through those widening cracks, leaving only stained memories, and other dark, nameless wounds?

'Let me tell you honestly, when Sheetal returned that day, I was scared that she had come to take Neha away from me. I clasped Neha to my chest and lay awake the whole night.' After a long, long silence, Bittu reflected, 'I still cannot find an answer to why Sheetal had to go to a stranger's house.' To Bittu, this incident demonstrated Sheetal's alleged infidelity. Having found tenable grounds, his suspicion was like the colour running off a wet cloth, seeping through each layer of his waking thoughts. It stained his days and nights, troubling him. 'If someone had told me back then, when we were falling in love, that such relationships change, I could have never believed them. How can our nearest ones become the most distant without us understanding why? Sometimes it felt like, whatever it was, we had overcome the impasse, coming close to a resolution; at other times, it felt like we were standing at the cliff's edge.' In a tone of bitter sadness, almost inaudibly, he said, 'The truth is that it was never the same again.

'We used to sleep on the terrace. She got up early to give Neha her medicine, and did not return. When I saw her hanging from the fan, I pulled the bed and reached up to her to pull her down. She was still breathing. I called 108, but all she did was mutter "uh" and look at me. That was the end. People have told me I will be accused for her death, but what could I do? Now it is all over, I feel I could have…' and then haltingly, 'If I could have done some things differently…' His voice, flat and expressionless, faltered and stopped. Just for a split second, I saw his masculinity slip off its mantle and well up in the lump in his throat. Swallowing hard, he pushed it back. Such displays of emotions are generally forbidden to men. Bittu, I assumed, had acquired the skill with some difficulty. Using it now, he deftly turned away from me and the subject. I wondered what it was that he hid.

Watching him, I was reminded of the first day he had come to the organisation. His gait and appearance had the alertness of a cat as he carefully scanned the place. He was accompanied by a male friend. Much later, when we were able to laugh together at the scenario, he explained, 'I was coming to a strange place in a new city. I needed someone who could speak on my behalf. I was afraid of hidden cameras. I had to take precautions.'

That was the first time that I saw hints of an untold story that lay underneath whatever had hit the headlines. There was something about Bittu that made me uneasy and continued to baffle me later. That first time, we just heard the bare bones of his story, no details. I sensed his loss. Sudden death can leave a person without a sense of closure. I wanted to reach out, but his terse narrative left me shaken. I turned my gaze away. But what I saw when I looked up took me by surprise: his eyes had an inexplicable intensity, a shine which I had not seen, and then it disappeared. In one quick moment, it had vanished. I wondered if that was my illusion, and yet, the thought persisted: was it an invitation? Like a skilled performer, he knew exactly how to win over his audience, so that not a grain of doubt remained about his story. Perhaps he saw his desired effect on me and allowed himself a small flicker of a victory, or was it a reflection of me gravitating towards him, or merely the evening ray of light that slanted in through the window and touched his eyes for a fraction of a second? How do I explain it? Gestures and expressions have sensations, but there are no words that can say exactly what they imply.

But that day, long after we had finished, a feeling that there was a lot more unsaid stayed with me. Before that meeting, our only knowledge of Bittu—minus a few brief telephone calls—was what the newspapers had said about him. Bittu recalled meeting us for the first time, 'I did not know you all, but I decided to come. I told myself: Go Bittu, and see for yourself who this woman whose voice sounds so sweet on the phone is. I came because I was curious.' Then laughing aloud and holding both his ears with a shake of the head, he continued, 'And now that I know her, I can tell you, her voice is such a contrast to her no-nonsense temperament!' This confession of his was shared after some time, when we had become close and confident enough to share such thoughts with one another. It did make me wonder though… Bittu had come to see us two months after Sheetal's death, and the reason was that he was 'curious' to see the woman whose voice sounded sweet! He couldn't have gotten over Sheetal that soon, surely.

'The best of relationships do not allow for a totality of truth-telling' was something that Bittu taught me.

As the group began to get to know Bittu better, our fondness for him grew. But there were challenging times too. His gestures, for example him drawing the figure of a woman in the air, or his syrupy sucking sound. He would simply curl his forefinger in a perfect round over his thumb, holding up the rest of his three fingers, widen his eyes, and unabashedly wink at us, alerting us not to miss the pretty sight. Never did he hesitate to openly acknowledge his desire, such an outpouring of which rarely has sanction in our society; it is sanitised, kept out of reach, locked even in one's own inner recess, assigned to particular rooms and relationships. Yet here was Bittu, proudly owning his desires, as if putting them out for display. According to him, admiring women other than one's own wife 'taints no eye'. Sometimes, he would let out this huge, exaggerated, and theatrical lovelorn sigh. Bittu's openness surrounding sex and sexuality challenged me, sometimes leaving me puzzled as I failed to understand how he had acquired it.

As Indian society would have it, a man and a woman declaring to be 'in love' could only be viewed as legitimate in an endogamous marriage. And if so, for a man to see another woman would be expressly prohibited, or in the event of such, society would forbid talking about it publicly in the manner that Bittu did. The rule of silence is applied to women even more particularly, and as for an attraction between two women, it is totally and utterly unspeakable.

Bittu, for various reasons, could not be classified as being part of 'mainstream' society. And nor is he a woman. I did wonder, however, how he could have remained untouched by the socialising he must have gone through during his youth, that

was spent being viewed as a girl. Men are given greater leverage. Had Bittu managed to leverage the same sanctions as men?
From where had he acquired this openness that was viewed as
'shameless' in women? What kind of society had Bittu socialised
in? Had this socialisation had an effect on the outcome of this
story?

As I fumbled for words, and questions began to form, I began to hear what was unsaid in Bittu's story, in both told and
untold narratives. I learnt to pass over some of the unanswered
questions, to listen and accept answers that were fragmentary,
sometimes contradictory. I knew full answers would not be possible, so I learnt to simply listen.

One Sunday, we travelled to the city where Bittu lived and
visited him in the office of the transport company where he slept
and worked. After walking down lanes that led to other lanes,
and after passing several trucks, we entered the two-storied office of the transport company. There was a staircase to the right,
under which lay a small room which gave off an odour that made
no secret of its identity as a toilet. The room exactly opposite the
stairs was where Bittu's boss sat. From the curtained window in
the room, a slight line of light revealed a small space outside the
room, perhaps a verandah. That was all that was visible; the rest
was all covered, deserted, and silent. An indefinable air of ambiguity hung about the place.

Bittu never told us anything other than him being an er-
rand fellow in the *seth's* office. When we went to visit him, it
was he who fetched the cups of tea. And while we sat sipping,
he was positioned outside of the circle of tables and chairs in
which we and his boss sat. When the tea was finished, it was
Bittu who collected the cups onto a tray. All perfectly normal,
except, for some reason, the mathematics of hierarchy between
employer and employee just didn't seem to add up. Perhaps it
was we who were unable to add up the numbers, but there was
something about Bittu's bearing and conduct that conveyed an

aggressive sense of self, undiminished by the nature of his work or the presence of his boss, who I noticed seemed to look at Bittu every now and then, as if seeking approval out of the corner of his eye.

Bittu's employer, whom he referred to as *seth*, was married. 'But he likes men,' Bittu confessed later. 'He is like me,' Bittu tried to explain. As we grew closer to Bittu, and the dramatic edge to his voice began to soften, he began to open up: 'I told you before and I'll tell you again, in my experience "no one does a favour without taking one in exchange". My *seth* and I have a give and take relationship. I fulfil some of his wishes in return for the place he has given me to stay.'

Bittu recalled his time living with the *seth*. 'This was during the time when I had just gone to the media so that I could keep my daughter. I paid a high price for speaking out. When the news broke, I could not return to my own house. The monsoon rains had started, and I could barely see through the thick curtain of rain. Flashes of lightning illuminated the streets and the thunder deafened me. It was cold and wet. I finally had a home in the city, but I felt as though I could not go there; there were far too many prying eyes. But I had to take care of Neha and earn a living. I moved out of the house and returned to the streets, an anonymous outsider in the city crowds. And then the *seth* let me stay in his office.

'This was also the time when I had started interacting more regularly with you and your organisation. Before that, I had no idea that there were other people like me, and so many! I couldn't believe it. I thought I was alone, but finding people like me and receiving their support really helped me.'

His stay with the *seth* ran into a year. But as months went by, we began to hear a disgruntled tone in his voice, and he no longer wanted to stay with the *seth*. When we suggested returning to his own house as an option, he completely ruled it out. 'I do not want to ever go there again. I want to sell it.' Bittu suggested we talk to Sheetal's brother, who was in the police. He would be able to negotiate a good deal. He had the capacity to clear the dues, and could also locate a suitable buyer. Bittu naturally could not talk to him directly, so he wanted us to talk for him. Having met Sheetal's mother, the family knew of us, and our presence helped to open a dialogue between the two parties. We managed to arrive at an understanding that Bittu would present the documents related to the house, and after the transaction was completed, the two would mutually share the proceeds. Sheetal's brother agreed to take some responsibility in selling the house. Our meeting stayed focused strictly on the subject in hand. No reference was made to Sheetal at all.

Whilst negotiations regarding the sale were underway, an intriguing news story drew our attention.

In December 2009, the year that Section 377 was read down by the Delhi High Court only to be reimposed by the Supreme Court few years later, a regional newspaper published a story about the marriage of two women in an interior village by the Arabian Sea. This news was special to us for many reasons. Above the headline, there was a photograph featuring a man and a woman. Although the paper had declared their marriage as being between two women (despite one party having a different gender orientation), the report stated that their marriage was solemnised in front of 200 guests. The story was both incredible and filled with contradictions. We wondered to what extent the incident narrated in the published story had been possible due to the recent decriminalisation. Our organisation decided to visit the village to get an insider's view of the couple's life and find out how they overcame opposing families and the other barriers placed before them.

Rather than hiring a driver, it made sense to ask Bittu to chauffeur us there. It was appropriate to have community amidst us; visible identifiers lead to silently recognising similarities, and thus assist in closing the gap between 'us' and 'them'. Bittu agreed to our proposition. Our group consisted of two other trans persons and I as the only lesbian woman.

The nature of our visit, and us as a group approaching unknown people in an unknown place—in a controversial context—created an anxiety that we had barely acknowledged. But as we set forth, laughing and talking amongst ourselves, our anxieties soon dissipated somewhere along the smooth highway; as the car's speed swept up swirls of dust and air, we saw the limitless sky of freedom. Trees, fields, houses, huts, and human settlements became a blur as we sped along with a song in our hearts. These golden moments allowed us to briefly overlook Bittu's driving abilities, though never for long. We held our breath several times, thanking our stars for surviving a direct hit or being almost thrown off the road. Before we departed, we had asked Bittu if he could drive, to which he immediately nodded in response. 'Yes,' he proclaimed in a resolute voice, proudly flashing his license before us.

Finally, we reached our destination unhurt but completely shaken. 'You said you knew how to drive...'

'I do.'

'Oh, you do!'

'No, no. Yes, I mean, I had practised, but not that much. But you know it, if I had told you all that, would you all have let me drive? No, right? And look, I drove you safely, didn't I? Nothing untoward happened, we are all safe.'

This is how Bittu is. There is no telling what he might do, putting himself and sometimes others at risk. He may talk a lot, but he tells little. When conversing, though, he often says more than he intends to; he is like an overloaded wardrobe, its doors pressing open and giving a sudden glimpse into its hidden interiors. As a bystander, the onus is almost upon you to look away when necessary, because Bittu would not have even realised that the closet had opened, and that you saw the chinks he did not want to show.

We had almost reached our destination. Bittu walked quietly beside us as we made our way to the infamous couple's house. After only the barest formalities of introductions, it soon seemed as if we had all known each other for years. The one who identified as a man had a secret masculine name, Brij, known and used by his partner, Vasanthi. Only a short distance from their home was the vast shore of the Arabian Sea, and it was there we went to find privacy. Walking along the shore, beneath the orange glow of the setting sun, we shared our stories. Our religions, caste, professions, the places we came from, all different; yet, each of our stories featured footprints of recognisable struggles. We parted with heavy hearts and a promise to see each other again soon. By the time we returned home, a new dawn was breaking ahead of us.

Then one day, the couple from the shores of the Arabian Sea came to see us. They came for two reasons. Ever since Brij had seen Bittu and Virat, his dream of physically changing his gender had been reignited, especially when he learnt that Virat had received his surgery almost free of charge in a civil hospital. He wanted the correct information before proceeding with surgery: the formalities required, such as the documents, pre- and post-surgery medicines, and how long the whole process would take.

The second reason for their visit took us completely by surprise: a marriage proposal for Bittu.

Vasanthi continued, 'The woman we have in mind is my elder sister Kokila. She has been married. She has a son. She has been living with our parents for some time now. Her husband did not earn anything, and he beat her.' As surprising as it was— casually framing these, until recently, criminalised relationships within the paradigm of heterosexual norms—we wondered if adhering to them would be thus reproducing the same structures of power and inequality?

On the surface, the couple appeared to fit into mainstream society's relationship ideals, but their orientations meant that they could not conform completely to these norms. Did the use of mainstream terminology conceal critical differences? How best can we create visibility of these new beginnings and partnerships that portend change? These were questions that often came up amongst us, but raising them there, and at that moment, was not a good idea. This was a decision that had to be entirely left to Bittu. He had already expressed his loneliness and desire to leave the *seth's* employment, and perhaps this opportunity could act as a catalyst for the change he was looking for. Of course, we were happy to pass on the message to him.

'Has she divorced her husband?' we quizzed the couple.

'No, would that create a problem?'

'Bittu may not like that. It is just that, what if her husband raises some kind of problem?'

'I am quite sure he will not do anything. Besides, what is there to tell? If anything at all, we will say she is working there.'

Bittu decided that he wanted to meet the potential wife. And so, we went to do just that.

The hut, with its roof and crown of hay and bamboo logs, stood humbly under an intensely blue sky; its walls made from the paste of mud and cow dung. Built amidst twittering birds and trees and without a wall to demarcate it from the undulating plains, it was skilfully crafted to match nature's own beauteous forms that surrounded it. The obvious persistence of poverty was a visible irony in contrast to the bountiful nature and human skills on display; the gap between rich and poor, rural and urban, continues to be both wide and stark.

We had come primarily to seek parental consent and meet with the woman. Over tea and snacks, we discussed the issue of marriage, assuming they would resist the idea, but it appeared that the parents were agreeable to the notion. However, they did want to follow the traditional, tribal custom of bride 'price', which had to be paid by the bridegroom. Bittu was disappointed.

While this development took us by surprise, in retrospect, we realise that we should have anticipated such a possibility; as a community lacking role models, the traditional systems laid out for us were the only ones that were known. Arguably, we had already embarked upon this path by following an arranged meet between the 'boy and girl'. Obviously, Bittu was beyond anxious about the money needed.

Bittu's first meeting with Kokila appeared to be a success. Bittu extended his stay, and Kokila missed a day of work and wages. As they got to know one another, Bittu's geniality, peppered with humour, created laughter and fun. His willingness to take on work, and expenditure on daily necessities from a shop further away from the house, only added to his popularity. Even Kokila's son took a liking to him and enjoyed it when he lifted him up and sat him on his motorbike. Bittu liked Kokila, and Kokila liked Bittu. They exchanged telephone numbers and agreed to keep in touch before parting.

Soon enough, the pair were building a close relationship over long telephone calls, a development that we were not aware of. In fact, we did not learn about the seriousness of their relationship until receiving an unexpected angry call from Brij and Vasanthi, saying, 'We trusted Bittu, and this is what you all have done!' Confused, we could hear their rage over the static, accusing us of having a hand in the pair's affair. 'Human decency demands you divulge the whereabouts of Bittu and Kokila!' The truth was, we had no idea what had transpired between them and we had no idea where they had gone, but our plea of ignorance failed to convince them.

It took a while to piece the story together: Bittu had been to Vasanthi and Brij's village twice. After his second visit, when he stayed only for one day, Kokila disappeared. It was assumed she had returned to her family's house, but she did not. Her absence made the family uneasy, her mobile was unreachable, and she wasn't at any of her usual spots. Her parents assumed the worst; she had fled with Bittu.

We had no idea of the events that followed, and nor could we have predicted how the whole thing would have unfolded —we were in the middle of a fair and reasonable marriage settlement, after all. But midway through the proceedings, Bittu had to decide to suddenly change course, and we were the only ones left to account for him. We were clueless as to where he could have gone; Bittu had no home, nor any relatives. We had been left in the dark just as much as Vasanthi's parents, and we could offer them nothing in terms of a potential location where they might be.

Several months passed before the mystery was solved. As it turned out, a couple who had earlier eloped from their homes helped Bittu in bringing Kokila from her village. It was in this couple's new home that Bittu and Kokila found their first refuge after fleeing from their respective places. That adventure of escape was shared much later in the group. There was a very heated exchange about the reasons for keeping this plan a secret from the rest of us. Each of us tried to defend our respective points of view; there was very little ground that we could agree on. Much later, we learnt what had happened in the tiny room, with scarce household materials and prying neighbours. The young couples recalled, 'That night, what a night it was! Just two sheets over us, one for each couple. That was all that separated us. It was a night-long struggle, tucking in one end of the sheet while keeping the other fastened to fingers, attempting to muffle the sounds and disguise all the goings-on inside. It was a night to remember!' The two couples lived together for a fortnight before the neighbours began to whisper: some said they were a 'strange' lot, all of them, whilst others claimed they were all women involved in some kind of suspicious activities. Either way, their strangeness was enough for the landlord to want to get rid of them.

Bittu returned to his city of origin, and the other couple rented a house in another locality. After the news of their location and other details were leaked to us, Bittu called, three months later. Although he agreed to inform Vasanthi's family that Kokila was fine, he refused to reveal where they were currently located—'not yet,' he argued. And bound by a promise of confidentiality, we were unable to tell them either. The cold war between ourselves and Vasanthi's family continued.

As information about their daughter's well-being reached them, Kokila's family became less and less angry when they called to ask about any information we might have gathered. Over time, her father was able to forget the lines that had been drawn between us. And finally, the couple agreed to disclose their location to Kokila's family. It was about this time that Bittu's house was sold, which meant he finally had a bit of money in his pocket. Bittu already wanted to relocate, and so our organisation intervened to help him do so, and introduced him to a bank in our city. The community assisted him by finding him a job in an office, along with an affordable place to rent. It was a spacious one-room apartment; the kitchen was divided by a plastic sheet; the water had to be fetched from the tap outside, and they had to go to the toilet outside, but Bittu and Kokila were satisfied. 'I have a foothold in the new city. I have a place with my partner. And soon, I will find a better paying job. Together, we will manage.' He looked at Kokila; lean and dark, with her hair plaited down to her waist, she twirled her sari *pallu* between her fingers and simply nodded in affirmation.

As the couple settled down, I began to see a change in Kokila. She learnt how to drive a two-wheeler, spoke Hindi, and no longer restricted her attire to saris. She began to wear different clothes, and her monosyllabic responses blossomed into layered dialogue and conversation. Alacrity marked her gait, and a new, alert expression matched these changes. She discovered the city's roads and found shortcuts to her daily destinations. As well as seeing the pair at meetings, we would also often bump into them on their way to fetch groceries and run other errands, especially at one intersection. Often, we found Kokila standing there alone, and upon asking if she needed any help, she would say, 'No, do not bother, I am waiting for Bittu to come and pick me up.' At other times, we simply acknowledged each other with a wave and went on our way. A year later, Bittu told us they had moved to a locality with running water. A wall and a door separated the kitchen from the main room, and there was a washroom in their flat. 'We both work now.'

But work alone did not resolve the couple's problems. One night, well past midnight, the ringing of the telephone cut across our rooms, pillows, and quilts. Jerking the household out of sleep, I could hear Indira drawl 'Hello…'

'Hello,' she repeated louder this time.

I heard the mumble from the room next door.

I walked across, and switching on the light, asked, 'Who is it?' I was curious.

'Who else?'

'Bittu?!'

He was calling from the police station, wanting us to talk to the police officer on his behalf. A cis couple had run away from home, and the families had put forward Bittu's name as a suspect, likely to know the whereabouts of the couple. We asked Bittu directly, in front of the officer in charge, if he knew anything, at which Bittu strongly argued his innocence, guaranteeing that the Bittu we had now known for several years could not be a party in matters such as these.

'Ah, we got off lightly that day,' Bittu recalled that particular night. 'But do you remember the other night, about a year after that one… the night of 15 January 2015. I remember the date so well because it was the night of *Uttrayan* (the kite flying festival). There was a huge fight between me and my neighbours, they had accused me of harassing their daughter. Of course, I didn't do anything! But all their relatives and people from their community gathered around us. We had nobody on our side. And then it got violent. I had to defend myself! The police were called; although they tried to settle the matter, it soon flared up again. So, they hauled us all into the police van. I called you both from the police station, remember?!'

Of course, we remembered.

'I anticipated trouble. People locally knew me as a man, but on paper, I was still a female. I had an awful feeling that the discrepancy between my appearance and my documents would create even more trouble. It was better to say that I was a woman from the get-go, to get it out there before they could start suspecting me of all kinds of things. I also knew that, as a woman, there would be some advantages, such as being taken to the station in the morning. I was on dangerous grounds, in a place where my choice of gender could be used against me. Although I severely hated the idea of labelling myself as a woman, that's what I told them I was. To which the neighbours protested, most ironically. "He is a man!" they scoffed at me, calling me a liar.

'I was shoved into the van and taken to the police station. We were all asked to get out, without a veneer of politeness. The tone soon became acidic as we were commanded to enter the room on the left. Yellow light from a naked bulb streamed down at us. I was blinded by the intensity and almost fell over as I was shoved into a far corner of the room towards a bare wooden bench. "Sit," I was told. I sat.'

We arrived to the policeman grumbling about having to work during the holidays before he pointed Bittu out to us. 'He says he knows you well. Those people there, standing behind you, they are his neighbours. They say he was harassing their daughter. When they tried to stop him, he abused them, and beat them up! But now he says that they beat him up, that he was merely defending himself. And, he even claims to be a woman, indeed, a woman!' Cursing under his breath, he went on, 'He knows your organisation, he says, that is why he called you people. We will have to verify his sex.'

Bittu remembers, 'I froze when I heard this. I do not know how, but I remember feeling that the light had grown more intense. Around me, all I heard was a babble of angry voices, loud laughter, and the shuffling of feet. And then suddenly, I recognised my neighbour's face as he surfaced over the crowd, menacingly pointing towards me, and saying, "We know him! And he is not a woman. We know that he lives with a woman!"

'After that, the scene transformed, like a spreading fire. Within seconds, a derisive collective laughter engulfed me with the choicest of abuses. I was seen as a man playing to be a woman! And that neighbour of mine, he would not stop, he went on and on, unravelling my story with his arms waving wildly: "But he lives with a woman in our neighbourhood, this woman here..." Everyone turned to look at Kokila, who had just entered the room. "With her! He claims to be a man. They have a child too! Would you believe, a woman indeed? Two women with a child?! Answer me that!"

'Then I saw the police inspector take the organisation's card that you handed him. I don't know what you said to him, but I heard what he said: "You work with women, madam? It is people like them..." The incomplete sentence bristled with an unnamed danger. "You do not know madam, what kind of..." He turned to look at me, "You do not know what these people are!" Then he went on to so arrogantly condemn me, so loudly, in front of everyone, "What do you think you are, dressed like a man, what kind of a woman are you? You tell me... or I will have to do the needful..." It was a threat that had a familiar, nauseous smell. And the chill it carried did not wane. We are the butt of jokes so often, but this was dangerous. We knew that.

Bittu pondered, 'You know, all my life, I have struggled to live by the identity that I strongly feel is mine. And there I was, pre-

senting myself as a woman, only to be disbelieved, to be tossed up
in jeers, derided, and laughed at. Even for self-protection, I could
not shed the male identity that made me who I am. I said a small
prayer to Sai Baba. The officer ordered us to come out. I saw my
neighbour with his crowd of supporters in close consultation, and
I could sense their mood for compromise.'

The policeman was eager to sort this out, then and there,
so as not to be left with a case on his hands, especially now that
he believed Bittu was in fact a woman, and a woman-to-woman
harassment case did not have the same significance. Proceeding further was only going to lead both parties into a long and
drawn-out battle in court, which neither wanted, or could afford.
And so, apologies and compromises were swiftly made.

'But do you remember?' I did remember. 'The policeman had
asked who Kokila was, and she tried to give the truthful answer,
"I am his partner..." but we had quickly interrupted her, saying
that she was just his friend!' I recalled that moment well. There
were several reasons for quickly stamping out Kokila's words before they had a chance to be imprinted upon the khaki uniform.
For that night, Bittu was a woman. Yes, the NALSA judgement
had been passed a year ago, but its effects were nowhere to be
seen, not here, nor at the state-level; our everyday lives continued
to be lived under the shadow of Section 377. Who was to know
how Bittu and Kokila's relationship could be construed? In an
act of panic, the two of us had hurriedly attempted to hide their
partnership.

Since that night, we have gone through that scene over and
over: the way the policeman looked at us, and how he went on to
say, 'I want to ask you something… something, you would know.
Is this relationship… would you know, I mean do you… think
they are…' He came up close. All four of us looked the other way,
not meeting each other's eyes. The word 'lesbian' resounded like
an abuse around us, eroding our identities; the word that was so
proudly claimed on the streets during the Pride marches lay be-

draggled when uttered in a low tone that hissed so venomously. We did not wait around to hear more. We hastily moved out of the policeman's proximity and out of his sight.

That night left us all intensely aware of the issues diverse gender identities and same-sex relationships are fraught with, even after NALSA. A year since the judgement, nothing had really changed. Though some rights may have been articulated, they did not yet exist in police stations, in lives that needed them.

Of course, we could rely on Bittu to philosophise the situation. 'There is one thing I want to tell you, and you write it for me, for everyone to read: Nothing may change in our lifetime. But there is one thing that I have learnt from my experience—whatever scares you the most, or is used to scare you, if you do that very thing, then there is no longer anything to fear. No, nothing. You can become fearless.'

Section 377

It was the same year we went to visit Mataji, 2009, when the Delhi High Court initially struck down Section 377, eight years after the Naz Foundation first filed the PIL case, and after a legal struggle lasting a decade. Although there hadn't been a single reported case of anyone charged for homosexual acts under Section 377 within the last fifty years,[54] the law's existence created and allowed for stigma that had detrimental effects on the queer community, whether it be the multiple cases of gay men being arrested, blackmailed, entrapped, and conned out of money by the police;[55] forbidding the distribution of condoms in prisons rife with HIV/AIDS;[56] or the discrimination faced at work and in other walks of life.

---

[54] Gupta, Alok. 'Section 377 and the Dignity of Indian Homosexuals.' *Economic and Political Weekly* 41, no. 46 (November 18, 2006).

[55] Ibid.

[56] Malik, Varun. 'Section 377 Of IPC Quit India: The Tension between the Human Rights of LGBT and Normative Values.' *International Journal of Research in Social Sciences* 3, no. 2 (May 2, 2013): 144–150.

It wasn't just socio-economic and health disparities that Section 377 manifested itself as; most poignantly, Section 377 had debilitating effects on the self-esteem and mental health of homosexuals, even though it involved not physical force but more, the subtle dynamics of representation.[57] Although one may have been able to knowingly and vocally object to the condemnation of homosexuality, the mere existence of the law still affected one's personal identity and relationship with the world and others around them.[58] So for the queer community, the reading down of Section 377 was symbolic and a call for celebration: now we could change public attitudes and erode stereotypes;[59] we could follow in the footsteps of other countries, by using it to influence public opinion to pave the way for future rights and legislation.[60]

Following the initial striking down of Section 377, there were stories of same-sex couples turning up at police stations asking for them to help attain their 'right to marry' after eloping from their families.[61] These couples were met with confused blank stares, and perhaps a laugh. No such rights existed. Decriminalisation created no rights. Any legal changes that undo discrimination without providing legal rights have very little impact for women.[62] There were swamps of grey areas and ambiguities that we were left to muddle through—the issue of child custody, for

---

[57] Suresh, Mayur. 'I'm Only Here to Do Masti.' In *Law Like Love: Queer Perspectives on Law*, edited by Alok Gupta and Arvind Narrain. Yoda Press, 2011.

[58] Ibid., 469.

[59] Aloni, Erez. 'Incrementalism, Civil Unions, and the Possibility of Predicting Legal Recognition of Same-Sex Marriage.' *Duke Journal of Gender Law and Policy* 18, no. 105 (2010). https://scholarship.law.duke.edu/cgi/viewcontent.cgi?article=1185&context=djglp.

[60] Waaldijk, Kees. 'Standard Sequences in the Legal Recognition of Homosexuality – Europe's Past, Present and Future.' *AUSTRALASIAN GAY AND LESBIAN LAW JOURNAL*, 1994.

[61] Thangarajah, Priyadarshini, and Ponni Arasu. 'Queer Women and The Law in India.' In *Law Like Love: Queer Perspectives on Law*, edited by Alok Gupta and Arvind Narrain. Yoda Press, 2011.

[62] Ibid.

example, which created a swell of debate when Bittu's story was splashed across the newspapers.

Politically, the repealing of Section 377 was a great feat. But for many of the queer women and trans men we knew, it didn't make anything easier; in fact, it was arguably more uncomfortable. Now that LGBT+ rights were a feature of public discourse, it created fear for those women who were 'not out'. Before all of this, walking around with short hair and in pants may not have turned heads, but now that 'gay' and 'lesbian' were words far more common in everyday conversations, could somebody recognise how they identified? This was a real fear. Would people be talking about them? Physical attributes that were once codes within the community could now be potential markers for the public to conspire about their sexual and gender identities.

It is commonly agreed that Section 377, pre and post its reading-down, had a disparate effect on women and men.[63] As homosexual acts between men were mostly carried out in the public sphere, it was they who bore the brunt of its punishments and could breathe a bit easier when it was gone. For women who could keep their same-sex acts and desires hidden in the private, the explosion of homosexuality into public discourse tore holes in the silences that allowed for them to live in some comfort. In a Vikalp survey of queer women and trans men, only 47 per cent even knew anything about Section 377.

A year after the judgement, when our office was pelted with stones and swarmed by a crowd of a hundred and fifty people shouting 'lesbians, lesbians!', there was no magic shield that Section 377 could materialise to protect us. Laws are merely abstract concepts in these situations. In order to receive police protection from the mob, we had to deny any allegations of sexuality; we

---

[63] Thangarajah, Priyadarshini, and Ponni Arasu. 'Queer Women and The Law in India.' In *Law Like Love: Queer Perspectives on Law*, edited by Alok Gupta and Arvind Narrain. Yoda Press, 2011.

had to use that old 'just friends' excuse. It was apparent that the erosion of stigma and stereotypes would be just that—an erosion, gradual and really, really slow.

17

No, No, We Are Not Hurt So Badly That We Cannot Move

In April 2010, two women contacted Sabrang/Vikalp, seeking protection against their families' attempts to separate them. It was Nikita's upcoming wedding, just a few months away, that compelled the couple to hasten their getaway, one month ahead of plan. Before this, Nikita had successfully dissuaded the other prospective husbands her parents made her meet. Whenever the parents allowed a separate meeting with the potential bridegrooms, she showed no interest in them. 'My behaviour was so utterly rude that it left them with no option. At times, I sat there with such a stubborn look on my face that my rejection of the proposal was obvious. I certainly did not present myself as a good woman brought up with an understanding of "tradition and honour". Once, I even wore makeup that made me look dark.' However, the wedding in July was fixed successfully. Having successfully resisted the earlier suitors, Nikita had felt confident that she would be able to do so again. But this time the family did not arrange for Nikita to meet the boy alone. She kept protesting, but her voice fell on deaf ears.

The dictates of 'family honour' destine marriage for the daughter of a family. The rule fits rigidly like a collar that could not be loosened, even if she was the only child. Allowing a woman to choose a husband for herself might threaten that so-called honour. But Nikita's parents had a different sort of problem at hand: Nikita's intimacy with another woman. Though this detail was never specifically spoken about, they saw marriage as an antidote for the situation. Nikita's parents did not overtly impose the marriage, nor did they directly confront their daughter or her 'friend', Avani. Instead, they made it seem as if they were going along with their daughter's choices.

In a desperate effort to avoid marriage, in her naïveté, Nikita confessed to her family that she wished to live with Avani. But they brushed it aside as a childish whim, telling her that 'such things are not possible'. But the family also acted as if they were understanding, and they assured her, saying, 'Meeting with a boy does not amount to marriage. We will go back home and decide.' Upon the family's return home from this meeting, she learned that the boy had agreed to marry her. Her family went ahead and began to plan her wedding. Nikita and Avani had planned to leave their homes once Avani had finished her exams, but now with a wedding approaching, their plan had to change.

It was at this point that they first contacted Sabrang, and it was made clear to them that, as adults, they had rights to take decisions about their own lives. Sabrang encouraged them to think through the consequences of their decision and carefully examine their plans to elope, and then aided them in their preparation and assisted in coming up with a strategy for how to proceed.

The idea of leaving home raised a number of issues. The actual act of leaving the house, for one. Travel would involve reservations, which could mean interactions at counters managed by familiar people. It did not matter whether they used real names or fake ones; that wouldn't take them very far. Buses and trains going through fixed routes could be intercepted. Information travels faster by word of mouth. The use of their mobiles would certainly lead to detection. Sabrang also advised them on which important documents to carry with them when they left. Withdrawal of money from bank accounts should be done without evoking suspicion. Even the bare necessities, when packed, added to the conspicuousness of two girls embarking on a journey. The exact time of exit becomes crucial in planning, and the inability to know that precisely is what makes the success of most exit plans unpredictable. In these conditions, getting out and arriving safely away from home was like finding a small dry patch amidst floods.

Sabrang suggested that they book tickets to Bombay and get off in Vadodara, but this was not feasible in this case as the train to Bombay left at a time when the girls could not reach the station. Earlier, when they had planned to get away, they were recognised at the station. Finally, it was planned that two members of Sabrang would drive there and pick them up at a convenient time and place. The son of one of the Sabrang members, a supporter in our work, would drive with Sabrang members, so that he could ride back in Avani's new motorcycle, one of her favourite things in the world. No one in the family used it besides her, and in her absence, the bike would simply be there, collecting dust and dirt, and would be ruined in its neglect. It simply made more practical sense to have one's own transportation in a new city.

The plans were all put in place and on the day of departure, just before taking the leap to leave home, the couple made one last attempt to dissuade the groom from marriage. If it worked, it would give them some time to better prepare themselves. They wrote letters to the boy and made anonymous calls saying that the bride was 'of a questionable character'. Certain that the groom would now turn away, the two women began slowly taking their clothes and other necessities from their homes to another place for safekeeping until the time for their getaway came. Unfortunately, the boy paid no attention to their efforts. Meanwhile, Nikita's family ran up the wedding preparation expenses to lakhs, and the two women scurried back and forth with their rainy-day grains. This went on until one day when Avani's mother spotted the bulging bag on her daughter's shoulder and asked what she was carrying to college. 'Just books and computers,' she said, but her mother was not satisfied.

Avani's mother disapproved of Nikita's daily presence in their house. She tried to discourage their friendship by preventing her daughter from hanging out with Nikita. Often, the excuse was Avani's mother's health. A diabetic with high blood pressure and heart troubles, her claim over Avani's time and her help in household chores stayed firm and in place. Having grown up under these circumstances, Avani had become quite adept at cooking and cleaning, in addition to all the odd jobs she did. She had also learned to drive. Her father depended on her too. While he held a government job and their son worked in Delhi, it was Avani who took care of the daily chores at home. She was the kind of student who did her exam preparations at the last minute and passed. Amidst all this, she also worked as a sales promoter in a company.

Even though Nikita's growing presence continued to annoy Avani's mother, things were getting along just fine up to a point. It all started with what was only a tiny speck in the routine which had carried no hint of the storm it would raise. It started small, when Avani's mother noticed her daughter's bulging bag and asked her husband to make sure that their daughter was indeed going to college. He found that the girls had not attended college for many days. But instead of telling his wife, he asked his daughter where she had been. The question alerted her. She realised that her father had gone to their college. Instead of being discouraged by this development, she responded aggressively, saying that she did not attend college because she had a lot of work to do and errands to run. Knowing that her father would not like having this conversation with his wife, she offered to talk to her mother and explain things to her. But he did not want that because he knew his wife would be upset. They left the matter there, but it rang an alarm for Avani and Nikita.

The women realised that they both were under parental scrutiny in different ways. While one was being forced to marry, the other one's mobility, which was already restricted, was now being closely monitored. Taking note of the suspicions and full vigilance they were being subjected to, they cancelled the plan with Sabrang. This was the third time that their getaway plan had been cancelled.

For us at Sabrang, it was hard to read and understand their intent from their updates over the phone. Even though it did not happen frequently, we at Sabrang did occasionally deal with the 'cries of wolf' so, we wondered if this was one such cry for help. The advance for renting the vehicle had been paid, and two Sabrang members were all set and waiting with the car that was to take them to Alwar with food, water, addresses, names, and numbers. Risky as it was, it still had the lure of the bond that is formed between people sharing similar struggles in life. We were one; however, that oneness lay dissipated, demolished just minutes before departure. The abruptness of such cancellations left a void. Then, the reflection began.

To be fair, all that the couple knew about Sabrang was through a widely read mainstream Hindi magazine, which did not have our number or address. Humsafar was the group that had the number and a name. It was from them that they had learned about us. We wondered what prevented the two from leaving. Was it the fear of stepping into the unknown? Or the fear of relying on us, the people at the other end of the phone calls, people with unknown identities, names, and addresses? After all, they had no means to verify the information they had about us. Or, perhaps, they had been caught and were not mere suspects, as they said? The weight of the endless possibilities settled in, leaving a lingering sadness.

Nikita's imminent marriage to a man hung like a sword over the couple. It could tear them apart. Hoping to be able to resolve things while still staying at home, they attempted once again to dissuade the boy from marrying Nikita. They wrote to the groom, casting aspersions on the bride-to-be's morals. This time, the boy was enraged, and he informed Nikita's parents of the letters and their contents. It was the last straw that pushed Nikita's family to hunt down the culprit who had posted the letters. The girl with short hair, dressed in jeans, was identified. All hell broke loose when Nikita's parents descended on Avani's house and expressed their outrage, shouting until they were hoarse. Avani's parents stood aghast. Nikita came to explain that since she was being forced to marry, it was she who had written the letters, not Avani. She had protested the marriage right from the beginning and was not about to pin the blame on her friend. The plan to elope, which they had recently abandoned, finally had to be picked up once again.

In the meantime, we at Sabrang thought that since there was uncertainty about the arrival of the couple, it was best to continue with the usual routine of work, which took us out into the rural area and put us farther away from Baroda. While in the field, the phone suddenly rang, flashing Avani's name. It was puzzling, because the last time we had communicated, she had said that she would be changing her number and that no matter how things panned out, she would not be available at that number any longer. So, who was it, we wondered?

I pressed the blue button, and from the other end came an urgent whisper.

'We have left.'

'What?'

'We are coming in my Alto.'

'Alto? Your car?'

'Yes. But we hit a divider somewhere near Bhilwada, I think. Our clothes are soaked in blood.'

'Blood? Are you hurt? How bad is it? You need to go to a hospital immediately. Where are you? We will come.'

'Somewhere near Jaipur. No, no, we are not hurt so badly that we cannot move. Both our noses are injured, and it hurts a lot...

we ended up slamming our noses against the dashboard when I had to brake. We were going full speed when the car ahead did not allow us to pass...We took a ride with someone who was passing by. He saw it all. We have transferred our luggage into his car.'

'And your car?'

'We will have to abandon it. The engine's stopped, it is torn apart from the bonnet, and the door has dented in. We were locked into the car and Nikita almost fainted; I somehow managed to open the door and get out. Now, we are on our way.'

'Let us know how you are doing there and inform us as soon as you know exactly how bad the injuries are and if we should come.'

'No, no. You stay there. We will keep you informed.'

It became imperative that we move closer to Baroda in case the girls decided to continue their journey or if we were needed there. As we drove back, it became clear over the next several hours that the girls were determined to continue their journey onwards to Gujarat, and specifically to Vikalp. After receiving some first aid and using semi-fake names for themselves, they boarded a bus for Baroda on the night of 1 June, giving us the name, number, and the time of arrival from the conductor's phone.

They reached Kala Ghoda Circle in Baroda around 4 a.m. that day. When they called, we rushed over to them. The streets were still asleep. There were no signs of travel-weary passengers, no buses, no luggage, and no two women, just silence. People who are compelled to live on the margins master the skill of merging into the background seamlessly. The dark light of the early dawn protectively covered the sharp and separate outlines of the world about us.

We called the number from the received calls and walked as directed. Peering down the empty road further away from Kala Ghoda, we spotted Avani emerging from the shadowy edges.

Short hair, shirt, and pant. Then we saw Nikita. She sat on a bag, her head turned towards us, anxious, tired, and waiting. They smiled, slightly restrained under their protruding, bandaged noses and the watchful eyes of the conductor. We quickly gathered up the luggage and sped past the public space and into the privacy of our exchanges.

Alienated and yet at home at last, they began to talk; 'We had the accident on the Bhilwada Highway. While we were sitting in the other guy's car, I kept feeling faint looking at the blood the way it was spurting out. But I kept talking to our saviours on the phone, and I did not want the man asking questions. We chose a private hospital for that reason. It works faster and identification would be harder,' they reasoned. 'The doctor there has advised a minor operation.'

We agreed that it was the first thing that needed attending. Much later, days after each of us had told our side of the story, they confessed, 'We did not expect such older women.' I thought to myself, grey hair like ours tells of the presence of people like us in times gone by. People don't know all the wounds we had to bandage to survive those times.

Later that day, everyone helped the pair settle in at Vikalp. Feeling safe and comfortable, they relaxed and slept after their long and stressful journey. We began to plan the next steps, thinking about homes of Sabrang members, as the space in Vikalp would be the first to come under the scanner. The first two or three days, we would have to be careful. What would our strategy be if the family came here looking for them? The police would be looking for them sooner or later. It would not be long before the calls would be traced to Baroda and finally, here. While hiding was not an indefinite possibility, it was useful for buying time to prepare legal protections. What would be the best options for availing those, the ones that were the safest and that would work?

We had asked the girls to get a proof of their age. We all agreed that something needed to be sent in writing to the police in Alwar, with documentary proofs of their age, saying that leaving their homes and families was necessitated by the coercion to get married. Of the two reasons for running away, only the latter needed to be revealed.

'But what about me? What do I say?' Avani asked.

One member of Sabrang suggested, 'You accompanied her as a supportive friend.'

Then we moved on to wondering if we should keep the Gujarat Police informed. Would that be safer? After all, as part of the state, they were duty-bound to protect, but the question that rattled us was, would they really do so? Even as we looked into various possibilities, we felt the need to connect with the larger community. They would understand this contradiction of walking one step forward and two steps back. We started contacting LBT groups, friends, and lawyers to think through and lay out a plan for the next few days. We turned again to Humsafar to see if they could post letters by the two women from Mumbai to keep their location concealed. We called the Alternative Law Forum Bangalore and the Human Rights Law Network to get a legal perspective. We also contacted Lesbians and Bisexuals in Action (LABIA) and Sangama for shelter for the couple, if the need arose. Throughout the planning process, we continually engaged with Nikita and Avani. We asked them about the likely steps their families would take and then thought about how we would potentially deal with that response. That night, we felt that the safest space for them to sleep was at a volunteer's flat in Alkapuri. A volunteer from Canada would never be suspected. Besides, they had a place where the girls could comfortably rest.

3 June

The office was quiet. No one was around. The girls were in a hospital in Vadodara. Avani was having surgery on her nose, and Nikita was getting stitches. Ankit, a member of Sabrang who was around the same age as the couple, stayed with them in the hospital. As their peer, she softened the rough edges of entering a new city and being at the hospital the very next day.

While the couple was away, the scene at Vikalp was slowly beginning to escalate. 'Someone has called,' a Sabrang staff member exclaimed. 'We don't know who it was. They asked where the girls are.'

The interlude was finally over. This was bound to happen sooner or later. The family had probably traced the calls that had been made during the time the getaway was being planned. Things became instantly hectic. The couple had just returned from the hospital when the news of the call electrified the atmosphere at Vikalp. Both of them stumbled down the stairs sleepily and joined the search for correct police phone numbers for Alwar on the computer, as everyone huddled around the buzzing screen. As planned, the police in Alwar had to be informed that the pair had come of their own free will and without any coercion. The names, numbers, and addresses of the Alwar police had to be searched and verified. But the search on the computer was only partly successful. Contacts within Rajasthan helped us get the numbers and the names, but we stuck with designations alone as Nikita and Avani wrote out the letters to the concerned police officials and to the police station under whose jurisdiction the houses of both girls fell.

To avoid being traced, a far-off city was chosen as the place to fax the letters from. It was not too far, but was far enough for no one to come searching around Vadodara. 'Come on then, let's go, hurry up.' With that general agreement, all of us piled into the car. The sun descended as we sped away cutting through the darkness on yet another crest, the end of which lay uncertain before us like the road we took.

On the way, we received a call from an unknown number. Something must have been up, so we pulled over so that the staff member who was driving could answer. As soon as the phone was answered, a man's voice immediately began speaking. We quickly came to know it was Avani's brother. He spoke loud and gruff; thanks to the pin-drop silence, everyone in the car could hear him. Pretending to be another staff member's brother, she claimed to know very little about the couple. She said her sister was 'strange, always up to something', fabricating a character. Telling half-truths, she played innocent, putting their worries at rest in order to buy time for strategising. She promised to keep him updated as soon as any new developments arose. It was also planned that the two should call their parents from the same place.

Once we reached our destination, we drove around looking for an STD/Fax shop. Finally, we pulled over somewhere, and Avani, Nikita, and Ankit got out to search on foot. The group decided it was best for the three to go alone to prevent and confuse further identification because the fax and calls would likely be traced and inquiries would follow. Furthermore, women who looked like men would be a dead giveaway.

We watched as they left the fax shop and walked across the street to another STD stand to call their homes. The faxes were sent successfully to:

The Superintendent of Police, in Alwar Rajasthan

The IG headquarters in Jaipur

The Police Inspector, Police Thana Rajat Nagar III

Proof of age for both was attached, sent from Shop Number 320, Bus Stand, National Plaza.

Avani told us that her mother tried to persuade both girls to come home. 'My mother said that they would accept Nikita into our home.'

Nikita's parents merely responded in monosyllables. She felt that they had given her up as the black sheep of the family and had severed all ties with her.

Sharing these responses and tallying one another's sense of what this translated into, we all quickly realised it was just a ploy to trick them into going home. Genuine approval of the couple

seemed highly unlikely for both families. Nikita's parents' acquiescence felt too ominous. It left us with an indefinable unease.
Avani's mother was willing to accept Nikita immediately after the
runaway. Such a complete change from the day-to-day vibes of
hostility that Nikita had experienced was unbelievable.

It was a reaction the script of which read: the offer of candy
will bring the child back home. A slight suturing would bring
it all back to normalcy again. Nikita's family was no better. Far
from the severance that Nikita read, it was a way to connect, lay
their hands on her, and get her married to a man of their choice.
After all, her marriage had been fixed, and as a woman, she had
chosen it of her own accord. Women are rarely allowed this freedom in practice. This choice in particular, of love and intimacy,
undid everything. Avani shared that her mother had advised Nikita's family not to allow her out at all after the incident of the
letters had blown up in their faces.

The responses by their parents, and what we heard, did not
look good. Both of them echoed our thoughts when they said,
'We will not go home. It is because they think we are on our way
to Mumbai; that is why they are so welcoming. It is one way to
stop us from going to Mumbai. We told them we have jobs and a
place to stay there.'

Silence, rife with speculations, filled the car as we rode back,
tension and exhaustion consuming us all. The two sat together, fingers interlocked, comforting each other with whispered
words. Once home, we all fell asleep instantly.

4 June

When we came to the office in the morning, Avani's brother
called. He spoke with the same activist, still believing she was
a staff member's older brother. 'The police received a fax last
night, sent from a town called Kalol. This is close to you, no? We
checked the number and called the STD stand to inquire; apparently there were three people… Do you know the third person?'
'No, I am not aware who that person is. All I know is the girls are

on their way to Bombay,' she replied. 'Yes, that is what Avani told me when she called as well.' They chatted for a while, and she assured him that the girls were in a safe place. 'They are smart, and as adults, they know what they are doing. Do not worry for their safety.' She then promised to keep him updated on their whereabouts and well-being as soon as she heard any news.

Letters were also sent by post to:

The Superintendent Police at Army Area, Alwar, Rajasthan

The Police Inspector Thana Rajat Nagar III

The letters were sent from Vadodara, using the address Shop Number 302, Bus Stand, National Plaza. This precaution was intentional for continuity and so that the girls' whereabouts would remain unknown.

Later that evening, they were in very good spirits. We cooked and ate together, and they shared their love story. 'I always attended extra sessions and games led by Nikita just to be near her. I started slowly by giving her mix CDs filled with romantic songs. Finally, we had our first date on Christmas Day.' Nikita responded with a small smile on her face, saying, 'We were both speechless that night. Neither of us had any words to express the connection we felt.' One week later, Nikita said 'I love you' and Avani's response came almost instantly: 'I love you too.' From that day on, they would meet regularly, passing the night away listening to each other's voices on the phone.

Avani continued to shower Nikita with affection, frequent gifts, and bouquets. As the days went by, their love grew; after more than three years of knowing one another, promises of commitment were exchanged. From day-to-day meetings, they began to now envision a shared future and fondly dreamed of co-parenting a child. 'Ayati if she is a girl, and Shubh if he is a boy,' they shared with us in a chorus of laughter, amidst all the uncertainty and the absence of affirmation from their families. During this crisis, away from comfort and security, they had each seen sides of their families and themselves that did not add up to what they had imagined. Revisiting these shared dreams aloud in affirmative spaces was a reminder of the place they had hoped to reach, to legitimise those dreams. It was a way of transitioning from home to another place. Memories scaffold us in a time of crisis, lending support to return to dreams and imagination, to give us the strength to renovate, innovate, and invent, and to finally allow us to stand up on our own.

Since arriving in Baroda, Avani had requested her family to send her schoolbooks several times. Facing life on her own had further convinced her that the completion of her exam opened up greater earning opportunities. Since both families did not appear to completely reject them, the two women continued to make an effort to rebuild relationships with their families. Even though the families spoke with a semblance of acceptance of the other partner, neither family genuinely tried to extend themselves unconditionally. Avani's books never arrived. Her father was too busy, her mother could not go out to post the books, and her brother had taken leave during the time that she had fled. He stood by his parents then. Though her brother expressed concern over his sister's safety and well-being, he did not think it fit to send money. The families feared that money and unconditional acceptance would validate the choices of their children that went against their own. They wanted Avani to come home so that the stigma of a runaway daughter would be erased. They hoped that once home, the girls would succumb to pressure from their parents. Refusing to grant adulthood to children, their assumption was that as kids, they would not be able to hold out in hardship. Avani's family cloaked their arguments for her return on the reasonable grounds of economy: the car company would be convinced that it was an accident in which no third party was involved. Her physical presence was a necessity, they said, to stall the monthly payments. Through the months, they gave several indisputably sound reasons for her return, yet they made no effort to support her in any way. They did not even provide resources for another medical intervention for her nose that the doctor had recommended.

Nikita's parents also worked with the same hope, but through a different method. They did not attempt to speak with her on the number given to them. On the contrary, they called organisational members and Sabrang leaders in the middle of the night, sometimes threatening, and at other times pretending to be long lost friends reaching out and getting information on the 'case'. They did not give up tracking the phones. When they did talk, the dialogue was mostly patient and rang of resignation rather than aggression.

The family did not respond to repeated requests to stop tracking calls. Any SIM card that the two purchased and used in their mobiles would not allow the call to go directly to the person concerned.

'Becoming One' by Nikita

Two little trees
born on two different ends,
each limited by their own borders
both growing at parallel and opposite sides

Many days and months passed by
many were the years of rain that came,
every day a new story,
told in their own words

Slowly they grew big and tall
stepping out of their boundaries,
and they hugged each other
becoming one

They shared their stories of sorrow and happiness
in the sunlight
their branches came close together despite the shadows
in winter, they tightly hugged each other

Becoming one
In the autumn, why did they separate?
Two little trees becoming one
and apart?

23 June
Over two weeks had passed, and Nikita and Avani's presence around the office now felt more than natural. They had both secured jobs in Vadodara just 15 days after their arrival. Through networking and organising interviews, Sabrang members worked to settle them into the city, enabling the couple to start an independent and secure life. Nikita said, 'It was very easy to settle into Vadodara. We felt at home here right away, like we were surrounded by family. I don't know how we would have done it without their help.'

That day in the office, however, things felt surprisingly tense. Nikita expressed her concern regarding a friend of the family living in Vadodara who might have been tracking them down.

Not long after, the girls quickly raced up the stairs. 'My relatives have come,' Nikita yelled. Just then, two men had come to the front door asking for two girls from Rajasthan. Both tried to forcefully push the door wide open to climb up the stairs to pick them up. An activist had the presence of mind to direct them to the back entrance, saying that the only way to access the stairs was through the back entrance. The activist had earlier noticed the chowkidar at the hotel across the street from the office point towards Vikalp as two men stood by showing him a paper. Thankfully, the girls were able to escape out of the room while they asked for two girls who had come from Alwar.

Before the two men covered the distance from the front to the back, we had time to collect our wits and to get a plan ready. With the two safely out of sight and out of reach, we had successfully avoided what could have been a violent confrontation.

When the relatives entered again through the back, pushing the door ajar just as they were ready to step in, a staff member immediately put herself between the door and them and said,

'Why are you here?'

'We want to meet the girl who has come from Alwar.'

'This is my house. You cannot enter without permission. Get out from here.' The unexpectedness of the aggression left them astounded. They protested, but caught off guard, they pulled back and the activist swiftly shut the door in their faces. Looking out of the window, we watched them retreat and head towards the front side.

Anticipating more aggression, we called a lawyer to discuss and disclose the recent events. He advised us to wait and watch; rather than calling the police station under whose jurisdiction Vikalp fell, his advice was to get an appointment with the Police Commissioner. The organisation was given an appointment later in the day at 12:30 p.m. In the meantime, a brief application was drafted stating the situation, the fears of an attack, and a request for protection was made for the couple and the organisation.

After the family had been turned away, there was no doubt they would return and try to take Nikita back. We tried to think of a way out for the couple, but every exit point seemed impossible. The family must have been watching and waiting. Upstairs, the women were briefed on the situation. They were found huddled close together in a corner on the roof, wide-eyed and scared half to death. Without a chance to speak, Avani first protested, 'Nikita's mother and father have come to take her away! Her whole family is here—look, they have surrounded the office!' Her scared eyes stared wide and unblinking as she pointed to the street below. More than the panic of being surrounded, it was the awful dread of separation that prevented Avani from listening. She insisted on peering over the ledge and pointed to the group of huddled individuals across the road.

'Relax, the lawyer has come. If anything untoward happens, the police will be contacted right away. Nothing will happen to you.' However, preparing them also was important: 'Whatever happens, remember to stand firmly against anyone who may question you. Demand police protection, and be sure to tell them that you are adults who are entitled to rights.'

At approximately 10:30 a.m., only moments after encouraging them, a loud smashing noise was followed by a shrill scream from the front of the office. Suddenly, we heard a flurry of footsteps, accompanied by loud voices and the sound of doors banging.

This time, it was not the voices of the activists alone; there were garbled sentences and words. Everyone rushed there to find glass strewn across the floor. Two activists were at the door and a whole gang of men had gathered around it. There was no doubt that Nikita's relatives had engineered the attack on the office. They had violently hurled a stone through the window, shattering the glass pane. In front of the office, a crowd of men had gathered, yelling insults at the staff members. Curious onlookers, neighbours, and some well-wishers wanted to know what happened, and some even volunteered to help. This was a moment of crisis, and we had to act in self-defence. Seizing this opportunity, some of the activists opened the door and went on an offensive. Calling out to the attackers to 'show their faces' instead of hiding in the crowd, they warned them of severe consequences if they dared to hit out again. Many others, who were supported by Nikita's relatives, continued to threaten us with abusive words. Questioning the organisation's legitimacy, accusations of acting immorally towards the girls were hurled in the air. For protection, the front door was half-closed while the fighting ensued. Having rebuked them for the damage and the unruly behaviour, the door was securely bolted. We then dialled the number 100, for police assistance, which is available 24 hours.

After what felt like forever, the police showed up to control the situation. Before they arrived, Nikita's family managed to flee the scene out of fear. The police dealt with dispersing the crowd and attempted to gather information from witnesses. Within seconds, the media arrived, hurling their cameras around as if they were guns. Fear rose again and the room felt tense. About 15 people entered the office with cameras and video and sound recorders. Eventually, the police pushed out the abrasive group. But they lingered outside within a close range. Their cameras focused relentlessly on the inside of the office, standing, strutting around, or sitting on their haunches before the broken pane, walking past the windows and peeping right in. They were doing just anything, absolutely anything, without concern for the limits of privacy and other boundaries. They were on a hunt that would yield them the picture of the twosome and their story of the day.

Depleted, everyone headed to the back room to sit down and discuss the case with three officers while one stood guard in the front. All of the relevant information was recorded by one of them as Nikita and Avani explained their case. Having discussed it earlier, not a word was spoken about their intimate relationship. Avani's role was merely that of the supportive friend who came to ensure the safety of Nikita on her journey from home.

The police, as well as a Vikalp activist, escorted the couple to see the Police Commissioner. Since the media was still clicking away out front, the back door was essential for their escape. This was how Nikita and Avani managed to evade the cameras; their anonymity was vital in public places for their protection.

'We see this a lot, and it is not uncommon amongst two boys, or even a girl and a boy,' the Police Commissioner said at the station. 'When two girls run away together, that's when problems arise. People start questioning. So, I will ask—are you two in an intimate relationship?' Responding instantly, the girls denied their love for strategic reasons and claimed to be 'just good friends'. Once the situation had been fully explained to the Police Commissioner, a letter was provided for further verification and he agreed to fully support the couple's decision to leave home with the assurance of his protection at all costs. Vikalp filed a case against the relatives.

After some time, everyone regrouped in the office. Nikita and Avani walked in with huge grins spread across their faces. Sitting, discussing, and sharing opinions of the events of the day, the mood was more relaxed—a weight had been lifted.

Next, an officer from the Criminal Investigation Department (CID) came for an inquiry. Retelling the story once again, it felt as if the events of the morning took place days ago. The number of media people calling had been steadily increasing, so Sabrang decided to write a press release stating the events of the day and to provide an organisational stance on the issue of forced marriage. Required to hide the couple's love for each other, Vikalp stated that Avani was Nikita's friend from home who had travelled with her for increased security and support. In an opportunity such as this, one wishes to speak out; however, absence of entitlements prevented us from saying the truth, which was no easy task.

By ten o'clock, we were all sitting around the table. A sharp rap on the door sounded louder than thunder and shook everyone from their chairs. The police officer had returned and brought Nikita's relatives back. While the argument ensued, Nikita and Avani hid in the next room. Encouraged to step out and speak her mind, someone came to nudge Nikita along. The room fell silent once Nikita entered. Becoming apologetic, the uncle clasped his hands together, asking for forgiveness for their violent attack. Nikita's face turned white. It was a struggle for her. She had been trained to be silent and accept all, yet this situation called upon her to stand up for herself. She stood firm and replied that as an adult, she was choosing to stay in Vadodara to avoid her marriage. The relatives left; defeated, they were held in a cell overnight, and were released on bail in the morning.

24 June

By the next morning, all of the newspapers had reported on the events at the Vikalp office. Some wrote fairly accurately, while others skewed events, judging the organisation on the basis of 'immoral acts'. The English newspapers reported what was sent in the press release; however, they failed to include some of the basic information that had been provided. The local Gujarati papers accused Vikalp of harbouring foreigners, suggesting dishonest behaviour and suspicious actions. Even the photos, which accompanied the headlines, were insinuating other things; the one white volunteer was shown with a transgender member of Sabrang, and the title read 'Two Suspected Lesbians'.

The article continued to say:

'Nikita and Avani, for the last several years, have been deeply in love. When the parents came to know about the relationship, they opposed it fiercely. These two women have taken shelter in Vikalp Women's Group Vadodara. A lesbian relationship is suspected between them, but what exactly is the relationship between these friends and what is the role of the organisation? Nothing is known about these two questions. Above the office of Vikalp, there is a residence. There were ten women, including two to three foreigners, staying there. When there was an attack by the family members today, these women were taken out from the back door.'

Where the article mentioned 'ten women, including two or three foreigners came out of the organisation,' it cleverly mimicked the wording so often used to describe a raid on sex workers.

The grotesque reporting of events had already created a reaction amongst the community. The Sabrang member who was shown in the photos returned to the office claiming that a shopkeeper had identified her. Upon requesting a receipt, the shopkeeper asked for the company name, so she replied 'Vikalp Women's Group.' Immediately, the man responded, 'The runaway

from Alwar?' Thankfully, neither Nikita nor Avani figured in any
of the photos on account of the back door exit, which allowed
them to avoid the cameras.

All of the articles failed to include any of Vikalp's press re-
leases regarding Nikita and Avani's right to live a life of dignity,
security, and freedom. There was no space for a discourse of entitlements.

These are the true words, which never got a line in the papers:

'Vikalp extends full support to the two women to exercise
their right to choice and live a life with dignity and security.
Especially in these times when women are being murdered in
the name of "family honour", as a women's organisation we feel
impelled to appeal to the families and the States to ensure their
protection and see to it that their fundamental rights as citizens
of this country are upheld in sprit and practice.'

Nikita and Avani decided to settle in Vadodara. Currently,
they are both holding steady jobs with employers and coworkers
who are quite understanding and accepting. They now look for a
permanent place to stay together. They are both in contact with
their families, and hopefully a time will come when their families
can accept them.

Revisiting Section 377

The Delhi High Court, in July 2009, held that criminali-
sation of consensual sex between adults in private violates the
Constitution's guarantee of dignity, equality, and freedom from
discrimination based on sexual orientation (Articles 21, 41, and
15).[64] Thus, the judges 'read down' Section 377 so that it no longer criminalises consensual sex between adults in private. But an
appeal to the Court's order led to its overturning by the Supreme
Court in 2013, re-criminalising LGBT lives. Many from the community who had begun to live life out in the open were suddenly

---

[64] Naz Foundation vs Government Of Nct Of Delhi, 2 July 2009.

forced back into a life of fear and uncertainty after the Supreme Court overturned the decision.

In September 2018, the Supreme Court reversed its decision once again. Homosexuality was, once again, no longer a criminal offence. The judgement brought hope that queer lives would find greater affirmation as society becomes aware and laws are framed in the spirit of the judgement.

But as we saw in the stories set during the first period of decriminalisation, it was hard—if not impossible—to see any tangible effect that the change in the law had had on the lives of real people. Couples still had to elope, we and others still had to make up fables to the police, and our office was still pelted with stones. The final story, of Prem and Rukaya, is the last and most recent to be recorded after the rereading down of Section 377. In it, we can read almost the same story as the many that came before them. Is it merely that more time is needed for new liberal ideas to trickle into families in every small village, big city, and throughout the land? Or is law valued less in a country that is so large, with such varying intersections of lived realities and identities, not just from state to village, but from caste to tribe to religion and beyond? Laws are merely concepts that can only exist when accepted as existing, so how can they exist in places where there is no knowledge of them, or in communities that live within layered social norms resisting the reach of the state? As we have seen, at times, the law can even have a negative effect on queer individuals who have managed to live as their true self within their unique pockets of these layers. In a country where the patriarchal family model is all-powerful, a law can seem so feeble in the face of the family who is considered to know best.

18

Fear of Family and Community
Holds Us from Living Our Lives Fully

Prem and Rukaya both lived in a block situated in the district of Jamnagar. Both joined work in a government office as contract workers while pursuing their post-graduation. Since Prem had joined earlier, he was given the responsibility of training Rukaya; working closely, the two became good friends. Soon, their friendship developed into love. Lunch breaks cemented the relationship. Prem, who had recently acquired a two-wheeler, was now seen picking up Rukaya after work and dropping her home. As time went by, Rukaya's parents pressurised her to marry, but she found reasons to decline the proposals. Her parents were alarmed, but they had no idea that there was something deeper and different brewing in her friendship with Prem. Satisfied that they were doing their duty in pursuing marriage for her, they continued using pressure tactics until Rukaya succumbed.

To pre-empt the coerced arrangement by the parents, the pair sought out a lawyer in a city far from their place of residence. 'It was a huge cost, 8,000 rupees,' Prem told us. 'The lawyer told me that since our relationship was illegal in the eyes of the state, we would have to take another route.' Recalling the incident, he paused and then continued, 'He advised a contract of Maitri Karaar (friendship bond) on a stamp paper of Rs 20. I did not know that this would not be valid in the court. That was the first time, in February 2017, that I heard about Section 377. Since I had gone alone to meet the lawyer, he told me the other person would also have to be present to sign the stamp paper. The next time, we both went. But she had a hard time getting out of the house.'

'Yes.' Rukaya continued where Prem had left, 'Since I had been engaged, my movements were restricted between home and office. Being absent from the office was risky in case someone from home called and they said I was not in—that would have been our undoing. So, I said I had to go to college, and Prem drove his two-wheeler very fast so that we could sign and return immediately afterwards. The whole time, I was sick with nervousness. What if we were caught? My brother used to go to the same city to study computers. There was some sense of safety in the dupatta that we women generally wear over our faces while driving. And then, countering my own fears, I thought that if I was spotted, I could say it was not me. But the thing was that my family, neighbours, and colleagues had seen me ride behind Prem so often that they would infer it was me. So on and so forth. Like the wind exploding against my ears, a jumble of thoughts plagued me, each vying with the other to take charge, each presenting itself as more valid than the other.'

Rukaya's engagement, though a one-time event, had extended into her daily life. 'My engagement imposed an expectation that I would participate in my fiancé's family festivities and rituals. I did not enjoy these restrictions. I tried several ways to end my engagement. Finding a moment of togetherness with my mother as I sat on the ground getting my hair oiled by her, I wondered aloud what would happen if she called off my engagement. My mother's hands stopped midway on my head; I knew she was shocked because the man was good by all standards. He earned well. His family was known to us, and so on. Concerned, she asked me what troubled me. But of course, I could not tell her. I did not know how to tell her. The matter did not end there. How could I tell her that the engagement had become a trap for me? Especially when he called my mother one day to meet her alone.

'I was so uneasy to hear this from my mother. Perhaps he heard something about us, I mean, about Prem and me. Because there was no doubt that we were often seen together by our colleagues and generally others in the neighbourhood. I felt like we needed to act immediately; I was afraid they would force me to marry. I told Prem that I would not return home that night. I would die but I refused to step back in there. I did not know what my mother would be told and what they would put me through.'

'So,' Prem picked up the narrative, 'as a precaution, one of the first things that we both did was to seek help from Rukaya's aunt, who herself had been in love with a woman many years ago until she was forced to marry. She understood us. She advised us to immediately throw out our SIM cards and to have our phones formatted so that no call data could be traced. After making sure that our cell phones were formatted, we left with a few of our belongings and reached the house of Rukaya's aunt. That very day, she sent us to her friend's house in another town.'

Rukaya intervened to add, 'We stayed there for 15 days, and just when we began to feel safe and were planning to shift into our own place, we got a call from my aunt. A news report about us had been published in a paper. It had our picture, the one that I had set as my DP, a selfie that I had taken of us together on Makar Sankranti. The report cited many details about us, with our names, our families, where we worked—showing us as close friends, it also mentioned that we were untraceable since the day we had left. It is a frightening experience to have your own photographs stare back at you in a paper that went public—an innocent picture of a fleeting moment between us was out there for everyone to see. Our story was published every day for three days until we were traced.

'The lawyer had told us our relationship was illegal, and though the paper did not directly talk about that, the way it described our lives left little to the imagination. It made me want to cover my face. Whether we would be recognised or not is besides the point, it is that constant lurking fear of being recognised on the streets... My stomach was in knots because of the uncertainty, and the chain of unpredictable events that would follow weighed upon us. My aunt warned us that the police would come after us soon. The police came, just like my aunt had said, but to her house. They had traced our calls to her when we were planning to get away, and they wanted her to tell them where we were. Both our families had filed a missing person report at the police station of our town. My aunt was threatened with being locked up if she did not divulge our whereabouts. She told us that all the police wanted was a statement from us in person at the station close to where we were, and that we could go our own separate ways after making the statement. Then, the matter with the police would end. We were left with no choice but to proceed towards the city to report.

'We reached there around two in the afternoon and were told we would have to go to the town where we came from. We protested, saying that we were told that we would be free to leave after our statement. But once you're in the police station, you can do nothing. We were told "since the FIR was filed there, we have to take you back to your town." From there, we were taken in a jeep with a PSI, a writer, and a constable. No, there was no woman constable with us.'

'On our way, they reprimanded us for our foolhardy behaviour, holding us responsible for a tense situation between our two communities in our town and of causing trouble between "your own two families". The drive took 45 minutes,' Prem recounted, 'and the whole time, question after question was thrown at us. In a roundabout way, they kept asking the same thing. They suspected us of being involved with men. They wanted the full truth or threatened us with arrest. "We know where all you went because we have all the call details." Some more crude questions followed, indicating that they wanted to verify if there was something physical that transpired during our escape. We stuck to our truth, carefully concealing our relationship. After all the questioning, I became their target of suspicion for being a mediator and taking Rukaya to her boyfriend.'

The police assumed and considered Prem to be a woman. 'It was inconceivable for them to even imagine that two women could love one another,' Rukaya explained to me. 'People do not know this. Even me,' she repeated, pointing at herself, 'Even me, I had no idea that two women can love and live with one another. The first time when Prem proposed, I laughed. We were friends and that is what I took our relationship to be. I was friendly to all my colleagues, and I had a special feeling for one of my male colleagues... yes, you can say a boyfriend or a BF, as some of us referred to our special male friends. I was not surprised at all that the policemen accompanying us had not the faintest idea about us, me and Prem, no idea at all. In a way that put us at ease. We had only recently learnt that what we sought and wanted was illegal—how and what it meant was still unclear. Before this episode, we had instinctively learnt to silence ourselves and conceal our love. And we continued to do so with the policemen until we reached the police station of our town.

'When we stepped into the police station, an overpowering stench of *daru* (liquor) hung in the outer room, where we waited for an hour before our family members arrived. We saw the dirty lock-ups and a man being beaten up for indulging in illicit liquor trade. Sitting there and waiting for our families, for the people who had turned against us, we felt like criminals, unable to quite comprehend what was happening to us and around us. A distance lay between us that seemed impossible to cross. So, we sat quietly. Occasionally mumbling about what the outcome would be, we had lost all control over the way events had unfolded.

'Then my whole family turned up. My parents, both my brothers and sisters. My married sister had even brought her daughter. Too innocent to understand the tension, she came up to me and sat right next to me, touching my face and tugging at me to turn towards her. It eased the tension a little, and then the torture began, the torture of false promises and resolutions of not ever forcing me to marry until I wished otherwise.

'The PSI got a chance to butt in, "Now that your parents are giving you their word of not getting you married, you can go back home." Closing the matter with immense satisfaction, he turned to me and said, "Now, there should be no problem." But no matter how many times I told them that I did not want to go back to my family, they would not listen. No one was listening. They were completely in favour of our families and insisted on sending us back to them. But I persisted, telling them, "It is with Prem that I wish to stay."'

'From Rukaya's family, everyone came. For me, only my brother came to the police station. My mother had died the year before; a snake bit her and before we realised that it was poisonous, she was gone. My father was too sick to come to the police station. But I knew he was my strongest supporter. Rukaya had met him and he had accepted her. He and my brother had fallen out over my relationship with her. When he came to the police station, I told him that I would not leave Rukaya, and he would not hear of it. We had said all that was to be said. Each of us was taken separately, and the whole point of the efforts was to somehow cajole us, talk us down, and insist enough to compel us to go back to our families. My brother and the police had had enough of me. So, I moved away and came to where Rukaya stood, adamant but quiet, surrounded by her family, still being pressured to return. I went and stood next to her kin. I saw the PSI frown. My brother pulled me away. The evening had grown darker against the lights that had been turned on inside, growing more luminous with each passing hour, but Rukaya's family was still badgering her to change her mind. But she was firm in her refusal. I felt a sense of relief.

'Finally, it was the police who decided that the matter should end. In a once-and-for-all tone, he told us that if we did not want to go to our respective families, they would have to put us both in a women's shelter. When we resisted, he said we had no choice in the matter. He said that all we needed to do was to write an application to the person in charge at the shelter, and then we could leave. But since it was Saturday night already, we would have to stay there until Sunday because no officials would be available on a non-working day. Taking his word to be the rule of law, we reluctantly went along with him, carrying the burden of our rupture with our families back to the jeep, and on to the shelter home.

'We reached the Nari Sanrakshan Gruh around nine in the night. A long road inside the compound led up to the shelter. Yes, this time a lady constable accompanied us. She told us, "Live properly here. You are educated, so if they need help with computers or the like, you can help them." Too shaken to immediately respond, it was much later that it struck me, why had she told us to help them if we were to stay only till Sunday?

'Our arrival at night foreclosed procedural formalities. We signed on a paper. The person in charge for the night told us, "Forms will be filled only on Monday, when the main person in charge comes," and then checked us one by one. I watched quietly, suffocating inside as her hands ran over Rukaya's body, her fingers pushing deep into her pockets to see what was there; then, it was my turn. I suffered the same fate. All our belongings, like the money, the change that we carried, the mobiles, the locket she was wearing, pen, diary, our watches—everything was taken from us. A list of those things was drawn up and we saw our possessions being put away under lock and key. Our belongings had gone out of our keeping into hands we did not know. They did not tell us that our possessions will be taken away. They did not tell us anything, nothing; rather, they said one thing and did another.

'We were then taken into a room, bereft of our possessions. I thought that if only I had known, I would have devised a way of keeping some money with me. But we did not know, and they did not tell us.'

'I must tell you about the shelter home,' Rukaya said leaning towards me. 'It was quite a place! On the outside, all was quiet and resting. But inside, when we stepped into the room where we had to sleep, it was not quiet and neither did we find it resting. There were six beds pushed against one another, and there was barely any space for someone to stand between them; the room looked cramped and dim. The faint light showed us some of the bare stained mattresses and pillows. On one of the beds, a girl sat up almost immediately, excited to see Prem. She may have been 16 or 17 years old, not able to talk, so she showed her preference through sounds and gestures that expressed her sexual desire. Some said she was dumb ever since she was a child, and others said she had been so traumatised that she lost her speech. This information came from a young-looking woman, allegedly from Bangladesh, who engaged in sex work. Put away, she was not able to continue her work, which in turn affected her family to whom she sent money. "They survived on the money I earned here. Now I worry about them." Another woman, who was around 70 years of age, was not in her right mind, often staring into nothing, mumbling half articulated words that were interspersed with a lost look. She would often scream in the night, startling me out of sleep. Then, there was a woman who had somehow managed to get her mobile inside and spoke to her boyfriend frequently. We heard that she had several cases registered against her, but she seemed so unperturbed by the rules or laws.

'That first night, when I saw the girl and her lewd gestures, I do not know why but I broke down. The day had been so long and we had been in places where we had not been before, and that night in the shelter home was the worst nightmare. I could feel my eyes were heavy, but I could not close them. They gave us something to eat but I do not remember what it was. My throat felt so constricted. I knew I would not be able to swallow it. Leaning on each other, we sat awake through the whole night. We consoled ourselves that this would be over in another day. No more.

'On Monday, when the person responsible for running the shelter home came and noted down our history, she told us "There is no reason for you to be here." We thought it was strange that she should say that. We had no answer to her question. Instead, we told her that we were due to leave that very day. She simply shook her head in a non-committal way and turned the pages which she had noted our names down in. We think that the police and the people at the shelter home may have talked and arrived at some understanding, because after that she neither asked us why we were there nor gave us pen and paper to write the application. Instead, she began calling us separately each day and telling us to go back to our families. She even offered to intervene with them and tell them to take care of us, advising us to study and make something better of our lives rather than wasting them in a friendship like ours; she did all this whilst also painting the other in poor light. We soon learnt that she was playing one up against the other. We argued that we were adults and had a right to live our lives the way we wanted to, but the pressure to return to our families did not let up. We wondered what we could do to escape their clutches. We had reached an impasse. We stayed there for more than fifteen days.

'As the days went on, we realised that it was a matter of routine that everyone had to get up at six and do the cooking, cleaning, sweeping, and washing. All the chores had to be done by those of us who stayed there. Khushi, the girl enamoured by Prem, was given the job of sweeping the road leading down to the gate, the road strewn with leaves, scraps of papers, and plastic wrappers. As days passed, I learnt to see life in a new light. It was heart-wrenching to see her sweep and to learn from others that she was found on a roadside and put away here.

'So we lived there like the rest, as outcasts, in conditions that could be cleaner and better so easily. There was dust everywhere. The bathrooms were dirty and a stench filled the area in its vicinity. There were no sinks where one could brush and wash one's hands. We had reached on Saturday night, but we were given soap only on Monday! We had no clothes except the ones we were wearing. They gave us old clothes, perhaps left there by previous inmates. Prem, who had not worn women's—'

Prem intervened angrily, 'Yes, yes, that is what I was given, some discarded feminine clothes. I had not worn women's clothes ever since I remembered. This was the worst ordeal for me, this compulsion to dress a certain way. We were virtually in a lock-up where nothing or no one could go out or come in. Some journalists had tracked us down—we know this because they made us sign a paper which said that we would not speak to the media. We thought that if we had been allowed, we may have had a chance to get out. Who knows...'

'Or maybe it would have been worse...' Rukaya added philosophically. 'One night, I felt sick but I was taken to the hospital only in the morning, and of course, Prem was not allowed to accompany me.

'This was a frightening experience for us. It set us thinking of how we could get out of this shelter that we did not need. The bold woman, who had criminal cases filed against her, told us, "You could be here for a lifetime unless you listen to what they are saying..."'

'On the sixteenth day, our families were called. My brother and Rukaya's parents came. But we refused to go with them. Someone higher up in the chain of authority was called to counsel us, but we refused to separate. By then, the people at the shelter home had also grown weary. We realised that getting out of there was the first thing we needed to do. Once outside, we could plan something, even if it had to be within the family.

'The second time around, when they called our families, it was a Saturday and only Rukaya's people came. We were both told that this was the last attempt at reconciliation, and if it failed, we would have to live there. Supporting the shelter home authorities, Rukaya's father went a step ahead, saying, "I will file a case against you, disowning you, which will imply that you will have to stay here." Realising that it would not be possible to get out of there, we decided to agree to go with our families the next time they were called.

'Finally, when Rukaya's parents came, she acted according to what we had previously decided. She agreed to go along with them, but after a show of reluctance, on the condition that they would allow the two of us to meet. They, in turn, asked us to give in writing that we would not run away again. Their condition made us cautious of rigidly imposing our own conditions on them. None of us wrote down our conditions; there was a verbal agreement.' Before they left, the shelter home authorities made Rukaya write on a stamp paper of Rs 20 that she was going with her parents, and her parents also had to give in writing that they were taking their daughter with them. The couple had to part.

'And I had to stay two nights and a day extra,' Prem said. 'My brother came on Monday, because the next day was Sunday and no formalities could be completed that day. Finally, when he came and my things were returned to me, he refused to give me my telephone. Being without mobiles deprived us of news of one another. We were both worried for one another. It was after a heated exchange that my brother returned my phone two days later. My brother's wife turned against me after my return. She made it clear to me that my relationship with Rukaya had disgraced the family, and she refused to even acknowledge me. I was the one who had offered to be with her in Indore when she was carrying. But all that was forgotten because of what I had done. And what had I done? Exactly what my brother had done, got married to the partner of his choice. As days passed, Rukaya managed to make a few quick calls. Then I was the one who had to call. Or sometimes she did too, whenever she got a chance.'

'...But the trouble was that we could not really talk, it was all done so hurriedly. I had to be really careful. But then Prem began to come to my house. That was our condition, so they could do nothing about it. Though we were not allowed to talk or meet separately, we could at least see one another. This was important. If we had been totally prevented from meeting one another, we may have taken a drastic step. Maybe you would not have seen us here at all.'

'We could not settle back in our homes, and as days and weeks fled by, our lives almost came to a standstill. It was such a jolt, and we could barely talk about it to one another. Then a small door opened, breaking the uncertainty. Each of us got an opportunity to work. Rukaya was employed in the office of the Jumayat Khana, and her family was reassured that she would work under the watchful eyes of people within the community, who would report immediately if they saw anything suspicious between us. I tried not to meet her at the workplace. We did not have any plan in mind then—it was simply a precaution. We had to be cautious. But as days passed, I felt the need to do something that would protect us. On the suggestion of some friends of mine, I went to the DSP, who was based in a town away from where we lived. I told him about our situation and sought protection from our families, particularly for Rukaya. But he said he could not help us in the matter. Finally, I consulted a lawyer, following which I wrote letters to district level police officers, clearly stating that Rukaya and I had a contract of friendship and as adults, we wanted to live with one another, but were being prevented to do so by our families. Then I waited for some response from them, something like an assurance or an intervention, but nothing came for days, and I gave up waiting.

'In the meantime, I had also taken up a job in a nearby town, which was better developed than our own block. Keeping in touch with one another was complicated but whenever we could, we talked furtively over our mobile phones. It was not as hard for me as it was for Rukaya—she had to look for a secluded place away from the gaze of her family. Our conversations were often muffled and abrupt. Nonetheless, we planned once again to get away. Since I was working in another town, I hired a one-room apartment and put together some household essentials in anticipation of an opportune time when we could get away and begin our lives. And we did just that.

'It was July 2018, the month of monsoon. The sky was overcast with unmoving black-grey clouds. It spelt rain, ready to burst out anytime. But I had my bike. It gave me a confidence that pushed away that nasty twinge of nervousness: "What if we are...," Rukaya settled in behind me, and as I turned on the ignition, I said, "We will make it before the rain catches us." We pulled out of our homes and onto the road, and then the rain began to pelt down upon us. I had to go fast because Rukaya's absence, if discovered, would put her family on high alert. While the tarred road made it easy for me to ride fast, it was impossible to speed up on the broken road that turned in from the highway close to the town I had rented the apartment in. I rode over puddles with rain streaming down my eyes. I was not wearing a helmet. Some raindrops found their way into my eyes, blurring my vision. You saw when I came here that I had long hair, and water streamed down to my back. Then, we were fully drenched. It did not matter; nothing mattered except to get away soon—soon, I told myself. I was driving at a speed of 80 kmph. An accident slowed me down. A crowd had collected on the road.

'I knew waiting would be dangerous. We just had a few miles to cover; impatient, I got off the road, made a slight detour, and then got back on the road. With all of these manoeuvres and with the rain blurring my vision, I missed Rukaya's father. He was coming from the opposite side. He must have seen us. It was our bad luck that we did not see him. Even though he had to take a U-turn to catch up with us, he managed to reach us. He drove alongside us, neck to neck, and nearly banged against us in his attempts to slow us down. He shouted at the top of his voice, "Stop, stop!" I tried to outpace him but then he raced ahead and screeched to a halt right in front of us. Completely blocking our way, he sat glowering on his bike.

'His black familiar scarf stuck around his neck, limp and wet, as did the rest of his clothes around his body, making him look gaunt and tall. Wiping the water off his face, he came up menacingly close and said, "Where do you think you are going?" I was tempted to say, "You know the answer." But the din of the traffic behind us helped us in our refusal to respond.

'He hissed, "Follow me." Craning his neck to look at Rukaya sitting behind me, he gave her a long, hard look.

'I turned to look at her. She looked forlorn and scared and shoved at me to follow him. I drove behind him. Turning off the main road, he drove along the side, close to us, and if he had to drive ahead to give way to other vehicles, he turned to look every now and then. We were prisoners on a moving road. There was no way that we could ride fast and disappear. The thought did cross my mind—to drive and simply vanish. But there I was, on unfamiliar terrain. Even if we managed to get away, I knew we would be recaptured. Besides, the dirt road that we were on was no easy ride. Being compelled to skirt puddles and cross ditches slowed our driving. He took us to his relative's house in the nearby village.

'More than me, here it was Rukaya who was put through tortuous inquisition, reminding her and me of the promise we had made of not attempting to get away. "We trusted you, didn't we, and this is what you give us in return?" Turning to Rukaya and pointing to her, he said, "And you?" He shook his head in utter disapproval. "Is this the way, this…running away like this? Is this how you repay your parents, and your family?" Then he tried to dissuade us, this time more gently in the name of not sullying the honour of our families, persuading us to live a "normal life". But when we showed our unwillingness to leave one another, he called Rukaya's brother and mother from our village to where we were held.

"You do not understand now, but I am telling you, a few months from now, you will regret this decision. Listen... Your mother and brother will come soon and we can all return together and put this all behind us."

'Failing to get Rukaya to comply with his wishes, he got angrier and began to make all kinds of allegations against me as the person responsible for poisoning his daughter's mind and misleading her. "We trusted you, let you come to our house when your mother died, and now you turn our daughter against us, the very people who stood by you. We let you come inside our house when you were in trouble, and you stabbed us in the back."

'This was true. They had let me stay with them. This was soon after my mother's death. I was depressed and upset, and Rukaya was a great support. She used to call me over and her family allowed me to spend nights in their house. Of course, at that time they did not know we were involved with one another. I had a girlfriend and Rukaya had a boyfriend. It was much later that we chose one another over other special relationships that we had. If we could, we would indeed become "normal" as Rukaya's father said. But you see, we cannot.

'When Rukaya's mother and brother arrived, they saw a defeated and angry man amongst other relatives who were convinced that the best way to deal with her and me was to simply beat this adamance out of us. Rukaya's mother had little patience. She threatened death if Rukaya did not come around. She was the kind who could carry out her threats. When she saw Rukaya, she began to abuse us, and then she hit her hard. Rukaya staggered.

I rushed to stop her from hitting out one more time. She lashed out at me also.'

'Then, I covered up for Prem,' Rukaya chimed in. 'Suddenly, the scene went out of control. More abuses poured in, feet shuffled here and there, and hands spread out to pull my mother and us away from each other. Sanity restored, a silence fell upon us, broken only by the incessant rain pelting outside and on the roof. The straight lines of water that fell endlessly down the windows made me teary. My father said that he would go to the court and put the onus of my welfare on Prem's family. If anything untoward were to happen to me, Prem and his family would be held responsible. We did not know what that meant. At that point, it did not even matter. Naturally, I did not want Prem and his family to get into trouble. I was too exhausted to fight back. My father pulled me roughly and I let myself be propelled in that direction.'

'But when we rode back, I made sure that Rukaya sat behind me. While her father rode ahead of us, her mother and brother followed close behind us. We were trapped. We rode in the rain, all of us. Immediately after reaching their house, Rukaya was taken into their custody and I drove straight to the police station to file a complaint against Rukaya's parents. She had been threatened with death and was beaten in front of me. Within the four walls of her home, they could do anything to her. I was worried that if they carried out the threat or harmed her, no one would know. At the police station, there was the same PI who had manipulated us into coming back to our town and had attempted to send us back to our families. He was surprised to see me. "Back again. What now?"

'I narrated the whole incident.

'"You will not listen, uh? So it is that girl again? Why do you not leave her alone?" the PI rebuked me.

'So on and so forth, he went on baiting me and refused to take my complaint; instead, he kept calling my brother, who did not take his call. Finally, he asked another constable to call my brother. Amidst all this, I kept reminding him of the likely danger that Rukaya was in and the urgency to act. Finally, my brother took the call. He was asked to come and so he did, fuming for being called again. The PI sent me back with him, telling me to return in the morning, summarily dismissing me, "I will look into the matter. You come tomorrow."

'As we turned away, my brother dashed back inside to talk to the PI and told him that he had nothing to do with me and my doings. He did not want to be a part of all this—he had had enough of me and did not want to be called the next time. I am sure this is what he told the PI because that is exactly what he told my father. The next day, I went right back to the police station and stood by, insistent that Rukaya and her family be called. Finally, when they did arrive, he turned towards me saying, "There, look. Here she is, what are you complaining about?"

"We want to live together."

'The PI threw up his hands in frustration, "Indeed." Turning to Rukaya and her parents, he asked, "Can you not manage this girl? This one here tells me they ran away again. Can you not control your daughter?"

'While all this was happening, the PI received the letter that we had written to the DSP. I recognised my writing. He read through it and laughed at us outright. "This is your letter, isn't it? You want to have a live-in relationship! Two girls!" The other constables heard it and looked at us and her family, smirking and mocking us. Rukaya's family looked away, unable to meet the gaze that censured us and them. One of them volunteered to articulate the hostility and hate, "We will make the *mandap* right here and get you both married to boys." More derisive loud laughter followed. We stood shamed and silenced.

"It is such a dishonour that you bring to yourself and your families... you two should die. If you do not have the money to buy the poison, we will give you the money… your deaths will not make a difference to anyone."

'The matter was closed. According to them, Rukaya was safe with her parents. The PI had said so and sent her with them. The letter lay there, as forlorn as I felt inside.'

'After that, I was locked up. I think I was beaten and locked up to break my resistance. I was not allowed to go up on the terrace either. My parents used to keep white pigeons up on the terrace, a whole flock of them. That used to be my favourite place. I loved to see them flutter their wings, cooing and cuddling, and when they slept with their necks rested on their fluffed up snowy bodies, I would sit with books and watch them for hours. Then one day when we were out, a cat climbed up over the walls and got them all. Things were not the same within our family after that.

'Now I felt like those pigeons… captured and torn to shreds. I grew up in my maternal grandmother's house. Our mothers had to work hard to feed us, but I think that Prem had a far rougher time. Growing up was not as conflicting for me; I was born a woman and since then, I have been a woman. As a child, I had another name, but my name was changed for very different reasons. I used to stay sick all the time—a fever, cold, chickenpox—so my *nani* took me to a *mullah*, who suggested that my name be changed. He held my hands and simply declared that from then on, my name would be Rukaya.

'My problems were different. I mostly grew up in different places until I was six or seven years of age, which of course had its own consequences. I vaguely remember a village where there were factories over factories, where my father and mother would go to work. My father did not have a steady job. He often had differences with his employers and would then walk out in some kind of protest. My father's arrogance put people off. He felt he knew everything better than everyone else. Now tell me, what kind of boss would tolerate that? Even his own parents threw him out of the family. He studied until tenth class and then stopped going to school. Right from the beginning, my father was not willing to take any responsibility. He loved to roam around and chatter with friends, like a vagabond, and perhaps that is why he became an alcoholic. For a short time soon after his marriage, he looked as if he was ready to settle down, but by then he had already fallen into a habit of indiscipline, leaving him jobless and disgruntled.

'As a result, the onus of running the home and taking care of us children fell entirely on my mother. She was the one who provided us with food, clothes, and care. She had to take up different jobs. Sometimes it was a job in a factory, at other times she would find no jobs. It was a hard life then. We were three sisters and two brothers. I am in the middle. My other two sisters are married. Five of us were young, and the age differences between us were small. There was no older sibling like you see in other families, someone who could mind us all. We would fight endlessly. One day, it so happened that I got into a squabble with my sister over some marbles. In the scuffle, my sister swallowed a marble or two, and this panicked my mother. My mother told us how they tried everything to make her cough up the marbles, but they had slid down too deep. The doctor advised us to wait until morning. As predicted, my sister was fine the next day—the marbles came out naturally. But my mother was distraught.

'My father's unpredictability in job ventures was not encouraging either, and we moved endlessly. I grew up shifting between cities and villages. When I was in eighth class, or maybe seventh, I took a great liking to a boy in the village, but then it was time for us to move again. I resented it so much that I jumped off the *chakkada riksha* to be able to stay there. The only predictable part of our lives was the unpredictability.

'We, as children, did not make life any easier for my mother. She had to manage single-handedly, and so she packed me off to my maternal grandparents' house. That is how I came to live with my *nani* from an early age. It was not all good. I had two uncles. The elder one molested me sexually. I remember the incident. It left me uneasy. I did not understand it, but I knew it was dirty. I resented him and kept away from him. I refused to sleep on the bed. Since we had only one bed, I said I wanted to sleep on the floor.

'When younger, and in some ways until I left home, I was perhaps my father's favourite child. Not that he looked after us, but in his own way, he was not a bad person. I happened to be the one he would listen to. Many times, I was the one who intervened between my mother and father. I have this memory of my mother being absent in our lives. She went away several times, and every time, there would be compromise. My father cried and apologised and we would start afresh. The problem was he had no money and wanted to drink. He ran up debts and my mother would refuse to give him the money. You can imagine the rest. We grew up seeing my father beat my mother. He would lock her in and hit her; I still carry that memory with me. It overpowers me sometimes, the sound of his footsteps and his angry voice and my mother's hands and voice of protest.

'Around the time I came into tenth class, my *dada* died and my father inherited the shop that his father owned. Since then, he is a changed person. In that shop, he is his own master and that suits his temperament. He was so rude and aggressive that my maternal grandparents feared him. I believe they did not want to keep me either, but their daughter's situation compelled them. My life has had all these twists and turns, so when days like these go by smoothly, I almost wait for some kind of trouble to appear.

'My grandparents took me to Gondal to see their parents. We went in a mini bus. It was packed beyond belief, and there were only three children, including me, amongst all the adult passengers. The driver was rash. One of the tyres did not even have enough air. Even when the people pointed it out, he paid no heed. He went on driving fast along the steep, winding road.

Suddenly, it turned sideways and rested dangerously for a minute or two on the edge of the parapet. As the bus heaved to a sudden halt, my *nana* snatched me from my grandmother's arms and threw me out from the window just as the bus hurtled down into the valley with all the passengers in it. A biker was coming along the side of the bus. He caught me just as I was flung out, safe and sound without a scratch. The other two children died, and all the passengers were hurt, as were my *nana* and *nani*.

'I have heard my grandparents say that it was the sheer thought of my father creating a big ruckus that prompted my grandfather to throw me out of the window to safety; it was to save me and also himself from my father's wrathful abuses. I was the miracle child. Having a tyrant as a father was not easy until I grew up and learnt to deal with him. So, both Prem and I have had our struggles. His struggle was a lot more on the inside, and mine somewhat on the outside.'

Prem shared, 'When I went back home, there was a resentment that simmered quietly. It was not as out in the open as Rukaya's punishment. My brother did not talk to me, and my *bhabhi* ignored me. She did not give me food. My father was the only support I had. He had taken early retirement from the Railways because of his illness, so he was mostly laid up in bed. But having him home was good for me. When he was hospitalised, I was the one who tended to him day and night. My brother remained aloof then, and now when my life was turned upside-down, he turned his back on me too. But not my father—we shared a bond.

'My brother and I became strangers. When we were growing up, he had looked after me. My mother worked as a nurse. She did two shifts with a break of few hours. It was my brother who used to plait my hair and get me ready; we would ride to school together. I do not know how much my brother remembers those days. I grew up in both my grandmothers' homes. I used to sleepwalk, which worried my mother, so she sent me to my *nana-nani's* house. My parents had separated for a few years, so then,

I lived in different places. When my *dada* would get his pension, he would take me out for ice cream and almond milk. The shop is still there. All these conversations bring back sweet and sour memories. Growing up was not easy as I struggled with my identity. The compulsion of female clothes in school...I did not know where to put myself. I did not feel what other girls felt, and neither was I a man according to the rest of the world. I withdrew into myself. I can recall the tension in our house at the time. My father, as the only son, had to take care of his parents. But he was an alcoholic. He ran up a huge amount of debt, and people would keep coming to our house and demanding money.

'At times, money used to be desperately short. At the best of times, we had enough, and we would be happy with that. My mother worked hard. We lived in a small town, so the payment for nurses is not as good as one gets in a city. She worked in Jamnagar for quite a few years. Now that she is no more, I miss her. She died of a snake bite. By the time we took her to the hospital, it was too late. She never awoke from her sleep. I miss her; she was accepting of my gender identity. She passed away by the time Rukaya and I grew close.

'After our second getaway, more than two months passed before we tried to get away again. It was the night of 6 September 2018. I was awake, wondering how to break out of the stalemate we had landed ourselves in. Around one in the morning, my friend called and told me to quickly turn on the television. Just a few months back, our lawyer had said that our relationship was illegal, but here the news was that Section 377, the law which criminalised us, was no longer applicable. "We are free!" people like us were saying on the TV screen, rejoicing and celebrating, many of them from various NGOs.

'But then I thought about our own situation... nothing had really changed. It's not like I could suddenly get Rukaya out of her house now, or even get my brother and my *bhabhi* to accept me. Perhaps it was too much of a change to expect overnight.

I wondered how long we would have to wait. Before this news broke, I hadn't even heard of, let alone known, people like us. But there are so many of us out there. Unbelievable! Suddenly, I felt lighter and more confident.

'I realised that Rukaya's family would never accept our relationship, and neither would my brother and his wife. Amidst this conflict churning inside me, I managed to call Rukaya and give her the good news. She was excited too. Once again, we planned to get away. But Rukaya cautioned, "What should we do to not get caught this time?" She sensed that the law alone would not keep us safe.

'I decided to get in touch with organisations working with people like us. Having found Vikalp through another organisation, I planned our getaway with their support. Before eloping this time, I visited the organisation and made sure of our safety and the support we would need.

'We have since settled in with new bank accounts and rented accommodation. But still, the fear of family and the larger community holds us from living our lives fully. Blending into a new city and earning a livelihood required a lot of untruths in concealing our real reasons for coming and our parental estrangements. Joining work requires various proofs and papers, which exacerbates the fear of being traced. Then, there is always the paranoia of running into some known community member or relative. We cannot even have our trans or queer friends come to visit. The landlord will wonder. They already ask, "How come none of your relatives ever come here?"

'And then the worst part was that when my father died, I could not go home. The one last time...'

Rukaya said, 'For me, home is out of bounds forever.'

Appendix I

Sex in the Field

As a community group, the issues Vikalp gets involved with can span a wide range. Women who live in the areas where Vikalp works often come to the organisation to seek help in claiming benefits due to them from the government. In the period between 1998 and 1999 in Chhotaudepur, we noticed an abnormally large number of women approaching the organisation to seek widow compensation. We wanted to find out why this was the case. As it turned out, many of those who had emigrated to Godhra to work in the stone-crushing factories had died soon after. The silica stone, which was being crushed at these factories, was causing the workers to develop silicosis, an occupational lung disease. Vikalp undertook awareness programmes, filed a Public Interest Litigation (PIL), and conducted door-to-door campaigns which led to many workers leaving their jobs, even those who had been working at factories that had not been using the dangerous silica stone. Consequently, the factory owners became aware of our work and suspicious of our organisation.

The HIV/AIDS pandemic broke the silence around sexuality, changing national and state attitudes and creating spaces where it could—and had to—be discussed. Our understanding of the issue began to develop, and so our work within the area of sexual health started progressing. We were able to gather data that showed that a large number of rural tribal women were infected with STIs, concretely demonstrating a reality that had been suspected but not yet documented. We had to stand against local political leaders who would prefer to deny these facts for purposes of 'saving community honour'. The more egalitarian bend of tribal life, as well as their special customs, are often looked down upon by mainstream society as 'backward' or 'immoral'. Thus, proclaiming that there is a high rate of STIs amongst these communities would only reinforce and solidify existing prejudices.

The factory owners' opinions about our organisation became a problem when we began working with HIV/AIDS since many employers were reluctant to let us interfere in their affairs once again. Although we had trodden on some toes owing to the bad publicity from the data we had produced, the government had appointed us as their partner organisation to work around sexual health, which forced them to cooperate. This was around the time we met Shashi. Other than being a labourer in one of these stone-crushing factories, she has played countless other roles that illustrate the tangled web of intersecting identities and alternate realities that exist within queer rural life.